900 Practice Questions for the Upper Level

SSAT® & ISEE®

2nd Edition

By the Staff of The Princeton Review

PrincetonReview.com

Penguin Random House

The Princeton Review
110 East 42nd St, 7th Floor
New York, NY 10017
Email: editorialsupport@review.com

Published in the United States by Penguin Random House LLC, New York, and in Canada by Random House of Canada, a division of Penguin Random House Ltd., Toronto.

Terms of Service: The Princeton Review Online Companion Tools ("Student Tools") for retail books are available for only the two most recent editions of that book. Student Tools may be activated only once per eligible book purchased for a total of 24 months of access. Activation of Student Tools more than once per book is in direct violation of these Terms of Service and may result in discontinuation of access to Student Tools Services.

ISBN: 978-0-525-56893-3
ISSN: 2333-9365

SSAT is a registered trademark of the Secondary School Admission Test Board, and ISEE is a registered trademark of the Educational Records Bureau, neither of which sponsors nor endorses this product.

The Princeton Review is not affiliated with Princeton University.

Editor: Sarah Litt
Production Editor: Emily Epstein White
Production Artist: Deborah Weber

Printed in the United States of America.

10 9 8 7 6 5 4 3 2 1

2nd Edition

Editorial

Rob Franek, Editor-in-Chief
David Soto, Director of Content Development
Stephen Koch, Survey Manager
Deborah Weber, Director of Production
Gabriel Berlin, Production Design Manager
Selena Coppock, Managing Editor
Aaron Riccio, Senior Editor
Meave Shelton, Senior Editor
Chris Chimera, Editor
Sarah Litt, Editor
Orion McBean, Editor
Brian Saladino, Editor
Eleanor Green, Editorial Assistant

Penguin Random House Publishing Team

Tom Russell, VP, Publisher
Alison Stoltzfus, Publishing Director
Amanda Yee, Associate Managing Editor
Ellen Reed, Production Manager
Suzanne Lee, Designer

Acknowledgments

The Princeton Review would like to thank Anne Cullens and Anne Goldberg-Baldwin for their work on this book. We would also like to thank Deborah Weber and Emily Epstein White for their contributions.

Contents

Get More (**Free**) Content

at **PrincetonReview.com/cracking**

As easy as **1·2·3**

1 Go to PrincetonReview.com/cracking and enter the following ISBN for your book:
9780525568933

2 Answer a few simple questions to set up an exclusive Princeton Review account. *(If you already have one, you can just log in.)*

3 Enjoy access to your **FREE** content!

Once you've registered, you can...

- Get our take on the upcoming changes to the SSAT or ISEE

- Get valuable advice about the college application process, including tips for writing a great essay and where to apply for financial aid

- Check to see if there have been any corrections or updates to this edition

Need to report a potential **content** issue?

Contact **EditorialSupport@review.com** and include:

- full title of the book
- ISBN
- page number

Need to report a **technical** issue?

Contact **TPRStudentTech@review.com** and provide:

- your full name
- email address used to register the book
- full book title and ISBN
- Operating system (Mac/PC) and browser (Firefox, Safari, etc.)

Look For These Icons Throughout The Book

 APPLIED STRATEGIES

 OTHER REFERENCES

Part I
So, You Want to Improve Your Score!

- Getting Started: Your Knowledge, Your Expectations
- Your Guide to Getting the Most Out of This Book

GETTING STARTED: YOUR KNOWLEDGE, YOUR EXPECTATIONS

Your route to a higher score on the SSAT or ISEE depends a lot on how you plan to use this book and its companion book *Cracking the SSAT & ISEE*.

Making your game plan starts with knowing where you are…and where you want to go.

1. Which test do you plan to take?
   (A) The SSAT
   (B) The ISEE
   (C) Both
   (D) I am…uh…what?

2. How many questions are you able answer correctly with respect to each of the following areas?

Synonyms	(A)	Lots! I can do it in my sleep.
	(B)	Some, but I should do better.
	(C)	I've got issues, dude!
	(D)	Uh…what?
Analogies	(A)	Lots! I can do it in my sleep.
	(B)	Some, but I should do better.
	(C)	I've got issues, dude!
	(D)	Uh…what?
	(E)	As if! I am taking the ISEE.
Sentence Completions	(A)	Lots! I can do it in my sleep.
	(B)	Some, but I should do better.
	(C)	I've got issues, dude!
	(D)	Uh…what?
	(E)	As if! I am taking the SSAT.
Numbers and Operations (fractions, decimals, percents, exponents, factors, multiples, and other math functions)	(A)	Lots! I can do it in my sleep.
	(B)	Some, but I should do better.
	(C)	I've got issues, dude!
	(D)	Uh…what?
Algebra (solving for x, inequalities)	(A)	Lots! I can do it in my sleep.
	(B)	Some, but I should do better.
	(C)	I've got issues, dude!
	(D)	Uh…what?
Geometry (triangles, quadrilaterals, circles, visual perception, and other geometric principles)	(A)	Lots! I can do it in my sleep.
	(B)	Some, but I should do better.
	(C)	I've got issues, dude!
	(D)	Uh…what?

Reading and Interpreting Data (mean, median, mode, range, probability, reading charts and graphs)	(A)	Lots! I can do it in my sleep.
	(B)	Some, but I should do better.
	(C)	I've got issues, dude!
	(D)	Uh...what?
Quantitative Comparisons	(A)	Lots! I can do it in my sleep.
	(B)	Some, but I should do better.
	(C)	I've got issues, dude!
	(D)	Uh...what?
	(E)	As if! I am taking the SSAT.
Reading Passages	(A)	Lots! I can do it in my sleep.
	(B)	Some, but I should do better.
	(C)	I've got issues, dude!
	(D)	Uh...what?

3. How do you expect to use this book? Circle all that apply to you.
   (A) I want to make sure I know content.
   (B) I want to make sure I know effective strategies.
   (C) I want to make sure I know content and effective strategies.
   (D) I am not sure yet.

YOUR GUIDE TO GETTING THE MOST OUT OF THIS BOOK

This book is designed to provide practice questions across as many—or as few—subject areas as is appropriate to help you improve your score. Read on to find out how to get the most out of this book based on your answers to the questions above.

Answer and Explanations

The answers and explanations in this book are designed with the following goals:

- to provide you a clear academic explanation for the correct answer—the way *your teacher* would do it
- where applicable, to provide you an alternative, strategic approach for answering the question correctly—the way *The Princeton Review* would do it

Almost all explanations begin with the academic explanation, indicated by the books icon.

 The books icon indicates *Your Teacher's Way*.

If The Princeton Review has a different, more strategic way to answer a question correctly, a second explanation will be given, indicated by the chess icon.

The chess icon indicates *The Princeton Review's Way!*

For a small number of questions, the only way to arrive at a solution is through strategy, so only the chess icon is shown.

Your Study Plan

1. If you have never taken a real or practice SSAT or ISEE before—or— if you answered *Uh...what?* to most or all questions above, do the following:
   a. Take a practice test in SSAT, ISEE, or both—from the back of this book or *Cracking the SSAT & ISEE.*
   b. Count how many questions you missed using the categories above.
2. Based on your subject-specific self-assessment, select the drills you will do. For each topic,
   a. do a drill.
   b. check the answers and explanations.
   c. *consider what you will do differently next time.*
   d. if available, do another drill for that topic.
   e. remember what you learned from the drill(s).

When you do more than *just* read an answer and explanation and instead think about *why* you got a question wrong and *what* you will do differently next time, you will answer more questions correctly!

   f. you may use *Cracking the SSAT & ISEE* for additional content and strategic support.
3. When you have completed your drills, take a practice SSAT, ISEE, or both—from the back of this book, *Cracking the SSAT & ISEE*, or a test in an official guide: *The Official Guide to the SSAT Upper Level* or *What to Expect on the ISEE Upper Level.*

FAQs

Q: How do I decide whether to take the SSAT or the ISEE?

A: If the schools to which you are applying will accept either test, respond to the following questions to help you assess which test is better for you:

- <u>Sentence Completions</u> / <u>Analogies</u> are easier for me
- Percent correct of SSAT Reading: ___
  Percent correct of ISEE Reading: ___
- Quantitative Comparisons questions are <u>No Sweat</u> /
  <u>Neither Here Nor There</u> / <u>A Nightmare</u>
- Percent correct of SSAT Math (both sections): __
  Percent correct on ISEE Multiple Choice Math (both sections): __

Q: May I use SSAT drills even though I am taking the ISEE (or ISEE drills even though I am taking the SSAT)?

A: While the tests are similar with respect to content, there are differences in emphasis, how certain questions and answers are constructed, and (of course) some question types. Even so, if you are looking for additional practice, you may follow these guidelines:

- If you are taking the SSAT, skip Sentence Completion drills and Quantitative Comparison questions.
- If you are taking the ISEE, skip Analogies questions.
- Use drills from the "other" test for content support, but remain aware that you may not see questions quite like those on the real test.
- If a question from the "other" test seems quite different from anything you have seen while practicing for your test, it likely will not appear on the real test.

Don't forget that the SSAT deducts one-fourth of a point for wrong answers, while the ISEE does not.

Q: Can I use this book for the Middle Level SSAT or Middle Level ISEE?

A: While this book is designed for Upper Level students—and therefore contains harder questions that would appear only on an Upper Level test—you may certainly use this book as part of your preparation. However, you should consult other resources, such as those described below, to determine whether certain types of questions would actually appear on a Middle Level Test.

Q: How do I learn about the structure and content of the SSAT or ISEE?

A: As the purpose of this book is to provide practice questions and explanations, it assumes you are familiar with the content and structure of the test you are taking, as well as the process for registering for that test. Other resources will provide the information you seek.

For information about the tests, you may use *Cracking the SSAT & ISEE* or visit PrincetonReview.com, www.ssat.org, or www.erblearn.org/parents/admission/isee.

Q: What if I need more help?

A: You may find *Cracking the SSAT & ISEE* useful. In addition, The Princeton Review offers courses and tutoring in SSAT and ISEE.

For more information, visit PrincetonReview.com or call 1-800-2REVIEW.

Your Schedule

Set yourself up for success by making sure you know what you are doing and when!

I will take a practice test <u>before</u> / <u>after</u> / <u>before and after</u> I use this book.

I will do drills in the following subjects (check all that apply):

__ Synonyms
__ Analogies
__ Sentence Completions
__ Fractions, Decimals, and Percents
__ Exponents and Roots
__ Factors and Multiples
__ Solving for x
__ Inequalities
__ Triangles, Angles, and Lines
__ Quadrilaterals
__ Circles and Cylinders
__ Miscellaneous Geometry and Visual Perception
__ Reading and Interpreting Data
__ Other Math Concepts
__ Reading: Finding Information

__ Reading: Understanding Purpose
__ Reading: Tone
__ Reading: Vocab in Context
__ Reading: Miscellaneous Reading
__ Reading: Full Passages
__ Writing

I will devote __ minutes to the SSAT/ISEE on each of the days below:

__ Sundays __ Mondays __ Tuesdays __ Wednesdays __ Thursdays __ Fridays __ Saturdays

I will / will not use *Cracking the SSAT & ISEE* to help me prepare.

I will / will not read the strategic advice in the answers and explanations.

FINAL THOUGHTS

By using this book, you have shown yourself to be someone who identifies goals and sets out to achieve them. Because you will increase your content knowledge, develop a more strategic approach, or both, you will become more confident in your ability to take the SSAT or ISEE. Sticking to a schedule and seeking help when you need it will only add to your potential to achieve. You are in control: have a seriousness of purpose, but also have some fun preparing. And above all, believe in your ability to improve!

Part II
Verbal

Synonyms

SSAT Synonyms Drill 1

1. INTEGRATE:
   - (A) bring together
   - (B) settle accounts
   - (C) press on
   - (D) create
   - (E) argue

2. PREDICAMENT:
   - (A) forecast
   - (B) plight
   - (C) sorrow
   - (D) regret
   - (E) dominance

3. RENDEZVOUS:
   - (A) response
   - (B) invitation
   - (C) score
   - (D) meeting
   - (E) memento

4. EULOGIZE:
   - (A) condemn
   - (B) preach
   - (C) flatter
   - (D) commend
   - (E) put down

5. PECCADILLO:
   - (A) instrument
   - (B) flavor
   - (C) dishonesty
   - (D) grave error
   - (E) minor offense

6. TITANIC:
   - (A) nautical
   - (B) romantic
   - (C) enormous
   - (D) mythical
   - (E) smooth

7. RAMBUNCTIOUS:
   - (A) dependent
   - (B) energetic
   - (C) disagreeable
   - (D) argumentative
   - (E) tame

8. DISDAIN:
   - (A) contempt
   - (B) appreciation
   - (C) descent
   - (D) fragile
   - (E) indifference

9. INVIGORATE:
   - (A) weaken
   - (B) import
   - (C) dispute
   - (D) stimulate
   - (E) delay

10. HAMPER:
    - (A) enclose
    - (B) restrict
    - (C) approve
    - (D) lower
    - (E) balance

Impede
Stalling

7/10

SSAT Synonyms Drill 2

1. SCOFF:
   (A) join
   (B) polish
   (C) seek out
   (D) wear out
   (E) make fun of

2. QUIP:
   (A) compelling reason
   (B) witty comment
   (C) loud call
   (D) innocent question
   (E) rude request

3. POTPOURRI:
   (A) assignment
   (B) assistance
   (C) accessory
   (D) assortment
   (E) allotment

4. ONEROUS: Burden
   (A) practical
   (B) deceitful
   (C) truthful
   (D) syncopated
   (E) difficult

5. FALLOW:
   (A) unused
   (B) tiny
   (C) worldly
   (D) widespread
   (E) youthful

6. AGGRAVATE:
   (A) eke out
   (B) settle down
   (C) make worse
   (D) pass by
   (E) go without

7. DEPRECIATED:
   (A) calmed
   (B) admitted
   (C) strengthened
   (D) accepted
   (E) devalued

8. QUIRK:
   (A) personal oddity
   (B) inquisitive mindset
   (C) faulty reasoning
   (D) impressive daring
   (E) innate bias

9. EMULATE:
   (A) imitate
   (B) sympathize
   (C) exclude
   (D) return
   (E) deter

10. LEGEND:
    (A) legal judgment
    (B) unanimous agreement
    (C) conventional belief
    (D) passive resistance
    (E) historical story

SSAT Synonyms Drill 3

1. MITIGATE:
   - (A) destroy
   - (B) pamper
   - (C) lessen
   - (D) study
   - (E) design

2. ONUS:
   - (A) completeness
   - (B) spirituality
   - (C) self-regard
   - (D) arrogance
   - (E) burden

3. IMPERATIVE:
   - (A) regal
   - (B) rushed
   - (C) alluring
   - (D) necessary
   - (E) thoughtful

4. POMPOUS:
   - (A) fast
   - (B) arrogant
   - (C) formal
   - (D) threatening
   - (E) reserved

5. ASSUAGE:
   - (A) increase
   - (B) insult
   - (C) critique
   - (D) soothe
   - (E) excite

6. MALICE:
   - (A) amusement
   - (B) intelligence
   - (C) pessimism
   - (D) hatred
   - (E) admiration

7. IMPROVIDENT:
   - (A) fortunate
   - (B) energized
   - (C) poor
   - (D) incomprehensible
   - (E) careless

8. PRISTINE:
   - (A) clean
   - (B) prudish
   - (C) adaptable
   - (D) important
   - (E) primitive

9. FLAUNT:
   - (A) show off
   - (B) flag
   - (C) hide from
   - (D) tease
   - (E) work with

10. WANE:
    - (A) brag
    - (B) cleanse
    - (C) enlarge
    - (D) fade
    - (E) react

SSAT Synonyms Drill 4

1. CONVENTIONAL:
   - (A) idealistic
   - (B) caring
   - (C) erratic
   - (D) sensitive
   - (E) typical

2. EXPECT:
   - (A) scuffle
   - (B) conceal
   - (C) demolish
   - (D) anticipate
   - (E) minimize

3. CONTRADICT:
   - (A) concur
   - (B) dispute
   - (C) underline
   - (D) accept
   - (E) acclaim

4. TURBULENT:
   - (A) tempestuous
   - (B) arduous
   - (C) meticulous
   - (D) fastidious
   - (E) hilarious

5. ADVISE:
   - (A) figure out
   - (B) lobby against
   - (C) offer recommendation
   - (D) make happen
   - (E) wander away

6. FLINCH:
   - (A) recoil
   - (B) unwind
   - (C) loosen
   - (D) fail
   - (E) tighten

7. HINDER:
   - (A) follow
   - (B) prevent
   - (C) exceed
   - (D) retract
   - (E) dissolve

8. DECADENT:
   - (A) sore
   - (B) elderly
   - (C) self-indulgent
   - (D) affluent
   - (E) plain

9. PUGNACIOUS:
   - (A) tiresome
   - (B) accommodating
   - (C) argumentative
   - (D) peaceful
   - (E) sophisticated

10. LINGER:
    - (A) delay
    - (B) grab
    - (C) throw
    - (D) release
    - (E) dismiss

SSAT Synonyms Drill 5

1. RESTLESSNESS:
   - (A) cleanliness
   - (B) discontent
   - (C) sharpness
   - (D) tenderness
   - (E) disagreement

2. DAINTY:
   - (A) complex
   - (B) crisp
   - (C) delicate
   - (D) hardy
   - (E) rude

3. IMPUDENT:
   - (A) powerless
   - (B) shy
   - (C) shameless
   - (D) clumsy
   - (E) reserved

4. EMBRACE:
   - (A) decorate
   - (B) reject
   - (C) dispense
   - (D) welcome
   - (E) comfort

5. EXPLOIT:
   - (A) mistake
   - (B) retirement
   - (C) adventure
   - (D) explanation
   - (E) decision

6. CANVASSED:
   - (A) fabricated
   - (B) polled
   - (C) clothed
   - (D) shamed
   - (E) purified

7. GAUDY:
   - (A) casual
   - (B) tasteful
   - (C) tacky
   - (D) obvious
   - (E) greedy

8. TENET:
   - (A) posture
   - (B) reputation
   - (C) experience
   - (D) obligation
   - (E) belief

9. PROPHECY:
   - (A) benediction
   - (B) credo
   - (C) profession
   - (D) collaboration
   - (E) prediction

10. CREDIBLE:
    - (A) naive
    - (B) believable
    - (C) suspicious
    - (D) fastened
    - (E) alike

ISEE Synonyms Drill 1

1. TERMINAL:

    (A) academic
    (B) final
    (C) formal
    (D) frequent

2. MASQUERADE:

    (A) ceremony
    (B) criminal
    (C) disguise
    (D) scandal

3. CHRONICLE:

    (A) account
    (B) commitment
    (C) disease
    (D) display

4. ADVOCATE:

    (A) actor
    (B) defender
    (C) enemy
    (D) model

5. RECTIFY:

    (A) build
    (B) comprehend
    (C) correct
    (D) depict

6. UNANIMITY:

    (A) agreement
    (B) argument
    (C) duty
    (D) fairness

7. APPENDIX:

    (A) accident ✗
    (B) attachment ✗?
    (C) collection ✗✗
    (D) introduction ✗

8. BRUSQUE:

    (A) abrupt
    (B) orderly
    (C) political
    (D) proper

9. VISCERAL:

    (A) instinctive
    (B) mutual
    (C) thoughtful
    (D) visual

10. HAZARD:

    (A) damage
    (B) obey
    (C) reverse
    (D) risk

ISEE Synonyms Drill 2

1. ABOLISH:

   (A) continue
   (B) fulfill
   (C) hasten
   (D) prohibit

2. CONCENTRATE:

   (A) cluster
   (B) include
   (C) replace
   (D) suffer

3. FLOURISH:

   (A) argue
   (B) explain
   (C) represent
   (D) thrive

4. DISTORT:

   (A) enclose
   (B) suffer
   (C) twist
   (D) warn

5. PARADIGM:

   (A) aide
   (B) example
   (C) extension
   (D) harshness

6. REVELATORY:

   (A) exhausted
   (B) first
   (C) pretentious
   (D) revealing

7. RECITE:

   (A) discard
   (B) narrate
   (C) question
   (D) trick

8. CALAMITY:

   (A) disaster
   (B) extension
   (C) humor
   (D) knowledge

9. VORACIOUS:

   (A) active
   (B) antique
   (C) docile
   (D) insatiable

10. DISPENSE:

    (A) convince
    (B) distribute
    (C) explain
    (D) organize

ISEE Synonyms Drill 3

1. MUTUAL:

    (A) clouded
    (B) essential
    (C) shared
    (D) sluggish

2. REPLICA:

    (A) copy
    (B) embodiment
    (C) program
    (D) viewpoint

3. TALLY:

    (A) count
    (B) describe
    (C) eliminate
    (D) examine

4. RIVAL:

    (A) competitor
    (B) coward
    (C) equilibrium
    (D) trick

5. CLARIFY:

    (A) delay
    (B) introduce
    (C) provoke
    (D) resolve

6. SERENITY:

    (A) calmness
    (B) insight
    (C) intelligence
    (D) resilience

7. EULOGY:

    (A) course
    (B) score
    (C) study
    (D) tribute

8. OBTUSE:

    (A) dense
    (B) distant
    (C) filling
    (D) porous

9. DOCILE:

    (A) dismissive
    (B) fleeting
    (C) studious
    (D) submissive

10. RECKON:

    (A) belabor
    (B) calculate
    (C) caution
    (D) redeem

ISEE Synonyms Drill 4

1. BELITTLE:

    (A) cleanse
    (B) criticize
    (C) describe
    (D) shrink

2. EXAGGERATE:

    (A) investigate
    (B) overstate
    (C) regret
    (D) request

3. CHIDE:

    (A) dominate
    (B) irritate
    (C) lecture
    (D) visit

4. CONSTRICT:

    (A) evade
    (B) inhibit
    (C) liberate
    (D) render

5. SEGUE:

    (A) composition
    (B) line
    (C) referral
    (D) transition

6. TRANSIENT:

    (A) moving
    (B) permanent
    (C) stubborn
    (D) temporary

7. AGITATE:

    (A) condemn
    (B) consider
    (C) disturb
    (D) satisfy

8. QUELL:

    (A) believe
    (B) demean
    (C) freshen
    (D) suppress

9. VANQUISH:

    (A) defeat
    (B) dictate
    (C) reduce
    (D) refute

10. BUOY:

    (A) advise
    (B) chasten
    (C) decorate
    (D) uplift

ISEE Synonyms Drill 5

1. DAMPEN:

   (A) discourage
   (B) enter
   (C) freshen
   (D) shackle

2. MUZZLE:

   (A) adopt
   (B) energize
   (C) incite
   (D) quiet

3. QUIVER:

   (A) depress
   (B) soothe
   (C) straighten
   (D) tremble

4. CONDONE:

   (A) admonish
   (B) excuse
   (C) impersonate
   (D) instruct

5. EXPEDIENT:

   (A) appropriate
   (B) distasteful
   (C) irresponsible
   (D) rushed

6. RUCKUS:

   (A) disaster
   (B) dismissal
   (C) disturbance
   (D) rite

7. BEDLAM:

   (A) chaos
   (B) escape
   (C) preserve
   (D) shelter

8. AMNESTY:

   (A) craft
   (B) pardon
   (C) tangent
   (D) testimony

9. GULLIBLE:

   (A) delicate
   (B) immediate
   (C) naïve
   (D) necessary

10. PALATABLE:

    (A) agreeable
    (B) believable
    (C) competitive
    (D) dangerous

Synonyms: Answers and Explanations

ANSWER KEY

SSAT Synonyms Drill 1		SSAT Synonyms Drill 2		SSAT Synonyms Drill 3		SSAT Synonyms Drill 4		SSAT Synonyms Drill 5	
1.	A	1.	E	1.	C	1.	E	1.	B
2.	B	2.	B	2.	E	2.	D	2.	C
3.	D	3.	D	3.	D	3.	B	3.	C
4.	D	4.	E	4.	B	4.	A	4.	D
5.	E	5.	A	5.	D	5.	C	5.	C
6.	C	6.	C	6.	D	6.	A	6.	B
7.	B	7.	E	7.	E	7.	B	7.	C
8.	A	8.	A	8.	A	8.	C	8.	E
9.	D	9.	A	9.	A	9.	C	9.	E
10.	B	10.	E	10.	D	10.	A	10.	B

ISEE Synonyms Drill 1		ISEE Synonyms Drill 2		ISEE Synonyms Drill 3		ISEE Synonyms Drill 4		ISEE Synonyms Drill 5	
1.	B	1.	D	1.	C	1.	B	1.	A
2.	C	2.	A	2.	A	2.	B	2.	D
3.	A	3.	D	3.	A	3.	C	3.	D
4.	B	4.	C	4.	A	4.	B	4.	B
5.	C	5.	B	5.	D	5.	D	5.	A
6.	A	6.	D	6.	A	6.	D	6.	C
7.	B	7.	B	7.	D	7.	C	7.	A
8.	A	8.	A	8.	A	8.	D	8.	B
9.	A	9.	D	9.	D	9.	A	9.	C
10.	D	10.	B	10.	B	10.	D	10.	A

SSAT Synonyms Drill 1

1. **A** *Integrate* means to *bring together* or incorporate parts into a whole.

2. **B** A *predicament* is an unpleasant or difficult situation or *plight*.

3. **D** A *rendezvous* is a French word that means an agreement to meet at a certain place or the *meeting* itself.

4. **D** *Eulogize* means to praise highly, or *commend*.

    The prefix *eu-* or *u-* comes from the Greek word for *perfect*, and the root *log* comes from the Greek word for thought or study.

5. **E** A *peccadillo* is a Spanish word for a very slight sin or *minor offense*.

6. **C** *Titanic* means huge or *enormous*.

    Everyone knows huge ships can't sink, right?

7. **B** *Rambunctious* means difficult to control or handle, wildly active and noisy.

8. **A** *Disdain* means a feeling of *contempt*, looking down on anything or anyone judged unworthy or inferior.

9. **D** To *invigorate* means to fill with energy and life or to *stimulate*.

10. **B** *Hamper* can be a noun or a verb, but since the answer choices are all verbs, the stem word must also be a verb. To hamper means to hold back, impede, or *restrict*.

SSAT Synonyms Drill 2

1. **E** To *scoff* means to *make fun of*.

2. **B** A *quip* is a *witty comment*.

3. **D** A *potpourri* is a mixture or *assortment* of any unrelated objects, but a common usage is for mixtures of dried fragrant flowers, leaves, and spices.

4. **E** *Onerous* means burdensome or *difficult*.

5. **A** *Fallow* means *unused* or inactive. It is most commonly used to describe land that is left uncultivated.

6. **C** To *aggravate* means to *make worse*. It is frequently misused as a synonym for *irritate*, but it should be used correctly to indicate worsening an already bad situation.

 Your little brother may have irritated you by poking you, but you aggravated the situation by punching him back.

7. **E** *Depreciated* means to have lost value or worth or *devalued*.

8. **A** A *quirk* is an individual peculiarity, or *personal oddity*.

9. **A** To *emulate* means to *imitate*, with a goal of equaling or surpassing the object of emulation.

10. **E** A *legend* is a story, neither documented nor proven, handed down by tradition and popularly accepted as a *historical story*.

SSAT Synonyms Drill 3

1. **C** To *mitigate* means to *lessen* or make less severe.

2. **E**  An *onus* is a difficult obligation, task, or *burden*.

3. **D** *Imperative* means absolutely *necessary* or required. The word comes from the same Latin word that gives us *empire*, *emperor*, *imperious*, and *imperial*.

4. **B** *Pompous* means to be very self-important or *arrogant*.

5. **D** To *assuage* means to ease, *soothe,* or make better.

6. **D** *Malice* means a desire to hurt or harm.

 The Latin root *mal* means *evil*. The most famous use of *malice* may be in the closing lines of President Abraham Lincoln's Second Inaugural Address: "With malice toward none, with charity for all, with firmness in the right as God gives us to see the right, let us strive on to finish the work we are in, to bind up the nation's wounds, to care for him who shall have borne the battle and for his widow and his orphan, to do all which may achieve and cherish a just and lasting peace among ourselves and with all nations."

7. E   *Improvident* means thoughtless or *careless*.

8. A   *Pristine* means <u>untouched</u>, <u>undisturbed</u>, or *clean*.

9. A   To *flaunt* means to *show off*.

10. D   To *wane* means to decrease in strength or intensity or to *fade*.

SSAT Synonyms Drill 4

1. E   *Conventional* means following or using accepted standards and rules, being ordinary and *typical*.

2. D   To *expect* means to look forward to or *anticipate*.

3. B   To *contradict* means to speak the contrary or opposite of a previous statement, to deny or *dispute*.

 Contra- is a prefix that comes from the Latin word for *against* and the root *dict* comes from the Latin word for *say*.

4. **A**  *Turbulent* means being agitated, disturbed, or *tempestuous*.

5. **C**  To *advise* means to provide advice or *offer recommendation*.

6. **A** To *flinch* means to physically react by drawing back or shrinking or to *recoil*.

7. **B** To *hinder* means to *prevent*.

8. **C** *Decadent* means being very *self-indulgent*, showing no restraint in fulfilling human appetites.

9. **C** *Pugnacious* means likely to fight or argue, inclined to being *argumentative*.

  The root *pug* comes from the Latin word for combat or fighting.

10. **A**  To *linger* means to stay longer than expected or to *delay*.

SSAT Synonyms Drill 5

1. **B** *Restlessness* means the inability to sit still or *discontent*.

2. **C** *Dainty* means *delicate*.

3. **C** *Impudent* means being fresh, as in a showing a lack of concern for insulting or offending anyone and a lack of respect.

 Shameless is a good synonym that is not as out of common usage as *impertinent*, *brazen*, or *saucy*, even if those are more fun to say.

4. **D** To *embrace* means to enclose something or someone physically in your arms, from which comes its figurative meaning: to accept gladly or *welcome*.

5. **C** An *exploit* is a spirited accomplishment or *adventure*.

6. **B** *Canvassed* means having your opinion solicited or being *polled*.

7. **C** *Gaudy* means tastelessly showy or *tacky*.

8. **E** A *tenet* is a *belief*.

9. **E** A *prophecy* is a *prediction*.

10. **B** *Credible* means *believable*.

 The root *cred* comes from the Latin word for believe.

ISEE Synonyms Drill 1

1. **B** *Terminal* means coming at the end or *final*.

2. **C** *Masquerade* means a *disguise*.

3. **A** *Chronicle* means a record of events or an *account*.

 The root *chron* comes from the Greek word for *time*.

4. **B** An *advocate* is someone who works to support or defend a person or cause.

 The prefix *ad-* means *to* or *toward* and the root *voc* comes from the Latin word for *voice*.

5. **C**   To *rectify* means to make right or to *correct*.

6. **A**   *Unanimity* is a state of consensus or *agreement* among all.

 The prefix *uni-* means *one* or *together* and the root *animus* comes from the Latin word for *mind* or *spirit*. There is a different prefix *un-*, which means *not*, but the word *unanimity* evolved to drop the *i* in the prefix *uni-*.

7. **B**   An *appendix* is additional material or an *attachment*, frequently found at the end of a book or document. In humans, the obsolete organ the appendix is attached to the large intestine.

8. **A**   *Brusque* means being very *abrupt*.

9. **A**   *Visceral* means being *instinctive,* in contrast to being *thoughtful* or rational.

 Viscera is a term to refer to the organs of the body, and thus a visceral reaction is one prompted by your gut, while a thoughtful reaction is one prompted by your brain.

10. **D**   To *hazard* means to *risk*.

ISEE Synonyms Drill 2

1. **D** To *abolish* means to outlaw, forbid, or *prohibit*.

2. **A** To *concentrate* means to group, bring to a common place, or *cluster*.

3. **D** To *flourish* means to grow dramatically or to *thrive*.

4. **C** To *distort* means to *twist*.

5. **B** A *paradigm* is a framework or model used as an *example*.

6. **D** *Revelatory* means showing, disclosing, or *revealing*.

7. **B** To *recite* means to repeat words in a lesson, poem, or story, or to provide an account of something, as in to *narrate* a story or event.

8. **A** A *calamity* is a great misfortune or *disaster*.

9. **D** *Voracious* means strongly craving or having an appetite that is *insatiable,* meaning it can't be satisfied, for large amounts of something such as food or knowledge.

10. **B** To *dispense* means to deal out or *distribute.*

ISEE Synonyms Drill 3

1. **C** *Mutual* means common or *shared.*

2. **A** *Replica* means a duplicate or *copy,* just as the verb *to replicate* means to copy or duplicate.

3. **A** To *tally* means to add up or *count.*

4. **A** *Rival* means a person who opposes in competition, therefore an opponent or *competitor.*

5. **D** To *clarify* means to explain, make clear, or *resolve.*

6. **A** *Serenity* means peacefulness or *calmness.*

7. **D** *Eulogy* means high praise or a *tribute* of high praise, most commonly thought of as a speech given at a funeral.

 The prefix *eu-* or *u-* comes from the Greek word for *perfect*, and the root *log* comes from the Greek word for thought or study.

8. **A** *Obtuse* means lacking in perception or intellect, or being *dense*.

 In geometry, an obtuse angle is greater than 90 degrees, while an acute angle is less than 90 degrees. Used figuratively, *acute* is the opposite of *obtuse*, describing a person as sharp, smart, and quick.

9. **D** *Docile* means *submissive*, easily managed or controlled.

10. **B** To *reckon* means to count or *calculate*.

ISEE Synonyms Drill 4

1. **B** To *belittle* means to point out, if not emphasize, flaws and weaknesses or to *criticize*.

2. **B** To *exaggerate* means to stretch the truth or *overstate*.

3. **C** To *chide* means to find fault, express disapproval, or *lecture*.

4. **B** To *constrict* means to cause a contraction or shrinkage, to hold back or *inhibit*.

5. **D** *Segue* means a smooth switch or *transition*.

 It is pronounced SEG-WAY, just like the two-wheeled scooter. The inventor of the Segway died riding one of his devices off a cliff.

6. **D** *Transient* means not lasting or *temporary*. The root *trans* comes from the Latin word for *across*.

7. **C** To *agitate* means to shake, move roughly, or *disturb*.

8. **D** To *quell* means to stamp down or *suppress*.

9. **A** To *vanquish* means to conquer or *defeat*.

10. **D** To *buoy* means to keep afloat or *uplift*. As a noun, a buoy is a flotation device.

ISEE Synonyms Drill 5

1. **A** To *dampen* means to depress or *discourage*. Its more obvious meaning is to make wet, so used figuratively it means to throw water on hopes and spirits.

2. **D**  To *muzzle* is to silence or *quiet*. As a noun, a muzzle means both the mouth of an animal (or a gun) and a device to keep the animal's mouth closed.

3. **D**  To *quiver* is to shake or *tremble*.

4. **B**  To *condone* means to overlook, pardon, or *excuse*.

5. **A**  *Expedient* means *appropriate*, suitable, or proper for a purpose. Don't forget to look up words you don't know, and remember that words can have more than one meaning.

6. **C**  A *ruckus* is a noisy commotion or *disturbance*.

7. **A**  *Bedlam* means a scene of wild confusion or *chaos*.

 The name comes from the popular nickname for St. Mary of Bethlehem, the psychiatric facility in London founded in the thirteenth century and called for centuries an insane (sometimes lunatic) asylum, long before enlightenment on the origins and treatment of mental illness.

8. **B**   *Amnesty* means an act of forgiveness or a *pardon*.

9. **C**   *Gullible* means being easily deceived or cheated, or being *naïve*. Did you know that gullible isn't in the dictionary?

10. **A**   *Palatable* means acceptable or *agreeable* in taste or concept.

    The palate is the roof of the mouth and also means the sense of taste.

Analogies
and Sentence
Completions

SSAT Analogies Drill 1

1. Agenda is to meeting as
   (A) plan is to purpose
   (B) mission is to journey
   (C) plot is to revenge
   (D) itinerary is to atlas
   (E) program is to play

2. Pork is to sausage as _category_
   (A) pig is to cow
   (B) toast is to bread
   (C) cheese is to grater
   (D) egg is to mayonnaise
   (E) sugar is to flour

3. Recording is to sounds as
   (A) filming is to celebrity
   (B) embroidery is to finesse
   (C) portraiture is to likenesses
   (D) photography is to journalism
   (E) easel is to painting

4. Abundance is to supply as
   (A) idol is to belief
   (B) posterity is to will
   (C) education is to class
   (D) affluence is to wealth
   (E) wish is to fulfillment

5. Professor is to lecture as pastor is to
   (A) sermon
   (B) thesis
   (C) robe
   (D) husbandry
   (E) congregation

6. Sheep is to weaver as
   (A) cattle is to tanner
   (B) butcher is to hogs
   (C) crop is to miner
   (D) electrician is to carpenter
   (E) dog is to cat

7. Trot is to gallop as _extreme_
   (A) prance is to strut
   (B) drain is to flood
   (C) echo is to sound
   (D) squall is to storm
   (E) breeze is to gale

8. Loquacious is to verbose as tranquil is to _verbal_
   (A) dull
   (B) heft
   (C) peaceful
   (D) submissive
   (E) fastidious

9. Barometer is to pressure as
   (A) odometer is to speed
   (B) colorimeter is to density
   (C) stethoscope is to galaxy
   (D) phonograph is to light
   (E) thermometer is to dew point

10. Gluttony is to craving as
    (A) pride is to fall
    (B) jealousy is to envy
    (C) droplets is to hurricane
    (D) essay is to eulogy
    (E) sloth is to movement

5/10

SSAT Analogies Drill 2

1. Buttress is to support as
   - (A) door is to jamb
   - (B) nest is to freedom
   - (C) sloop is to marina
   - (D) placemat is to table
   - (E) food is to nourishment

2. Expel is to school as
   - (A) accept is to academy
   - (B) beguile is to charm
   - (C) testify is to court
   - (D) erect is to bridge
   - (E) disqualify is to competition

3. Suspended is to fired as fostered is to
   - (A) dealt
   - (B) adopted
   - (C) inspired
   - (D) derided
   - (E) elevated

4. Prevaricate is to lie as
   - (A) procrastinate is to demonstrate
   - (B) intimidate is to wander
   - (C) implicate is to guess
   - (D) dawdle is to delay
   - (E) doodle is to hurry

5. Deed is to ownership as
   - (A) fact is to trial
   - (B) license is to permission
   - (C) embargo is to trade
   - (D) rite is to passage
   - (E) pact is to secrecy

6. Mar is to destroy as
   - (A) paint is to pose
   - (B) smear is to clean
   - (C) buff is to polish
   - (D) admire is to venerate
   - (E) edit is to shorten

7. Hoarding is to stockpile as
   - (A) overhearing is to testimony
   - (B) overseeing is to ignorance
   - (C) overlooking is to omission
   - (D) overpaying is to admission
   - (E) overbooking is to concession

8. Foul is to smell as
   - (A) sour is to sight
   - (B) wrong is to right
   - (C) soft is to touch
   - (D) fair is to play
   - (E) rancid is to taste

9. Solicitous is to caretaker as
   - (A) duplicitous is to ally
   - (B) pompous is to cheerleader
   - (C) wise is to sage
   - (D) patience is to doctor
   - (E) brief is to pundit

10. Insulation is to cooling as antibiotic is to
    - (A) dehydration
    - (B) infection
    - (C) distinction
    - (D) reflection
    - (E) correction

5/10

SSAT Analogies Drill 3

1. Recalcitrance is to mischief as
   - (A) indifference is to praise
   - (B) refusal is to hesitation
   - (C) remonstrance is to remorse
   - (D) cardinal is to ordinal
   - (E) disinterest is to opinion

2. Axle is to wheel as
   - (A) crank is to winch
   - (B) joist is to jib
   - (C) rope is to slat
   - (D) candle is to power
   - (E) lead is to pencil

3. Entrée is to menu as
   - (A) word is to lexicon
   - (B) oboe is to reed
   - (C) résumé is to skill
   - (D) psalm is to church
   - (E) paragraph is to stanza

4. Hint is to proclaim as
   - (A) aggravate is to irritate
   - (B) sip is to guzzle
   - (C) taste is to sample
   - (D) portend is to warn
   - (E) hit is to strike

5. Flurry is to blizzard as
   - (A) drench is to water
   - (B) parch is to quench
   - (C) day is to month
   - (D) seep is to deluge
   - (E) flourish is to fade

6. Obfuscate is to enlighten as
   - (A) dictate is to teach
   - (B) imbibe is to drink
   - (C) enervate is to waste
   - (D) dim is to darken
   - (E) indulge is to abstain

7. Cloying is to odor as
   - (A) raunchy is to language
   - (B) historical is to romance
   - (C) gaudy is to fashion
   - (D) emotive is to cinema
   - (E) maudlin is to sentiment

8. Ballet is to dance as
   - (A) café is to eatery
   - (B) finale is to play
   - (C) cliché is to criticism
   - (D) bouquet is to flowers
   - (E) cachet is to rank

9. Table is to postpone as
   - (A) display is to restrain
   - (B) seat is to shuffle
   - (C) shelve is to shove
   - (D) plug is to promote
   - (E) wave is to crest

10. Peel is to apple as
    - (A) leaf is to spinach
    - (B) skin is to potato
    - (C) seed is to watermelon
    - (D) stone is to peach
    - (E) split is to banana

6/10

SSAT Analogies Drill 4

1. Baton is to conducting as
   - (A) prod is to shepherding
   - (B) wand is to blessing
   - (C) laser is to taming
   - (D) knife is to scooping
   - (E) flag is to protesting

2. Enmity is to hostility as chauffeur is to
   - (A) poet
   - (B) greed
   - (C) cobbler
   - (D) chef
   - (E) driver

3. Plumage is to cardinal as
   - (A) coat is to leopard
   - (B) army is to ants
   - (C) mink is to collar
   - (D) wool is to blanket
   - (E) mange is to dog

4. Tsunami is to ocean as
   - (A) hurricane is to lantern
   - (B) sushi is to seafood
   - (C) avalanche is to mountain
   - (D) tournament is to playground
   - (E) sudoku is to KenKen

5. Rival is to competition as ally is to
   - (A) avarice
   - (B) folly
   - (C) affiliation
   - (D) affection
   - (E) constriction

6. Peculiar is to bizarre as
   - (A) anxious is to relaxed
   - (B) brave is to jealous
   - (C) verbose is to shy
   - (D) plain is to austere
   - (E) homely is to pretty

7. Muffler is to neck as
   - (A) lock is to head
   - (B) radiator is to ankle
   - (C) mitten is to hand
   - (D) shroud is to wrist
   - (E) spear is to finger

8. Microphone is to announcer as camera is to
   - (A) starlet
   - (B) singer
   - (C) model
   - (D) physician
   - (E) photographer

9. Whirlpool is to eddy as
   - (A) candor is to honesty
   - (B) tornado is to gust
   - (C) spat is to war
   - (D) cyclone is to water
   - (E) freezer is to cooler

10. Imply is to insinuate as
    - (A) apply is to evaluate
    - (B) deploy is to attack
    - (C) infer is to deduce
    - (D) coach is to induce
    - (E) assign is to attenuate

SSAT Analogies Drill 5

1. Stout is to obese as
   - (A) hale is to hearty
   - (B) slender is to slim
   - (C) generous is to charitable
   - (D) adequate is to outstanding
   - (E) intentional is to purposeful

2. Worry is to dread as
   - (A) joy is to gladness
   - (B) glee is to jubilation
   - (C) grief is to concern
   - (D) sadness is to anguish
   - (E) loyalty is to fidelity

3. Seldom is to frequent as intermittent is to
   - (A) independent
   - (B) consistent
   - (C) strident
   - (D) persistent
   - (E) obedient

4. Lithium is to titanium as
   - (A) nickel is to platinum
   - (B) granite is to cement
   - (C) tar is to pavement
   - (D) gold is to metal
   - (E) silver is to coin

5. Grimace is to pain as
   - (A) wince is to pleasure
   - (B) flinch is to approval
   - (C) scowl is to anger
   - (D) yawn is to sympathy
   - (E) whisper is to scream

6. Silo is to wheat as
   - (A) fork is to road
   - (B) warehouse is to merchandise
   - (C) missile is to bomb
   - (D) pod is to whales
   - (E) lake is to salt

7. Request is to demand as
   - (A) blank is to white
   - (B) proposal is to marry
   - (C) buy is to sell
   - (D) desire is to grant
   - (E) advise is to order

8. Idle is to obsolete as
   - (A) ornate is to fancy
   - (B) evil is to handy
   - (C) adore is to appreciate
   - (D) tentative is to certain
   - (E) boring is to tedious

9. Logo is to company as
   - (A) emblem is to country
   - (B) face is to book
   - (C) target is to shop
   - (D) copyright is to claim
   - (E) gift is to card

10. Bowl is to tureen as cup is to
    - (A) mug
    - (B) catcher
    - (C) pitcher
    - (D) fondle
    - (E) glass

ISEE Sentence Completions Drill 1

1. The ------ of such innovations as the phonograph, the motion picture camera, and the
   light bulb, Thomas Edison contributed to
   the creation of new industries such as sound
   recording, motion pictures, and electric light.

   (A) builder
   (B) inventor
   (C) protégé
   (D) villain

2. The medicinal use of leeches dates back thousands of years, common in many civilizations
   including ancient India and Greece; although
   the practice declined with the rise of modern
   medicine, it has ------ in recent decades as
   leeches have proved useful for microsurgeries.

   (A) disappeared
   (B) rebounded
   (C) remained
   (D) responded

3. The tutor's directions were so ------ that the
   student could not offer the excuse that the
   directions were confusing.

   (A) explicit
   (B) fictional
   (C) heartfelt
   (D) mysterious

4. The singing show applicant looked embar-
   rassed by the applause after her audition, as
   if she ------ that her efforts had clearly fallen
   short.

   (A) acknowledged
   (B) emphasized
   (C) imagined
   (D) rejected

5. By 2014, individual devices such as digital
   cameras, GPS navigators, and MP3 players,
   which had seemed so ------ a few years earlier,
   had become less necessary as smart phones
   performed all those functions in a single gadget.

   (A) genuine
   (B) indispensable
   (C) unfashionable
   (D) vibrant

6. The mayor's decision to fund the pre-school
   program was ------ by his gratitude for the
   public support his family received when he
   was young and his ------for those struggling to
   escape poverty.

   (A) contradicted . . . admiration
   (B) revealed . . . understanding
   (C) shaped . . . empathy
   (D) shown . . . contempt

7. Like many ------ cities, Atlanta struggles with
   sprawl and the ------ traffic such development
   creates.

   (A) booming . . . snarling
   (B) growing . . . smooth
   (C) minor . . . tangled
   (D) shrinking . . . transparent

8. Although many people have ------ habits of
   eating healthy and exercising regularly, the
   appeal of tasty fast food and a comfortable
   sofa still ------ many others.

   (A) abandoned . . . appalls
   (B) adopted . . . lures
   (C) developed . . . repels
   (D) renounced . . . tempts

9. In the nineteenth century, those fighting for the abolition of slavery did not always agree with those fighting for women's rights: while some activists ------ each other's goals, others believed victory for one side would spell ------ for the other.

   (A) championed . . . defeat
   (B) encouraged . . . success
   (C) rejected . . . doom
   (D) understood . . . escape

10. New research has indicated that children's food inclinations develop in the womb: when pregnant women ------ lots of leafy green vegetables, their babies will show a ------ for leafy green vegetables throughout childhood.

    (A) consume . . . preference
    (B) cook . . . dismissal
    (C) ingest . . . hatred
    (D) avoid . . . taste

ISEE Sentence Completions Drill 2

1. Despite its fearsome reputation and intimidating looks, the American Staffordshire terrier is very ------ and is aggressive only when threatened.

   (A) amiable
   (B) contrite
   (C) energetic
   (D) solitary

2. One of the first cable series to earn critical ------ was HBO's *The Sopranos*, a groundbreaking drama whose success influenced dozens of shows on both cable and network TV.

   (A) acclaim
   (B) condemnation
   (C) persistence
   (D) precedence

3. Facial expressions such as rolled eyes and a begrudging vocal tone will ------ the sincerity of an apology.

   (A) balance
   (B) bolster
   (C) exaggerate
   (D) undermine

4. The grandchildren spent carelessly and unwisely, essentially ------ the family fortune built up over the two prior generations.

   (A) amassing
   (B) capitalizing
   (C) obstructing
   (D) squandering

5. The fans loved their favorite movie star with a worship that approached ------.

   (A) dismissal
   (B) embarrassment
   (C) permanence
   (D) veneration

6. A ------ of several musical forms including the blues, gospel, and Western swing, rock and roll ------ the idea of America as the great melting pot.

   (A) clash . . . explains
   (B) combination . . . belies
   (C) fusion . . . epitomizes
   (D) selection . . . shocks

7. Although over-the-counter pain medications such as Advil, Excedrin, and Tylenol cannot cure the underlying illness, they can ------ the symptoms and provide some ------.

   (A) alleviate . . . relief
   (B) eradicate . . . diagnosis
   (C) heighten . . . distraction
   (D) intensify . . . peace

8. Like many other movies ------ from popular novels, the blockbuster received mixed reviews from loyal fans of the book; some fans loved the film while others ------ it.

   (A) adapted . . . panned
   (B) appropriated . . . lauded
   (C) derived . . . trumpeted
   (D) deviated . . . rejected

9. If people drove in the snow with more ------ and employed fewer ------ maneuvers, there would be fewer accidents.

    (A) caution . . . reckless
    (B) emotion . . . rational
    (C) excess . . . generous
    (D) excitement . . . desperate

10. A ------ ear for languages can identify similarities and ------ the differences among several languages that descend from a common source.

    (A) deft . . . blunt
    (B) keen . . . discern
    (C) restrained . . . isolate
    (D) skilled . . . reserve

ISEE Sentence Completions Drill 3

1. A combination of healthy eating, a full night's sleep, and regular handwashing is the ------ offered by most doctors as the best way to avoid getting the flu.

   (A) counsel
   (B) distraction
   (C) enigma
   (D) limitation

2. When outbreaks of the disease pellagra spread throughout the American South in the early 1900s, doctors mistakenly ------ blame to a germ or toxin; by the 1920s, doctors understood the condition was caused by a deficiency of Vitamin A.

   (A) ascribed
   (B) catered
   (C) cleared
   (D) provoked

3. The holidays remind us each year that relationships with family and friends, not wealth or material goods, ------ true happiness.

   (A) complicate
   (B) demean
   (C) foster
   (D) recognize

4. Fats and carbohydrates, which were ------ by different diet fads in the 1990s and 2000s, are now recommended as part of a healthy eating regimen as long as they are consumed in moderate amounts.

   (A) denounced
   (B) extended
   (C) influenced
   (D) irritated

5. Granite, which resists stains and scratches, is a better choice for kitchen countertops than marble, which is easily ------.

   (A) absorbed
   (B) marred
   (C) recognized
   (D) repelled

6. Despite her ------ about her uncertain future, the graduate ------ in the praise that the ceremony celebrated.

   (A) apprehension . . . basked
   (B) concern . . . fretted
   (C) glee . . . wallowed
   (D) optimism . . . reveled

7. When people follow too ------ a budget throughout the year, they are likely to lose control and ------ on vacation and return home to a stack of unpayable bills.

   (A) frugal . . . stint
   (B) indulgent . . . repent
   (C) lax . . . celebrate
   (D) strict . . . splurge

8. Because the actress was known for choosing ------ characters to portray, critics praised her latest role as the villain, a ------ departure sure to surprise her fans.

   (A) despicable . . . welcome
   (B) sentimental . . . soothing
   (C) sympathetic . . . fearless
   (D) volatile . . . predictable

9. If voters used ------ instead of ------ to cast their ballots, the public would enjoy a more logical government.

    (A) contemplation . . . consideration
    (B) deliberation . . . impulse
    (C) emotion . . . apathy
    (D) prejudice . . . pride

10. Agreeing to the sponsors' ------, the speaker ------ the presentation and ended the event early.

    (A) entreaty . . . extended
    (B) legacy . . . dispatched
    (C) request . . . suspended
    (D) whim . . . resumed

ISEE Sentence Completions Drill 4

1. When the dictator launched a brutal crack-down on democracy demonstrations, his actions were ------ by human rights supporters.

   (A) applauded
   (B) decried
   (C) endorsed
   (D) tolerated

2. The enemy's surprise counter-attack ------ a change in tactics if the allies were to maintain their advantage.

   (A) contracted
   (B) imagined
   (C) necessitated
   (D) prevented

3. After mounting pressure from the international community and years of economic sanctions, South Africa ------ its oppression of the black majority and system of whites-only government known as apartheid.

   (A) depicted
   (B) enforced
   (C) recognized
   (D) renounced

4. In 1964, the surgeon general issued the first ------ on cigarettes, telling people that smoking was one of the leading causes of lung cancer.

   (A) advertisement
   (B) portrayal
   (C) position
   (D) warning

5. After several noisy disruptions, the judge ordered the trial closed to the public, effectively ------ protestors in her courtroom.

   (A) barring
   (B) exonerating
   (C) foreseeing
   (D) inviting

6. Like many ------ diseases, mononucleosis is easily transmitted from person to person; thus, if a patient stays away from others after falling ill, the ------ can be contained.

   (A) chronic . . . symptoms
   (B) communicable . . . outbreak
   (C) curable . . . epidemic
   (D) infectious . . . recovery

7. Jesuit institutions are ------ on principles that are committed to academic excellence and that ------ coordinated collaboration and shared resources.

   (A) dependent . . . dispute
   (B) determined . . . deter
   (C) founded . . . advocate
   (D) razed . . . condemn

8. The meteorologist had an uneven record of success for the week: while she ------ the path of the blizzard, she ------ the amount of accumulation.

   (A) bungled . . . misjudged
   (B) directed . . . lionized
   (C) pinpointed . . . botched
   (D) predicted . . . assessed

9. Even though polio has been largely ------ in the United States, instances of the disease still ------ in the developing world.

    (A) beaten . . . diminish
    (B) eliminated . . . persist
    (C) exposed . . . arise
    (D) immunized . . . exercise

10. While I attended the reunion with ------, I reconnected with old classmates and attended the various events and parties with a feeling that was positively ------.

    (A) detachment . . . unfeeling
    (B) excitement . . . transitory
    (C) nostalgia . . . vindictive
    (D) trepidation . . . jubilant

ISEE Sentence Completions Drill 5

1. Many of the jokes on *The Simpsons* are so ------ that only the most widely read viewers can understand them.

   (A) esoteric
   (B) functional
   (C) hilarious
   (D) offensive

2. Unlike otters, which build their dens aboveground, badgers are ------, emerging only to hunt for food.

   (A) endangered
   (B) omnivores
   (C) predators
   (D) subterranean

3. Many people believe lack of knowledge is the same as stupidity, as if intelligence is ------ on education alone.

   (A) practiced
   (B) predicated
   (C) rehabilitated
   (D) repudiated

4. By the middle of the twentieth century, the United States, which was once mostly ------, was considered an urban country because the majority of people lived in towns and cities.

   (A) abundant
   (B) partisan
   (C) rural
   (D) unpopular

5. Social media and texting ------ the innate human instinct to communicate, connect, and interact with each other.

   (A) derail
   (B) enrage
   (C) exemplify
   (D) ignore

6. Because the couple had conducted a ------ courtship, the announcement of their ------ shocked even their closest friends.

   (A) clandestine . . . betrothal
   (B) fanciful . . . bequest
   (C) romantic . . . nuptials
   (D) traditional . . . ceremony

7. Had she shown more ------ and used a more contrite tone when she made her apology, her friends would have been more likely to have ------ her.

   (A) authority . . . ignored
   (B) compassion . . . dismissed
   (C) condescension . . . believed
   (D) remorse . . . forgiven

8. The ------ investor knows better than to buy stocks in only one type of industry and instead will build a ------ portfolio that reflects a multitude of sectors.

   (A) adept . . . permanent
   (B) inquisitive . . . challenging
   (C) novice . . . profitable
   (D) savvy . . . diversified

9. Eleanor Roosevelt was a vocal ------ of the rights of minorities and oppressed peoples, leading President Harry Truman to call her the First Lady of the World for her ------ to human rights.

    (A) antagonist . . . dedication
    (B) defender . . . commitment
    (C) opponent . . . access
    (D) supporter . . . indifference

10. The darkening clouds and gusts of wind were a clear sign of the ------ storm, and the sudden loud thunder clap ------ the storm's arrival.

    (A) departing . . . announced
    (B) fading . . . missed
    (C) impending . . . indicated
    (D) waning . . . marked

Analogies and Sentence Completions: Answers and Explanations

ANSWER KEY

SSAT Analogies Drill 1	SSAT Analogies Drill 2	SSAT Analogies Drill 3	SSAT Analogies Drill 4	SSAT Analogies Drill 5
1. E	1. E	1. B	1. A	1. D
2. D	2. E	2. A	2. E	2. D
3. C	3. B	3. A	3. A	3. B
4. D	4. D	4. B	4. C	4. A
5. A	5. B	5. D	5. C	5. C
6. A	6. D	6. E	6. D	6. B
7. E	7. C	7. E	7. C	7. E
8. C	8. E	8. A	8. E	8. D
9. A	9. C	9. D	9. B	9. A
10. B	10. B	10. B	10. C	10. C

ISEE Sentence Completions Drill 1	ISEE Sentence Completions Drill 2	ISEE Sentence Completions Drill 3	ISEE Sentence Completions Drill 4	ISEE Sentence Completions Drill 5
1. B	1. A	1. A	1. B	1. A
2. B	2. A	2. A	2. C	2. D
3. A	3. D	3. C	3. D	3. B
4. A	4. D	4. A	4. D	4. C
5. B	5. D	5. B	5. A	5. C
6. C	6. C	6. A	6. B	6. A
7. A	7. A	7. D	7. C	7. D
8. B	8. A	8. C	8. C	8. D
9. A	9. A	9. B	9. B	9. B
10. A	10. B	10. C	10. D	10. C

SSAT Analogies Drill 1

1. **E**   An *agenda* is a list for a *meeting*. A *program* is a list for a play.

 If you don't know the meaning of *agenda*, work backward. *Mission* and *journey*, *plot* and *revenge*, and *itinerary* (travel plans) and *atlas* are not by definition related, so you can eliminate (B), (C), and (D). A *plan* is designed to achieve a *purpose*. Could something be designed to achieve a *meeting*? Maybe, so keep (A). A *program* is a list for a *play*. Could something be a list for a meeting? Yes, so keep (E). You should always guess when you are down to two.

2. **D**   *Sausage* is made from *pork*. *Mayonnaise* is made from *egg(s)*.

3. **C**   *Recording* captures *sounds*. *Portraiture* captures *likenesses*.

4. **D**   *Abundance* is an excess of *supply*. *Affluence* is an excess of *wealth*.

 If you don't know the meaning of *abundance*, work backward. *Idol* and *belief*, *posterity* (future generations) and *will*, and *wish* and *fulfillment* are not by definition related, so you can eliminate (A), (B), and (E). A *class* exists for *education*. Could *supply* exist for something? Probably not in a dictionary sense, so eliminate (C).

5. **A**   A *professor* delivers a *lecture*, and a *pastor* delivers a *sermon*.

6. **A** A *weaver* creates from part of a *sheep*. A *tanner* (leather maker) creates from part of a *cow*.

 Even if you don't know the meaning of *tanner*, select (A) because none of the other answers match the defining sentence for *weaver/sheep*.

7. **E** A *trot* is a lesser version of a *gallop*. A *breeze* is a lesser version of a *gale*.

8. **C** *Loquacious* (talkative) is the same as *verbose* (talkative). *Tranquil* (peaceful) is the same as *peaceful*.

 If you don't know the meaning of either *loquacious* or *verbose*, or you don't know the meaning of *tranquil*, you should skip this question without guessing. If you know *tranquil*, work backward. The only answer that relates in a dictionary sense is *peaceful*.

9. **A** A *barometer* measures *pressure*. An *odometer* measures *speed*.

 If you don't know the instruments in this question, it is difficult to answer, even with strategy. Skip it without guessing.

10. **B** *Gluttony* is an excess of *craving*. *Jealousy* is an excess of *envy*.

 If you don't know the meaning of *gluttony*, work backward. *Pride* and *fall*, *droplets* and *hurricane*, and *essay* and *eulogy* (praise) are not by definition related, so you can eliminate (A), (C), and (D). *Jealousy* is an excess of *envy*, while *sloth* is an avoidance of *movement*. Could something be an excess or an avoidance of craving? Yes, so guess between the two. If you were not able to eliminate three answers, you may wish to leave this question blank.

SSAT Analogies Drill 2

1. **E** A *buttress* provides *support*. *Food* provides *nourishment*.

 If you don't know the meaning of *buttress*, work backward. *Nest* and *freedom* are not by definition related, so eliminate (B). A *jamb* is part of a *door*. Could *support* be part of something? Probably not, so eliminate (A). A *marina* (boat dock) is a *home* for a *sloop* (a type of boat). Could *support* be a home for something? No, so eliminate (C). A *placemat* protects a *table*. Could something protect *support*? Probably not, so eliminate (D). *Food* provides *nourishment*, and something can provide *support*.

2. **E** To *expel* is to remove from *school*. To *disqualify* is to remove from a *competition*.

3. **B** *Suspended* is a temporary version of *fired*. *Fostered* is a temporary version of *adopted*.

 If you don't know the meaning of *fostered* and do not make the connection to foster care, skip this question without guessing.

4. **D**   *Prevaricate* is the same as *lie*. *Dawdle* is the same as *delay*.

 If you don't know the meaning of *prevaricate*, work backward. None of the answer pairs other than (D) are by definition related, so you can eliminate (A), (B), (C), and (E).

5. **B**   A *deed* is document showing *ownership*. A *license* is a document showing *permission*.

 If you don't know the meaning of *deed*, work backward. *Fact* and *trial*, *rite* and *passage*, and *pact* and *secrecy* are not by definition related, so you can eliminate (A), (D), and (E). A *license* is a document showing *permission*. Could there be a document showing ownership? Yes, so keep (B). An *embargo* is a restriction of *trade*. Could there be a restriction of permission? Yes, so guess between (B) and (C).

6. **D**   *Mar* is a lesser version of *destroy*. *Admire* is a lesser version of *venerate*.

 If you don't know the meaning of *venerate*, you should still select (D) as none of the other answers match the defining relationship between *mar* and *destroy*.

7. **C**   *Hoarding* is to make a *stockpile*. *Overlooking* is to make an *omission*.

 If you don't know the meaning of either *hoarding* or *stockpile*, you should skip this question without guessing.

8. **E**   *Foul* describes an awful *smell*. *Rancid* describes an awful *taste*.

 Even if you don't know the meaning of *rancid*, you should still select (E) as none of the other answers match the defining relationship between *foul* and *smell*. While *foul* can be a noun, the first words of the answer choices are adjectives, which means *foul* is intended as an adjective.

9. **C**   *Solicitous* (concerned about others) is a characteristic of a *caretaker*. *Wise* is a characteristic of a *sage* (a person of great wisdom).

 If you don't know the meaning of *solicitous*, work backward. None of the answer pairs other than (C) are by definition related, so you can eliminate (A), (B), (D), and (E). If there are words you do not know in the answer pairs, but you can use process of elimination to get to two or three answers, guess.

10. **B**   *Insulation* works to prevent *cooling*. An *antibiotic* works to prevent an *infection*.

SSAT Analogies Drill 3

1. **B**   *Recalcitrance* (extreme disobedience) is a greater version of *mischief*. *Refusal* is a greater version of *hesitation*.

If you don't know the meaning of *recalcitrance*, work backward. *Indifference* and *praise*, *remonstrance* (protest) and *remorse* (regret), and *cardinal* and *ordinal* (both types of numbers) are not by definition related, so you can eliminate (A), (C), and (D). Refusal is a greater version of hesitation. Can something be a greater version of mischief? Yes, so keep (B). *Disinterest* is not showing an *opinion*. Can something be not showing remorse? Maybe, but (B) is more likely. If you don't know some of the words in the answers, you may need to guess after process of elimination or even skip this question.

2. **A**   An *axle* works to turn a *wheel*. A *crank* works to turn a *winch*.

Several of the answers contain technical or mechanical terms that you may not know. However, you can eliminate (D) and (E), as those answers do not share a relationship with the original pair. Thus, you may end up guessing from (A), (B), and (C).

3. **A**   An *entrée* (main course) is part of a *menu*. A *word* is part of a *lexicon* (the words in a language).

Even if you don't know the meaning of *lexicon*, select (A) because none of the other answers match the defining sentence for *entrée/menu*.

4. **B** *Hint* is a lesser version of *proclaim*. *Sip* is a lesser version of *guzzle*.

5. **D** *Flurry* is a lesser version of *blizzard*. *Seep* (flowing slowly) is a lesser version of *deluge* (flooding).

 Even if you don't know the meaning of *seep* and/or *deluge*, select (D) because none of the other answers match the defining sentence for *flurry/blizzard*. If you don't know all the words in the answers, you may need to guess after process of elimination.

6. **E** *Obfuscate* (confuse) is the opposite of to *enlighten* (educate). *Indulge* (give in to a desire) is the opposite of to *abstain* (refuse to give in to a desire).

 If you don't know the meaning of either *obfuscate* or *enlighten*, you should skip this question without guessing. If you know one of the words, you can try to work backward, but the answers may have several words you don't know as well. Don't spend too much time on questions with several difficult words.

7. **E** *Cloying* describes an unpleasantly excessive *odor*. *Maudlin* describes unpleasantly excessive *sentiment*.

 If you don't know the meaning of *cloying*, work backward. *Historical* and *romance*, as well as *emotive* and *cinema*, are not by definition related, so you can eliminate (B) and (D). *Raunchy* is obscene language. Can something be an obscene odor? No, so eliminate (A). *Gaudy* is tasteless fashion. Can something be tasteless odor? No, so eliminate (C). Even if you do not know *maudlin*, (E) is the only remaining answer.

8. **A** *Ballet* is a type of *dance*. *Café* is a type of *eatery*.

9. **D** To *table* is to *postpone*. To *plug* is to *promote*.

 You may have thought table was a noun at first, but the answer choices contain verbs as the first words. If you don't know the verb form of *table*, work backward. None of the answer pairs other than (D) are by definition related, so you can eliminate (A), (B), (C), and (E).

10. **B** The *peel* is the outside layer of an *apple*. The *skin* is the outside layer of a *potato*.

SSAT Analogies Drill 4

1. **A** A *baton* is used for *conducting*. A *prod* is used for *shepherding*.

2. **E** *Enmity* is the same as *hostility*. *Chauffeur* is the same as *driver*.

 If you don't know the meaning of *enmity* (which is related to enemy), work backward. *Chauffeur* relates by definition only to *driver*, so select (E).

3. **A** *Plumage* is the outside covering of a *cardinal*. *Coat* is the outside covering of a *leopard*.

4. **C** A *tsunami* is a storm in an *ocean*. An *avalanche* is a storm on a *mountain*.

5. **C** A *rival* is a person in a *competition* (a contest). An *ally* is a person in an *affiliation* (an association).

 Even if you don't know the meaning of *affiliation*, select (C) because *ally* does not relate by definition to the other answers.

6. **D** *Peculiar* is a lesser version of *bizarre* (extremely out of the ordinary). *Plain* is a lesser version of *austere* (severely simple).

 Even if you don't know the meaning of *austere*, you should still select (D), as none of the other answers match the defining relationship between *peculiar* and *bizarre*. If you don't know all of the words in the answers, you can guess after process of elimination.

7. **C** A *muffler* (a scarf) is used to warm the *neck*. A *mitten* is used to warm the *hand*. A *mitten* differs from a glove by separating only the thumb but enclosing the four fingers together.

 If you don't know the meaning of *muffler*, work backward. None of the answer pairs other than (C) are by definition related, so you can eliminate (A), (B), (D), and (E). If you don't know *shroud*, guess between (C) and (D).

8.　**E**　　An *announcer* uses a *microphone*. A *photographer* uses a *camera*.

9.　**B**　　A *whirlpool* is a stronger version of an *eddy* (a small circular current of water). A *tornado* is a stronger version of a *gust*.

　If you don't know the meaning of *eddy*, work backward. *Spat* and *war*, *cyclone* and *water*, and *freezer* and *cooler* are not related by definition, so eliminate (C), (D), and (E). *Candor* is the same as *honesty*. Could a *whirlpool* be the same as something? Yes, so keep (A). A *tornado* is a stronger version of a *gust*. Could a *whirlpool* be a stronger version of something? Yes, so keep (B). Guess between (A) and (B). If you don't know *candor*, you would still guess between (A) and (B).

10.　**C**　　*Imply* (suggest) is the same as *insinuate*. *Infer* (conclude) is the same as *deduce*.

　If you don't know the meaning of either *imply* or *insinuate*, you should skip this question without guessing. If you know one of the words, you can try to work backward, but the answers may have several words you don't know as well. Don't spend too much time on questions with several difficult words.

SSAT Analogies Drill 5

1. **D** *Stout* is a lesser version of *obese*. *Adequate* (sufficient) is a lesser version of *outstanding* (superior or excellent).

2. **D** *Worry* is a lesser version of *dread*. *Sadness* is a lesser version of *anguish*.

    Even if you don't know the meaning of *anguish*, you should still select (D), as none of the other answers match the defining relationship between *worry* and *dread*. If you don't know all of the words in the answers, you can guess after process of elimination.

3. **B** *Seldom* (happens rarely) is the opposite of *frequent*. *Intermittent* (happens randomly) is the opposite of *consistent*.

    If you don't know the meaning of *intermittent*, you should skip this question without guessing.

4. **A** *Lithium* and *titanium* are both metals, and *nickel* and *platinum* are both metals.

5. **C** A *grimace* is a facial expression showing *pain*, and *scowl* is a facial expression showing *anger*.

6. **B** A *silo* is a structure that holds *wheat*, and a *warehouse* is a structure that holds *merchandise*.

7. **E** To *request* is a polite version of *demand*. *Advise* is a polite version of *order*.

8. **D** *Idle* (not currently in use) is a lesser version of *obsolete* (never to be used). *Tentative* is a lesser version of certain.

 If you don't know the meaning of either *idle* or *obsolete*, you should skip this question without guessing. If you know one of the words, you can try to work backward, but the answers may have several words you don't know as well. Don't spend too much time on questions with several difficult words.

9. **A** A *logo* is the sign or symbol of a *company*, and an *emblem* is a sign or symbol of a *country*.

10. **C** A *bowl* is a small *tureen*. A *cup* is a small *pitcher*.

 If you don't know the meaning of *tureen*, work backward. Usually when one of the answer words is next to the stem pair rather than in the answer choices, there is only one possible defining relationship. Here, however, you can argue that *cup* relates to (A), (C), and (E), although (E) is particularly weak. In this case, you should guess between (A) and (C).

ISEE Sentence Completions Drill 1

1. **B** *Innovations* and *creation* require *invention* as the answer.

2. **B** *Although the practice declined* requires *rebounded* (came back) as the answer.

 Even if you do not know the word *rebounded*, you can eliminate the other answers because the correct answer must be the opposite of *declined*.

3. **A** *Not confusing* requires *explicit* (stated clearly) as the answer.

 Even if you do not know the word *explicit*, you can eliminate the other answers because the correct answer must be the opposite of *confusing*.

4. **A** *Her efforts had clearly fallen* short requires *acknowledged* (admitted) as the answer.

5. **B** *Less necessary* than *years earlier* requires *indispensable* (required) as the answer.

 While the vocab is harder here, you can easily eliminate (C) because the correct answer must be the opposite of *less necessary*. You might also have realized the words beginning with "vi" often relate to life (vitality, vivacious), in which case you can eliminate (D). You may need to guess down to two or three.

6. **C** The first blank must mean *caused*, while the second blank must mean *feeling*, thus requiring *shaped* and *empathy* (feeling) as the answer.

 Do one blank at a time. The second blank, which might seem easier, must mean *feeling*, so you can eliminate (A), as well as (D) if you know the word. The first blank must mean *caused*, so you can eliminate (A), (B), and (D). The Latin root *path* means feeling.

7. **A** The first blank must relate to *sprawl* and *development*, while the second blank must relate to *struggle* with *traffic*, thus requiring *booming* (rising quickly) and *snarling* (difficult) as the answer.

 Do one blank at a time. The second blank, which might seem easier, must relate to a *struggle* with *traffic*, so you can eliminate (B) and (D). Even if you don't know the word *sprawl*, the fact that there is *traffic* and *development* suggests that the problem is large. So, eliminate (C).

8. **B** The first blank must relate to those who follow *healthy habits*, while the second blank must relate to those who can't resist the *appeal of tasty fast food*, thus requiring *adopted* and *lure* (tempt) as the answer.

 Do one blank at a time. The second blank, which might seem easier, must relate to the *appeal of tasty fast food*, so you can eliminate (A) and (C) if you know those words. The first blank must relate to following *healthy habits* so eliminate (A), as well as (D) if you know the word. You may need to guess after eliminating one or two answers.

9. **A** The two blanks must run in contrasting directions, requiring *championed* (supported) and *defeat* as the answer.

 It is not possible to do one blank at a time, because you need one blank in order to know the other blank. However, the contrast between *while some* and *others* indicates that the blanks must run in contrasting directions. So, you can eliminate (B) and (C) because the words run in a similar direction and (D) because the words do not relate.

10. **A** The two blanks must run in a similar direction, requiring *consume* and *preference* as the answer.

 It is not possible to do one blank at a time, because you need one blank in order to know the other blank. However, the statement that *preferences develop in the womb* indicates that the blanks must run in a similar direction. So, you can eliminate (C) and (D) because the words run in contrasting directions and (B) because the words do not relate.

ISEE Sentence Completions Drill 2

1. **A** *Despite* and *fearsome* require *amiable* (friendly) as the answer.

 Even if you do not know the word *amiable*, you can eliminate (C) and (D), as well as (B) if you know the word, because the correct answer must be the opposite of *fearsome*. Also, the root *ami* means friend.

2. **A** *Groundbreaking*, *success*, and *influenced* require *acclaim* (praise) as the answer.

 Even if you do not know the word *acclaim*, you can eliminate the other answers if you know the words, because the correct answer must be consistent with *groundbreaking* and *influenced*. You may need to guess if you cannot eliminate the three wrong answers.

3. **D** *Rolled eyes* in contrast to *sincerity* requires *undermine* (weaken) as an answer.

 Even if you do not know the word *undermine*, you can eliminate (A) and (C), as well as (B) if you know the word, because the correct answer must reflect how the *rolled eyes* show a lack of *sincerity*. You may need to guess if you can eliminate only two wrong answers.

4. **D** *Spent carelessly* and *unwisely* requires *squandering* (wasting) as the answer.

 Even if you do not know the word *squandering*, you can eliminate the other answers if you know the words because the correct answer must reflect the result of *spending carelessly and unwisely*. You may need to guess if you cannot eliminate the three wrong answers.

5. **D** *Worship* requires *veneration* (high respect) as the answer.

 Even if you do not know the word *veneration*, you can eliminate the other answers because the correct answer must mean *worship*.

6. **C** The first blank must mean combination (of *musical forms*), while the second blank must mean contribute to (the *idea*), requiring *fusion* (combining) and *epitomizes* (perfectly represents) as the answer.

 Do one blank at a time. The first blank, which might seem easier, must mean combination (of *musical forms*), so you can eliminate (A) and (B). The second blank must mean contribute to (the *idea*), so eliminate (D).

7. **A** *Although cannot cure* requires that the first blank mean *reduce* and the second blank mean help, requiring *alleviate* (lessen) and *relief* as the answer.

 Do one blank at a time. The first blank, which might seem easier, must mean *reduce* because of *although cannot cure*, so you can eliminate (C) and (D), as well as (B) if you know the word. The second blank must mean *help* for the same reason, so eliminate (B).

8. **A** The first blank should mean *taken from* and the second blank should be opposite of the clue *loved the film*. Therefore, that second blank should be something similar to *disliked*. Start with one blank at a time, and perhaps the second blank is easier here: eliminate (B) and (C) since these do not mean *disliked*. Now look at the first blank: eliminate (D) because *taken from* does not mean *deviated from*. The correct answer is (A).

9. **A** The first blank must mean *care*, while the second blank must mean *careless* to ensure *fewer accidents*, requiring *caution* and *reckless* (careless) as the answer.

10. **B** The first blank must mean *capable* (of *identifying similarities*), while the second blank must mean *recognize* (*the differences*), requiring *keen* (sharply smart) and *discern* (figure out) as the answer.

 Do one blank at a time. The first blank, which might seem easier, must mean *capable* (of *identifying similarities*), so eliminate (C). The second blank must mean *recognize* (*the differences*), so eliminate (A) and (D).

ISEE Sentence Completions Drill 3

1. **A** *Offered by doctors* requires *counsel* (advice) as the answer.

 Even if you do not know the word *counsel*, you can eliminate (B) and (D), as well as (C) if you know the word, because the correct answer relates to what a *doctor offers,* such as a *recommendation.* If you watch shows like *Law & Order*, you may have noticed that lawyers are often referred to as counselors, because a counselor is an advisor.

2. **A** *Doctors mistakenly understood* requires *ascribed* (referred to as) as the answer.

 Even if you do not know the word *ascribed*, you can eliminate (B), (C), and (D), because the correct answer relates to what a *doctor mistakenly understood.*

3. **C** *Relationship* and *happiness* require *foster* (support) as the answer.

 Even if you do not know the word *foster*, you can eliminate (A), (B), and (D), because the correct answer must mean *cause* as *relationships* cause *happiness*.

4. **A** The contrast with *now recommended* requires *denounced* (criticized) as the answer.

 Even if you do not know the word *denounced*, you can eliminate (B), (C), and (D), because the correct answer must be the opposite of *now recommended*. The Latin word *nunci* means to state and gives us the words announce and pronounce. The prefix *de* means again. So, to *denounce* is to state against something.

5. **B** The contrast with *resists stains and scratches* requires *marred* (harmed) as the answer.

 Even if you do not know the word *marred*, you can eliminate (A), (C), and (D), because the correct answer must be the opposite of *resists stains and scratches*.

6. **A** The first blank must relate to *uncertain* (of the future), while the second blank must relate to *celebrate*, requiring *apprehension* (concern) and *basked* (enjoyed) as the answer.

 Do one blank at a time. The first blank, which might seem easier, must relate to *uncertain*, so you can eliminate (C) and (D). The second blank must relate to *celebration*, so eliminate (B).

7. **D** The first blank must relate to the opposite of *losing control* of a *budget*, while the second blank must relate to *losing control* of the *budget*, requiring *strict* and *splurge* (spend a lot) as the answer.

 Do one blank at a time. The second blank, which might seem easier, must relate to *losing control* of a *budget* so you can eliminate (C), as well as (A) and (B) if you know the words. The first blank must be the opposite of the second blank, so eliminate (B) if you know the word. You may need to guess after process of elimination.

8. **C** The first blank must mean the opposite of a *villain*, while the second blank must relate to *praise* and *surprise*, requiring *sympathetic* and *fearless* as the answer.

 Do one blank at a time. The first blank, which might seem easier, must be the opposite of *villain*, so you can eliminate (A), as well as (D) if you know the word. The second blank must relate to the *praise* and *surprise*, so eliminate (B) and (D).

9. **B** The first blank must mean *logical*, while the second blank must be the opposite of the first, requiring *deliberation* (consideration) and *impulse* (emotion-based decision) as the answer.

 Do one blank at a time. The first blank must mean *logical*, so you can eliminate (C) and (D). The second blank must be the opposite of *logical*, so eliminate (A).

10. **C** The first blank must be something one can *agree to*, while the second blank must mean *ended*, requiring *request* and *suspending* as the answer.

 Do one blank at a time. The second blank, which might be easier, must mean *ended*, so you can eliminate (A) and (D), as well as (B) if you know it. The first blank must be something one can *agree to*, so eliminate (B).

ISEE Sentence Completions Drill 4

1. **B** The contrast between *brutal dictator* and *human rights supporters* requires *decried* (criticized) as the answer.

 Even if you do not know the word *decried*, you can eliminate (A), (C), and (D), because the correct answer must reflect what *human rights supporters* would say about a *brutal dictator*.

2. **C** The *surprise attack's* relation to *change in tactics* requires *necessitated* (required) as the answer.

3. **D** *Pressure* about *oppression* requires *renounced* (refuse to support) as the answer.

 Even if you do not know the word *renounced*, you can eliminate (A), (B), and (C), because the correct answer must mean *ended*.

4. **D** *Telling* about *cancer* requires *warning* as the answer.

5. **A** *Closing* the *trial* requires *barring* as the answer.

 Even if you do not know the word *barring*, you can eliminate (C) and (D), as well as (B) if you know the word, because the correct answer must mean *stopping* in light of the *trial's closure.*

6. **B** The first blank must mean *easily transmitted*, while the second blank must relate to a desire for *containing* the presence of a disease, requiring *communicable* and *outbreak* as the answer.

 Do one blank at a time. The first blank, which might seem easier, must mean *easily transmitted*, so you can eliminate (C), as well as (A) if you know the word. The second blank must relate to a desire for *containing* the presence of a disease, so eliminate (A) and (D).

7. **C** The first blank must reflect that Jesuit institutions have certain *principles*, whereas the second blank must reflect that the institutions are *committed* to those principles, requiring *founded* (created an organization) and *advocate* (argue for) as the answer.

 Do one blank at a time. The second blank, which might seem easier, must relate to the fact that Jesuit institutions are *committed* to certain principles, so you can eliminate (A), as well as (B) and (D) if you know the words. The second blank must relate the fact that the institutions have those *principles*, so eliminate (D) if you know the word. You may need to guess after eliminating.

8. **C**   The two blanks must run in contrasting directions, requiring *pinpointed* and *botched* as the answer.

 It is not possible to do one blank at a time, because you need one blank in order to know the other blank. However, *uneven record of success* and *while* indicate that the blanks must run in contrasting directions. So, you can eliminate (A) and (D) because the words run in a similar direction and (B) because the words do not relate.

9. **B**   The two blanks must run in contrasting directions, requiring *eliminated* and *persist* (continue) as the answer.

 It is not possible to do one blank at a time, because you need one blank in order to know the other blank. However, *even though* and *still* indicate that the blanks must run in contrasting directions. So, you can eliminate (A) and (C) because the words run in a similar direction and (D) because the words do not relate.

10. **D**   The first blank must be the opposite of feeling *positively*, whereas the second blank must relate to feeling *positively*, requiring *trepidation* (nervousness) and *jubilant* (joy) as the answer.

 Do one blank at a time. The second blank, which might seem easier, must relate to feeling *positively*, so you can eliminate (A), as well as (B) and (C) if you know the words. The second blank must be the opposite of feeling *positively*, so eliminate (B), as well as (C) if you know the word. You may need to guess after process of elimination.

ISEE Sentence Completions Drill 5

1. **A** *The most widely read viewers* requires *esoteric* (known by only a few) as the answer.

 Even if you do not know the word *esoteric,* you can eliminate (B), (C), and (D), because the correct answer must relate to something that only *widely read viewers* can understand.

2. **D** *Unlike aboveground* requires *subterranean* (underground) as the answer.

 Even if you do not know the word *subterranean,* you can eliminate (A) and (C), as well as (B) if you know the word, because the correct answer must mean something that is *unlike aboveground.* The root *sub* means under, and the root *terra* means earth.

3. **B** *Lack of knowledge* and *as if* requires *predicated* (based on) as the answer.

 Even if you do not know the word *predicated,* you can eliminate (A), as well as (C) and (D) if you know the words, because the correct answer must mean *based on,* given *lack of knowledge* and *as if.* You may need to guess after process of elimination.

4. C   *Once mostly* and *urban* require *rural* (country or farm, not city) as the answer.

   Even if you do not know the word *rural,* you can eliminate (D), as well as (A) and (B) if you know the words, because the correct answer must mean *not urban*. You may need to guess down to two or three.

5. C   *Social media and texting* and *need to communicate* require *exemplify* (represent) as the answer.

   Even if you do not know the word *exemplify,* you can eliminate (A), (B), and (D) because the correct answer must mean relate to, given the connection between *social media and texting* and *need to communicate*.

6. A   *Courtship, announcement,* and *shocked* require *clandestine* (secret) and *betrothal* (engagement) as the answer.

   Do one blank at a time. The first blank, which might seem easier, must mean *secret* because the *announcement shocked* the friends, so you can eliminate (B), (C), and (D). While you do not need to address the second blank at this point, that blank must mean *engagement*, which would follow a *courtship*.

7. **D**   *More*, *contrite*, and *apology*, as well as the contrast between *had* and *would have*, require *remorse* (regret) and *forgive* as the answer.

  Do one blank at a time. The first blank, which might seem easier, must relate to her lack of an *apologetic* tone, so you can eliminate (A) and (B), as well as (C) if you know the word. The second blank relates to her friend's reaction to an *apology* that did *not* seem *apologetic*, so you can eliminate (A) and (B). You may need to guess after process of elimination.

8. **D**   *Knows better* and *multitude* require *savvy* (clever) and *diversified* (mixed) as the answer.

  Do one blank at a time. The second blank, which might be easier, must relate to *multitude*, so you can eliminate (A), (B), and (C). While you do not need to address the first blank, it must relate to *knows better*.

9. **B**   *First Lady of the World* and *human rights* require *defender* and *commitment* as the answer.

  Do one blank at a time. The first blank, which might be easier, must relate to support for *human rights* because the president honored Roosevelt by calling her First Lady of the World, so you can eliminate (C), as well as (A) if you know the word. The second blank must have a similar meaning, so eliminate (D). If you need to guess between (A) and (B), your safer guess is (B) because the root *ant* means *against*.

10. C   *Darkening clouds* and *gusts of wind*, followed by *loud thunder clap*, requires *impending* (about to happen) and *indicated* as the answer.

 Do one blank at a time. The second blank, which might be easier, must mean *signaled*, because there was a *sudden loud thunder clap*, so you can eliminate (B). The first blank must mean *coming* because of the *darkening clouds* and *gusts of wind*, so eliminate (A), as well as (D) if you know it. You may need to guess after process of elimination.

Part III
Math

Fractions, Decimals, and Percents

 _ 5 mi/h

SSAT Fractions, Decimals, and Percents Drill 1

1. Identify the fraction that is less than $\frac{3}{8}$.

(A) $\frac{4}{9}$

(B) $\frac{5}{14}$

(C) $\frac{6}{11}$

(D) $\frac{9}{20}$

(E) $\frac{7}{16}$

2. $\frac{3}{4}$ of $\frac{4}{5}$ is what fraction?

(A) $\frac{2}{3}$

(B) $\frac{5}{8}$

(C) $\frac{3}{5}$

(D) $\frac{4}{3}$

(E) $\frac{5}{2}$

3. Evaluate $\frac{1}{4}+\frac{1}{5}+\frac{1}{6}=$

(A) $\frac{37}{60}$

(B) $\frac{48}{60}$

(C) $\frac{72}{60}$

(D) $\frac{1}{15}$

(E) $\frac{3}{20}$

4. If a chess team contains 8 girls and 4 boys, approximately what percent of the team are girls?

(A) 75%
(B) 67%
(C) 57%
(D) 43%
(E) 25%

5. Jack has $450 in the bank. If he takes out 30%, how much money will he still have in the bank?

(A) 135
(B) 150
(C) 270
(D) 315
(E) 350

6. 16 is what percent of 80?

(A) 10%
(B) 20%
(C) 25%
(D) 30%
(E) 40%

7. Which number represents three thousand five and twelve thousandths?

(A) 35,000.12
(B) 3,500.012
(C) 3050.12
(D) 3005.012
(E) 3005.12

8. Divide 155.8 by 8.2.

(A) 0.19
(B) 1.9
(C) 2.2
(D) 19
(E) 22

9. Each of Chris's golf balls weighs 0.045 kilograms. A bag containing 12 golf balls weighs 0.62 kilograms. How many kilograms does the bag weigh by itself?

(A) 0.045
(B) 0.080
(C) 0.575
(D) 0.581
(E) 0.728

$0.045 \times 12 = 0.54$

$62 - 54$ ⑧

10. $544.1 + 87.3 + 28.4 + 166.2 =$

(A) 628
(B) 650
(C) 700
(D) 816
(E) 826

7 min

SSAT Fractions, Decimals, and Percents Drill 2

1. Archie purchased 3 peppers, 2 onions, 8 carrots, 6 potatoes, and 1 head of kale. What was his ratio of onions to all food purchased?

(A) 2:19
(B) 2:23
(C) 1:10
(D) 1:11
(E) 1:18

2. Find the ratio of 48 minutes to 2 hours.

(A) 24:1
(B) 4:3
(C) 1:2
(D) 2:5
(E) 3:5

3. The softball team lost 18 games out of 27 games played. Find the ratio of games won to games lost.

(A) $\frac{1}{3}$

(B) $\frac{1}{2}$

(C) $\frac{3}{5}$

(D) $\frac{2}{3}$

(E) $\frac{3}{2}$

4. Estimate the total amount of snow that fell during 8 hours of a snowstorm, according to the table.

Snowstorm

Hour	in of snow
1	0.6
2	0.8
3	2.4
4	4.5
5	5.2
6	6.5
7	3.4
8	0.4

(A) 8 in
(B) 12 in
(C) 14 in
(D) 20 in
(E) 24 in

5. If 20% of a number is 90, then 60% of that same number is

(A) 60
(B) 180
(C) 270
(D) 450
(E) 540

6. A farmer sold 30% of his corn crop to an ethanol plant. He then sold 10% of the remainder of his crop to a grocery store chain. What percent of his original crop does he now have?

(A) 70%
(B) 65%
(C) 63%
(D) 60%
(E) 50%

7. If 80 percent of x is 9, what is 40 percent of $2x$?

(A)   3
(B)   6
(C)   9
(D)   12
(E)   18

$$\frac{9}{8} \cdot \frac{{\overset{5}{\cancel{40}}}}{1} = \frac{45}{4}$$

8. A ribbon $6\frac{1}{3}$ feet long can be cut into how many pieces each 4 inches long?

(A)   9
(B)   12
(C)   15
(D)   19
(E)   21

9. $0.050 \times 1,000.00 =$

(A)   0.05
(B)   0.5
(C)   5.0
(D)   50
(E)   500

10. Find the quotient of 7.2 and 1.8.

(A)   40

(B)   4

(C) $\dfrac{1}{4}$

(D) $\dfrac{1}{40}$

(E) $\dfrac{1}{400}$

10 min

ISEE Fractions, Decimals, and Percents Drill 1

1. Which of the following is NOT equal to $\frac{5}{6}$?

    (A) $\frac{0.5}{0.6}$

    (B)   0.833333

    (C) $0.8\overline{33}$

    (D) $\frac{7.5}{9.0}$

2. An actor has increased his Twitter following of 1,200 by 45%. How many followers does he now have?

    (A)   2,400
    (B)   2,000
    (C)   1,820
    (D)   1,740

3. Which is the largest fraction?

    (A) $\frac{3}{7}$

    (B) $\frac{4}{9}$

    (C) $\frac{6}{11}$

    (D) $\frac{7}{15}$

4. If the length of a rectangle is increased by 20% and the width is decreased by 40%, what is the percent decrease in the area of the rectangle?

    (A)   60%
    (B)   30%
    (C)   28%
    (D)   20%

5. What is the value of 4.2 + 5.6?

    (A) $10\frac{5}{8}$

    (B) $10\frac{1}{4}$

    (C) $9\frac{4}{5}$

    (D) $9\frac{2}{3}$

6. In the numeral 2.3145, what is the value of the digit 4?

    (A)   4

    (B) $\frac{4}{10}$

    (C) $\frac{4}{100}$

    (D) $\frac{4}{1,000}$

7. 9 is what percent of 6?

   (A) 33%
   (B) 66%
   (C) 133%
   (D) 150%

8. A $12 T-shirt is discounted by 40%. What is the amount saved in the purchase of the T-shirt?

   (A) $4.80
   (B) $7.20
   (C) $8.00
   (D) $16.80

9. What is the value of $11.25 - 4.67$?

   (A) 6.58
   (B) 7.42
   (C) 7.58
   (D) 7.68

10. What number is halfway between $\frac{2}{5}$ and $\frac{3}{8}$?

   (A) $\frac{31}{40}$
   (B) $\frac{31}{60}$
   (C) $\frac{5}{13}$
   (D) $\frac{31}{80}$

5 min

ISEE Fractions, Decimals, and Percents Drill 2

Directions: Using all information given in each question, compare the quantity in Column A to the quantity in Column B. All questions in Part Two have these answer choices:

    (A) The quantity in Column A is greater.
    (B) The quantity in Column B is greater.
    (C) The two quantities are equal.
    (D) The relationship cannot be determined from the information given.

In September, oranges were selling for $1.25 a pound. In October, the price of oranges was 10% higher than the September price. In November, the price of oranges was 10% lower than the October price.

Column A	Column B
$1.25	The price of oranges in November

C
1.

	Column A	Column B
	$\dfrac{5}{8}$ $\quad \dfrac{15}{24}$	$\dfrac{16}{24}$ $\quad \dfrac{2}{3}$

B
2.

Column A	Column B
10% of 100	20% of 50
10	10

C
3.

4. *A*

Column A	Column B
$-\dfrac{3}{4}$	$-\dfrac{2}{4} - \dfrac{1}{2}$

A house that was purchased in 2006 for $100,000 was sold in 2010 for $80,000.

Column A	Column B
The percent decrease in the house's value	25%

B
5.

20%

A house that was purchased in 2010 for $80,000 was sold in 2014 for $100,000.

Column A	Column B
The percent increase in the house's value	20%

C **6.**

20%

	Column A	Column B
7.	$\dfrac{7.2}{2.4}$ $\dfrac{72}{24}$	3

C

$\dfrac{36}{12}$ $\boxed{23}$

	Column A	Column B
8.	$\dfrac{13}{20}$	0.70

$\dfrac{7}{10}$ $\dfrac{14}{20}$

B

	Column A	Column B
9.	$\dfrac{1}{4}+\dfrac{1}{3}+\dfrac{1}{2}$	$\dfrac{4}{15}+\dfrac{5}{14}+\dfrac{7}{13}$

B

A flat-screen TV, regularly priced at $400, is on sale for 10% off, before sales tax of 10% is charged.

	Column A	Column B
10.	The price of the discounted TV, including tax.	$400

B

Fractions, Decimals, and Percents: Answers and Explanations

ANSWER KEY

SSAT Fractions, Decimals, and Percents
Drill 1

1. B
2. C
3. A
4. B
5. D
6. B
7. D
8. D
9. B
10. E

SSAT Fractions, Decimals, and Percents
Drill 2

1. C
2. D
3. B
4. E
5. C
6. C
7. C
8. D
9. D
10. B

ISEE Fractions, Decimals, and Percents
Drill 1

1. B
2. D
3. C
4. C
5. C
6. D
7. D
8. A
9. A
10. D

ISEE Fractions, Decimals, and Percents
Drill 2

1. A
2. B
3. C
4. B
5. B
6. A
7. C
8. B
9. B
10. B

SSAT Fractions, Decimals, and Percents Drill 1

1. **B** Compare the decimal values for each fraction in the answers to the decimal value of $\frac{3}{8}$, 0.375. Only (B), with a value of 0.357, is less.

 As $\frac{3}{8}$ is less than a half, first look to see which fraction are not less than a half. In fact, they all are. However, most of the fractions are fairly close to a half, while (B) is closer to one-third. As it is the smallest fraction, it must be the correct answer.

2. **C** Translate the English into a mathematical equation, replacing *of* with a multiplication sign and *is* with an equal sign. $\left(\frac{3}{4}\right) \times \left(\frac{4}{5}\right) = \frac{3}{5}$.

3. **A** Add the three fractions, first converting each to the lowest common denominator 60: $\frac{15}{60} + \frac{12}{60} + \frac{10}{60} = \frac{37}{60}$.

4. **B** Fractions represent a part to a whole, while ratios represent a part to a part. As the ratio of girls to boys is 8 to 4, the fraction of girls is $\frac{8}{12}$, or $\frac{2}{3}$. It is useful to know that $\frac{2}{3}$ as a percent rounds to 67. You can also set up the proportion to determine the percent: $\frac{2}{3} = \frac{x}{100}$.

5. **D** First take 30% of $450: $450 \times \dfrac{30}{100} = \$135$. As the question asks for the remaining amount, subtract $135 from $450: $315.

6. **B** Set up a proportion: $\dfrac{16}{80} = \dfrac{x}{100}$. Cross multiply: $1600 = 80x$. Divide both sides by 80: $x = 20$.

 Translate the English into a mathematical equation, replacing *is* with an equal sign, *what percent* with $\dfrac{x}{100}$, and *of* with a multiplication sign. $16 = \dfrac{x}{100} \times 80$, and solve for $x = 20$.

7. **D** *Three thousand five* is represented by 3,005. *Twelve thousandths* is represented by 0.012.

8. **D** Set up the division: $8.2\overline{)155.8}$. Move the decimals: $82\overline{)1{,}558}$. As two times 82 is greater than 155, start with a 1 over the second 5, multiply by 82, find the difference, bring down the 8, and determine how many times 82 goes into 738:

$$
\begin{array}{r}
19 \\
82{\overline{)\,1{,}558}} \\
-82 \\
\hline
738 \\
-738 \\
\hline
0
\end{array}
$$

 Set up a fraction and move the decimals: $\dfrac{1{,}558}{82}$. Reduce by 2: $\dfrac{779}{41}$. As 41×10 is 410, we know the result must be (D) or (E). Test (D): $41 \times 19 = 779$.

9. **B**   First determine how much 12 golf balls weigh: $12 \times 0.045 = 0.54$. Then, subtract that weight from the combined weight of the bag and the 12 balls for the weight of the bag: $0.62 - 0.54 = 0.08$ kilograms.

10. **E**   Stack the numbers so that the decimals are aligned. Then add normally. The result is 826.

SSAT Fractions, Decimals, and Percents Drill 2

1. **C**   A ratio represents a part to a part, although in this case the question is asking for a comparison of a part to a whole (usually called a fraction). As there are 20 vegetables and onions, the ratio of onions to vegetables is 2:20, or 1:10.

2. **D**   Convert the hours to minutes for an apples to apples comparison: 2 hours = 120 minutes. Thus, the ratio of 48 minutes to 120 minutes is 48:120, which reduces to 2:5.

3. **B**   A ratio represents a part to a part, while a fraction represents a part to a whole. As 18 games were lost out of a total of 27 played, 9 games won. Thus, the ratio of wins to losses is 9:18 or 1:2.

4. **E**   Calculate the total amount of snow by adding all of the values in the table. Add the inches, aligning by the decimal. Over 8 hours, it snowed 23.8 inches.

  Take advantage of the question's invitation to estimate. Start by adding up only the numbers to the left of the decimal. You already have 20 inches, and you have not included the decimal values. Thus, the total snow must be greater than 20, leaving only (E).

5. **C**   First, to find the number, set up a proportion, cross multiply, and divide by 20: $\frac{20}{100} = \frac{90}{x}$, $20x = 9{,}000$, and $x = 450$. Then find the answer by following the same procedure: $\frac{60}{100} = \frac{x}{450}$, $100x = 27{,}000$, and $x = 270$.

  You can use logic. 60% of a number is three times greater than 20% of the number. Thus, simply multiply 90 by 3.

6. **C**   Let x represent the value of the original crop. As he first sold 30%, he had 70% left, so he currently has $0.70x$. He then sold 10% of that remaining amount, so he had 90% of the amount left. Therefore, he now has $(0.90)(0.70)x$. Multiply the two numbers for a result of $0.63x$. This is 63% of the original amount.

  On percent questions without an original amount, you can plug in for the original amount. 100 is a good number. If the farmer sold 30% of his corn, he sold 30, leaving 70. If he then sold 10% of what is left, he sold 7. There are 63 left, or 63% of the original 100.

7. C Set up a proportion to solve for x, cross multiply, and divide by 80: $\frac{80}{100} = \frac{9}{x}$, $900 = 80x$, and $x = \frac{90}{8}$ or $\frac{45}{4}$. The next proportion calls for $2x$, which is $\frac{90}{4}$ or $\frac{45}{2}$. Follow the same procedure: $\frac{40}{100}$ or $\frac{x}{\frac{45}{2}}$, $900 = 100x$, and $x = 9$.

 If you cut a percent in half and double the number, the result will be the same.

8. D Convert the feet into inches, so you can easily divide: $6\frac{1}{3}$ feet is 6 feet and 4 inches, and 6 feet is 72 inches. So, you have 76 inches. Divide 76 by 4 to determine how many pieces will result.

9. D When you multiply by 1,000 you move the decimal over three places to the right. Thus, $0.050 \times 1,000.00 = 50$.

10. B Set up long division, and move the decimals: $18\overline{)72}$. Determine how many times 18 goes into 72. The answer is 4 without a remainder. Translate the English into a mathematical expression, replacing the *quotient* with a division sign. $7.2 \div 1.8 = 4$.

 Put 7.2 over 1.8, move the decimals, and reduce in steps: $\frac{7.2}{1.8} = \frac{72}{18} = \frac{36}{9} = 4$.

ISEE Fractions, Decimals, and Percents Drill 1

1. **B**   Choice (A) is the same as $\frac{5}{6}$, as you can move the two decimals. Choice (D) reduces to $\frac{5}{6}$. If you divide 6 into 5, you will get a repeating decimal, consistent with (C). As the decimal in (B) terminates, the value is not equal to $\frac{5}{6}$.

 Numbers divided by 3, 6, 7, and 9 generate repeating decimals. If you know this fact, you can select (B) without additional work.

2. **D**   Multiply 1,200 by 0.45 and add the result to 1,200, for a total of 1,740.

 A 45% increase is slightly less than an increase by half. An increase by half would add 600 followers for a total of 1,800. Thus, the answer must be a bit less than 1,800. Choice (D) is the only option.

3. **C**   Convert each fraction to a decimal or create common denominators for the fractions, so you can compare the numerators. Choice (C) is the largest.

 Notice that the numerators in (A), (B), and (D) are less than half of their denominators, which means each fraction is something less than one-half. In (C), the numerator is greater than half of its denominator, which means that it is something greater than one-half.

4. **C**   Assign x and y to the lengths of the rectangle. The original rectangle has an area of xy. If you add 20% to the length x, you will have a length of $1.2x$. If you reduce the length y by 40%, you will have a length of $0.6y$. Thus, the new area will be $0.72xy$, meaning the area was reduced by 0.28 or 28%.

 Plug in values for the length and width of the rectangle. Because a square is a type of rectangle and 10 is a great number for percent questions, use 10 for the length and width. The original area is 100. The larger side (20% greater than 10) is now 12 and the smaller side (40% reduction from 10) is now 6. Thus, the new area is 72, meaning there was a decrease of 28. As the original area was 100, 28 out of 100 is 28%.

5. **C** $4.2 + 5.6 = 9.8$. As 0.8 is equivalent to $\frac{4}{5}$, the answer is $9\frac{4}{5}$.

6. **D**   The digit 4 is in the thousandths place, which means its value is $\frac{4}{1,000}$.

7. **D**   Set up a proportion and cross multiply: $\frac{9}{6} = \frac{x}{100}$, so $x = 150$.

 Translate English into Math. *Is* means =, *what* means x (variable), and *of* means (times), so $9 = \frac{x}{100} \times 6$. Thus, $x = 150$.

8. **A**   To obtain the discount, or amount saved, multiply \$12 by 40% or 0.4. The result is \$4.80.

9. **A**   Stack the decimals and work carefully when borrowing tens. 11.25 − 4.67 = 6.58.

10. **D**   To find the number halfway between two fractions, you should find the average of the fractions. You will need to create a common denominator to add the fractions: $\frac{2}{5}+\frac{3}{8}=\frac{16}{40}+\frac{15}{40}=\frac{31}{40}$. Now, you can divide the sum by 2: $\frac{31}{40}\div 2=\frac{31}{40}\times\frac{1}{2}=\frac{31}{80}$.

ISEE Fractions, Decimals, and Percents Drill 2

1. **A**   The September price of $1.25/lb rose after a 10% increase in October to $1.38/lb, after rounding up: 0.10 × $1.25 = $0.125, and $1.25 + $0.125 = $1.375 ($1.38). In November, the price dropped after a 10% decrease to $1.24/lb, after rounding down: 0.10 × $1.38 = $0.138, and $1.38 − $0.138 = $1.242 ($1.24).

 In this type of question, the original price does not matter, so plug in $100 to keep things simple. Adding 10% brings the price to $110. Subtracting 10% brings the price to $99. Thus, increasing a price by a percent and then decreasing the price by the same percent will yield a price lower than the original amount.

2. **B**   Convert both fractions to decimals: $\frac{5}{8}=0.625$. $\frac{2}{3}=0.\overline{6}$. Alternatively, create common denominators: $\frac{15}{24}$ and $\frac{16}{24}$.

3. **C** 10% of 100 = 10 (0.10 × 100 = 10), and 20% of 50 = 10 (0.20 × 50 = 10).

 If you double the percent (10% to 20%) and halve the amount (100 to 50), the result will be the same.

4. **B** A negative closer to 0 is larger than one farther away.

5. **B** Percent change is calculated as follows: $\dfrac{\text{difference}}{\text{original}} \times 100$, so the house value decreased by 20%. $\dfrac{100,000 - 80,000}{100,000} = \dfrac{20,000}{100,000} \times 100 = 20\%$.

6. **A** Percent change is calculated as follows: $\dfrac{\text{difference}}{\text{original}} \times 100$, so the house value increased by 25%. $\dfrac{100,000 - 80,000}{80,000} = \dfrac{20,000}{80,000} \times 100 = 25\%$.

7. **C** Reduce the fraction in Column A in steps and stages: $\dfrac{7.2}{2.4} = \dfrac{3.6}{1.2} = \dfrac{1.8}{0.6} = \dfrac{0.9}{0.3} = \dfrac{0.3}{0.1} = 3$

 To make reducing easier, move the decimal over by one in the numerator and by one in the denominator: $\dfrac{7.2}{2.4} = \dfrac{72}{24}$.

8. **B** Convert Column A to a decimal for the comparison: $\dfrac{13}{20} = 0.65$.

9. **B**   You can add the fractions in each column by finding the common denominator for each column, but this will be terribly difficult for Column B. You can also convert each fraction into a decimal before adding them, which will make Column B a bit easier to deal with.

 This question is much easier if you think creatively about the fractions. As $\frac{4}{16} = \frac{1}{4}, \frac{4}{15} > \frac{1}{4}$. Similarly, as $\frac{5}{15} = \frac{1}{3}, \frac{5}{14} > \frac{1}{3}$. Likewise, as $\frac{7}{14} = \frac{1}{2}, \frac{7}{13} > \frac{1}{2}$.

Thus, the sum of the fractions in Column B is greater than the sum of the fractions in Column A.

10. **B**   The TV is discounted by 10% first: $0.10 \times \$400 = \$40$, and $\$400 - \$40 = \$360$. The tax is calculated on the sale price: $0.10 \times \$360 = \$36$, and $\$360 + \$36 = \$396$.

 In this type of question, the original price does not matter, so plug in $100 to keep things simple. Subtracting 10% brings the price to $90. Adding 10% brings the price to $99. Thus, decreasing a price by a percent and then increasing the price by the same percent will yield a price lower than the original amount.

Exponents and Roots

7 min

SSAT Exponents and Roots Drill 1

1. $\sqrt[3]{x^8} =$

   $\sqrt[3]{x \cdot x \cdot x \cdot x \cdot x \cdot x \cdot x \cdot x}$

   (A) $(x^2)^3 \sqrt[3]{x^2}$ $x^2 \sqrt[3]{x^2}$
   (B) x^{24}
   (C) x^5
   (D) x^2
   (E) $24x$

2. Simplify the variable expression: $\dfrac{13 f^4 t^9 u}{52 f^2 t^8 u}$

   (A) $\dfrac{tu}{4}$

   (B) $\dfrac{4}{ft}$

   $\dfrac{ft}{4}$

   (C) $\dfrac{ft}{4}$

   (D) $\dfrac{f^5 t^9 u^2}{4}$

   (E) $\dfrac{ft}{4u}$

3. $\left(-\dfrac{6}{5}\right)^3 =$ $-\dfrac{6}{5} \cdot -\dfrac{6}{5} \cdot -\dfrac{6}{5}$

   (A) $\dfrac{216}{125}$

   (B) $\dfrac{18}{15}$ $-\dfrac{216}{125}$

   (C) $-\dfrac{18}{125}$

   (D) $-\dfrac{18}{15}$

   (E) $-\dfrac{216}{125}$

4. Calculate $3a - b^2$ when $a = 6$ and $b = 4$.

   (A) 0
   (B) 1
   (C) 2 $3(6) - b(4)^2$
   (D) 14 $18 - 16$
   (E) 34 $= 2$

5. If $\left(x^a\right)^3 = x^{15}$ and $\dfrac{x^b}{x^2} = x^7$, then $b - a =$

   (A) -4 $a = 5$
   (B) -2 $b = 9$
   (C) 2
   (D) 4
   (E) 14

6. If $abc \neq 0$, $a^0 + b^0 + c^0 =$

   (A) abc $1 + 1 + 1$
   (B) 0
   (C) 1
   (D) 3
   (E) It cannot be determined from the information given.

7. If $0 < x < 1$, which of the following inequalities is correct?

   (A) $\sqrt{x} < x < x^2$
   (B) $x^2 < x < \sqrt{x}$
   (C) $x < x^2 < \sqrt{x}$
   (D) $\sqrt{x} < x^2 < x$
   (E) $x < \sqrt{x} < x^2$

8. $(2.4 \times 10^x)(3.0 \times 10^y) =$ $7.2 \times 10^{x+y}$

   (A) $72 \times 10^{x+y}$
   (B) $7.2 \times 10^{x+y}$
   (C) $7.2 \times 10^{x+y+1}$
   (D) 7.2×10^{xy}
   (E) 72×10^{xy}

9. $100,000 + (4.0 \times 10^3) =$

   (A)   4,000
   (B)   10,040
   (C)   10,400
   (D)   100,400
   (E)   104,000

10. $\left(\sqrt{27}\right)\left(\sqrt{3}\right) =$

   (A) $3\sqrt{3}$
   (B)   9
   (C) $9\sqrt{3}$
   (D)   18
   (E)   81

5 min

SSAT Exponents and Roots Drill 2

1. Simplify the variable expression: $(-2x^2y^5)^3$

   (A) $-2x^5y^8$
   (B) $-2x^6y^{15}$
   (C) $-6x^6y^{15}$
   (D) $-8x^6y^{15}$
   (E) $8x^6y^{15}$

2. Calculate $a^2b - ab^2 + (ab)^2$ when $a = 5$ and $b = 2$.

   (A)   20
   (B)   50
   (C)   100
   (D)   130
   (E)   170

3. Simplify the variable expression: $\dfrac{(2x^3y^2)^3}{4x^6y^9}$

   (A) $4x^3y^{-3}$

   (B) $2x^3y^{-3}$

   (C) x^3y^{-3}

   (D) y^{-3}

   (E) $\dfrac{1}{2}x^{-3}y^{-7}$

4. $(\sqrt[3]{x})^5 =$

   (A) $(x)\left(\sqrt[3]{x^2}\right)$

   (B) x^{15}

   (C) x^2

   (D) $\sqrt[15]{x}$

   (E) $\left(x^2\right)\left(\sqrt[3]{2x}\right)$

5. $\left(-\dfrac{4}{3}\right)^2 =$

   (A) $-\dfrac{16}{9}$

   (B) $-\dfrac{8}{6}$

   (C) $\dfrac{16}{9}$

   (D)   9

   (E)   16

6. $\sqrt[3]{8} \times \sqrt[2]{4^3} =$

   (A)   64
   (B)   32
   (C)   16
   (D)   8
   (E)   4

7. Simplify the variable expression: $\dfrac{(ab)^3 c^0}{a^3b^4}$

   (A) $\dfrac{1}{a}$

   (B) $\dfrac{1}{b}$

   (C) $\dfrac{c}{b}$

   (D) a

   (E) b

8. Calculate $(x)(x^2)$ when $x = -4$.

    (A) 64
    (B) 16
    (C) 4
    (D) −16
    (E) −64

9. $(5)\left(2^{\frac{1}{2}}\right)^2 =$

    (A) 25

    (B) 10

    (C) $5\sqrt{2}$

    (D) $\sqrt{10}$

    (E) $\dfrac{1}{10}$

10. Simplify the variable expression: $\dfrac{a^5b^{14}}{a^3b^6}$

    (A) a^2b^8

    (B) a^8b^3

    (C) a^8b^{20}

    (D) a^2b^5

    (E) $\dfrac{1}{a^2b^8}$

6 min

ISEE Exponents and Roots Drill 1

1. What is the value of the expression
$$\frac{2\left(2^2 + 2^3\right)}{8\left(2 + 4\right)}?$$

$\dfrac{2^3 + 2^4}{16 + 32}$

   (A) $\dfrac{1}{4}$

   (B) $\dfrac{1}{2}$

   (C) 2

   (D) 4

2. What is the value of the numerical expression $5.3 \times 10^6 + 6.2 \times 10^4$?

   (A) 6.152×10^4
   (B) 5.92×10^5
   (C) 5.362×10^6
   (D) 1.25×10^{10}

3. Which expression is equivalent to the expression $\sqrt{36x^{12}}$?

   (A) $18x^3$
   (B) $18x^6$
   (C) $6x^3$
   (D) $6x^6$

4. $\dfrac{6^8}{6^4} =$

   (A) 6^2
   (B) 6^4
   (C) 6^{16}
   (D) 6^{32}

5. $(-2x^2y^3)^4 =$

   (A) $-16x^8y^{12}$
   (B) $-16x^6y^7$
   (C) $16x^6y^7$
   (D) $16x^8y^{12}$

6. If $81^3 = 3^x$, then $x =$

   (A) 9
   (B) 12
   (C) 27
   (D) 30

7. $\dfrac{(ab)^4 c^0}{a^5 b^4} = ?$

   (A) 0

   (B) 1

   (C) $\dfrac{1}{a}$

   (D) $\dfrac{c}{a}$

8. Which expression is equivalent to the expression shown?

$$\frac{24\left(\sqrt[4]{16} + \sqrt{36x^2}\right)}{\sqrt{64}}$$

   (A) $12 + 18x$

   (B) $36x$

   (C) $\dfrac{12x\sqrt{14}}{17}$

   (D) $30x^2$

9. The approximate distance around the equator of the Earth, which is 2.5×10^4 miles, is about how many times the approximate distance from Detroit, MI, to Cleveland, OH, which is 5.0×10^1 miles?

(A) 2.0×10^6
(B) 5.0×10^4
(C) 2.0×10^4
(D) 5.0×10^2

10. $\dfrac{7.2 \times 10^6}{4.5 \times 10^{-2}} = ?$

(A) 1.6×10^{12}
(B) 1.6×10^8
(C) 1.6×10^7
(D) 1.6×10^4

$(3 \times 3 \times 3 \times 3)^3 = 3^x$

$3^{12} = 3^x$

8 min

ISEE Exponents and Roots Drill 2

1. If x and y are both integers, what is $(8.0 \times 10^x)(6.0 \times 10^y)$ expressed in scientific notation?

    (A) 48.0×10^{xy}
    (B) $4.8 \times 10^{x+y+1}$
    (C) $4.8 \times 10^{x+y}$
    (D) 4.8×10^{xy}

Directions: Using all information given in each question, compare the quantity in Column A to the quantity in Column B. All questions in Part Two have these answer choices:

(A) The quantity in Column A is greater.
(B) The quantity in Column B is greater.
(C) The two quantities are equal.
(D) The relationship cannot be determined from the information given.

	Column A	Column B
2.	$(1.5 \times 10^5)+(2.6 \times 10^{-3})$	$(9.8 \times 10^4) + (8.7 \times 10^{-2})$

	Column A	Column B
3.	$(6.0 \times 10^2)(7.0 \times 10^2)$	$\dfrac{4.2 \times 10^9}{4.2 \times 10^5}$

	Column A	Column B
4.	x	x^2

5.

Column A	Column B
$\dfrac{2^{16}}{2^{-4}}$ 2^{20}	$2^4 \times 2^5$ 2^9

Ⓐ

6.

Column A	Column B
27^5	$\dfrac{3^{15}}{\times 3}$ 27^5

Ⓒ

7.

Column A	Column B
$(0.8)^{11}$	$(0.8)^{12}$

Ⓐ

8.

Column A	Column B
$\left(\dfrac{1}{12}\right)^4$ $\dfrac{1}{12^4}$	$\left(\dfrac{1}{13}\right)^4$ $\dfrac{1}{13^4}$

Ⓐ

9.

Column A	Column B
$\sqrt{\dfrac{1}{12}}$	$\sqrt{\dfrac{1}{13}}$

Ⓐ

10.

Column A	Column B
$\sqrt{3.7}$ Ⓑ	$\sqrt{4.7}$

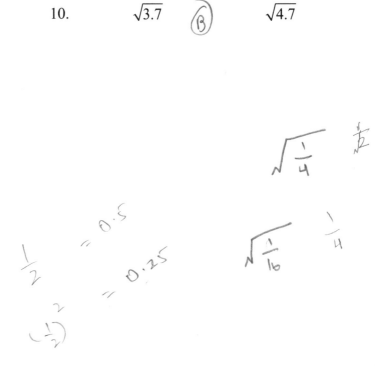

$\sqrt{\dfrac{1}{4}}$ $\dfrac{1}{2}$

$\sqrt{\dfrac{1}{16}}$ $\dfrac{1}{4}$

$\dfrac{1}{2} = 0.5$

$\left(\dfrac{1}{2}\right)^2 = 0.25$

Exponents and Roots: Answers and Explanations

ANSWER KEY

**SSAT Exponents
and Roots
Drill 1**

1. A
2. C
3. E
4. C
5. D
6. D
7. B
8. B
9. E
10. B

**SSAT Exponents
and Roots
Drill 2**

1. D
2. D
3. B
4. A
5. C
6. C
7. B
8. E
9. B
10. A

**ISEE Exponents
and Roots
Drill 1**

1. B
2. C
3. D
4. B
5. D
6. B
7. C
8. A
9. D
10. B

**ISEE Exponents
and Roots
Drill 2**

1. B
2. A
3. A
4. D
5. A
6. C
7. A
8. A
9. A
10. B

SSAT Exponents and Roots Drill 1

1. **A** To simplify a cube root, find any cubes and remove them. x^3 appears twice within x^8, so you can pull out x^2. There will still be two x values under the root, so leave x^2 there: $(x^2)\sqrt[3]{x^2}$.

 You can expand the expressions out. x^8 becomes $(x)(x)(x)(x)(x)(x)(x)(x)$. As we are dealing with cubes, combine the x terms to $(x^3)(x^3)(x^2)$. Therefore, there are two cubes to remove from the cube root (each one becoming x), and x^2 is left behind. Outside of the radical, all roots are multiplied. Thus, $(x^2)\sqrt[3]{x^2}$.

2. **C** Simplify the number terms first. $\frac{13}{52} = \frac{1}{4}$. Simplify the variables, using the rules of exponents: When like bases are divided, subtract the exponents. $\frac{f^3}{f^2} = f^{3-2} = f$; $\frac{t^5}{t^4} = t^{5-4} = t$; $\frac{u}{u} = u^{1-1} = 1$. This yields $\frac{ft}{4}$.

3. **E** Cube the numerator and the denominator. Remember that the cube of a negative base will be negative. $\left(-\frac{6}{5}\right)^3 = -\frac{216}{125}$.

4. **C** Replace the variables in the expression with the values provided. $3(6) - (4^2) = 18 - 16 = 2$.

5. **D** Solve for the variables by applying the rules of exponents. When an exponential expression is raised to another power, multiply the exponents. Therefore, $(x^a)^3 = x^{3a} = x^{15}$. Therefore, $3a = 15$, and $a = 5$. When exponential expressions with like bases are divided, subtract the exponents. Therefore, $\frac{x^b}{x^2} = x^{b-2} = x^7$. Therefore, $b - 2 = 7$, and $b = 9$. $9 - 5 = 4$.

6. **D**   Any number (other than 0) raised to a power of 0 is 1. Therefore, the value of the expression is 3.

7. **B**   When a fraction between 0 and 1 is raised to a power greater than 1, the fraction becomes smaller. Likewise, when a root is taken of a fraction between 0 and 1, the fraction becomes larger. Thus, $x^2 < x < \sqrt{x}$.

  Plug in a number for x. If $x = \dfrac{1}{4}$, then $\sqrt{\dfrac{1}{4}} = \dfrac{1}{2}$, and $\left(\dfrac{1}{4}\right)^2 = \dfrac{1}{16}$. Only (B) provides the correct range of the values.

8. **B**   Multiply the number terms inside the scientific notation first: $2.4 \times 3.0 = 7.2$. Multiply the exponential expressions with a base of ten. With like bases, add the exponents when you multiply the bases. $(10^x)(10^y) = 10^{x+y}$.

9. **E**   Expand the scientific notation: $4.0 \times 10^3 = 4{,}000$. Add to 100,000 for a total of 104,000.

10. **B**   You can multiply roots together, even if the numbers under the roots are different. Thus, $\sqrt{27} \times \sqrt{3} = \sqrt{27 \times 3} = \sqrt{81} = 9$.

SSAT Exponents and Roots Drill 2

1. **D**   The power applies to everything within the parentheses. A negative number raised to an odd power yields an odd result: $(-2)^3 = -8$. When exponential expressions are raised to a power, multiply the exponents. Thus, $(x^2)^3 = x^6$, and $(y^5)^3 = y^{15}$.

2. **D**   Replace the variables in the expression with the values provided and calculate. $(5^2)(2) - (5)(2^2) + (2 \times 5)^2 = 50 - 20 + 100 = 130$.

3. **B**   Start with the numerator. The power applies to all terms within the parentheses. Deal with the number first: $2^3 = 8$. When exponential expressions are raised to a power, multiply the exponents. Thus, $(x^3)^3 = x^9$, and $(y^2)^3 = y^6$. Now address the denominator, starting with the numbers: $\frac{8}{4} = 2$. When exponential expressions with the same base are divided, subtract the exponents: $\frac{x^9}{x^6} = x^{9-6} = x^3$, and $\frac{y^6}{y^9} = y^{6-9} = y^{-3}$.

4. **A**   According to PEMDAS, you can move the exponent under the root: $\left(\sqrt[3]{x}\right)^5 = \sqrt[3]{x^5}$. There is one x^3 included in x^5, so you can pull that out as x. Remaining under the root is x^2: $x\sqrt[3]{x^2}$.

 You can expand out the expression: $(\sqrt[3]{x})^5 = (\sqrt[3]{x})(\sqrt[3]{x})(\sqrt[3]{x})(\sqrt[3]{x})(\sqrt[3]{x})$, or $\sqrt[3]{(x)(x)(x)(x)(x)}$. This can be expressed as $\sqrt[3]{(x^3)(x^2)}$. Therefore, there is one cube to remove from the cube root, but x^2 is left behind: $x\sqrt[3]{x^2}$.

5. **C** The exponent applies to the numerator and denominator. A negative term raised to any even power will yield a positive result. Thus, $\left(-\dfrac{4}{3}\right)^2 = \dfrac{16}{9}$.

6. **C** As you cannot combine a square root and a cube root, simplify the different roots first: $\sqrt[3]{8} = 2$, and $\sqrt[2]{4^3} = \sqrt[2]{64} = 8$. $2 \times 8 = 16$.

7. **B** First, raise the term within the parentheses to a power of 3. $(ab)^3 = a^3 b^3$. When you divide exponential expressions with the same base, subtract the exponents. $\dfrac{a^3}{a^3} = a^{3-3} = a^0$, and $\dfrac{b^3}{b^4} = b^{3-4} = b^{-1}$ or $\dfrac{1}{b}$. As any number other than 0 raised to a power of 0 equals 1, $a^0 = 1$, and $c^0 = 1$.

8. **E** Replace the variables in the expression with the values provided and calculate. $(-4)(-4^2) = (-4)(16) = -64$.

9. **B** When exponential terms are raised to a power, multiply the exponents. $\left(2^{\frac{1}{2}}\right)^2 = 2^1 = 2$. Thus, $5 \times 2 = 10$.

10. **A** When you divide exponential expressions with the same base, subtract the exponents. $\dfrac{a^5}{a^3} = a^{5-3} = a^2$, and $\dfrac{b^{14}}{b^6} = b^{14-6} = b^8$.

ISEE Exponents and Roots Drill 1

1. **B** The exponential terms in the parentheses can't be simplified, so solve them: $2^2 = 4$, $2^3 = 8$, and $4 + 8 = 12$. Simplify the resulting fraction to $\frac{1}{2}$.

 Remember to divide before you multiply when dealing with fractions. Reducing first avoids large products.

2. **C** Convert each term to a decimal before adding them: $3 \times 10^6 = 5,300,000$ and $6.2 \times 10^4 = 62,000$. Stack them by their digits correctly to get the sum of $5,362,000$, which is 5.362×10^6.

3. **D** The square root of 36 is 6. For the variable, you must use the rules of exponents. If the bases are the same, add the exponents when you multiply the terms. The term x^{12} represents a base of x that was squared, i.e., multiplied by itself. Thus the two exponents added were the same value and produced a sum of 12. $(x^6)(x^6) = x^{12}$. To find the square root, divide the exponent in half. $\sqrt{x^{12}} = x^6$.

 The square root of an exponent will be one-half of the exponent.

4. **B** The terms in the numerator and denominator have the same base, so follow the rules of exponents. Subtract the exponents when the terms are divided. $\frac{6^8}{6^4} = 6^4$.

5. **D** Follow the rules of exponents. The power applies to all terms inside the parentheses. A negative base raised to an even power like 4 produces a positive result, in this case 16. When an exponential term is raised to a power, multiply the exponents. $(x^2)^4 = x^8$ and $(y^3)^4 = y^{12}$.

6. **B** Simplify 81^3 to a base of 3 so the terms have the same base. $81 = 3^4$ so $81^3 = (3^4)^3$. When an exponential term is raised to a power, multiply the exponents. $(3^4)^3 = 3^{12}$. Thus, $x = 12$.

7. **C** Any base to the zero power equals 1. So $c^0 = 1$, so c will not appear in the simplified answer. When an exponential term is raised to a power, multiply the exponents. The power applies to both terms inside the parentheses. $(ab)^4 = (a^4)(b^4)$. With like bases, subtract the exponents when the terms are divided. $\frac{(a^4)(b^4)}{(a^5)(b^4)} = a^{-1}$ or $\frac{1}{a}$.

8. **A** Simplify the roots first. $\sqrt{16} = 4$, $\sqrt{36x^2} = 6x$, and $\sqrt{64} = 8$. Terms that are unlike (4 and $6x$) can't be added. Reduce. $\frac{24}{8}$ to 3. Last, distribute the 3 by multiplying it by 4 and $6x$ to get a product of $12 + 18x$.

9. **D** *How many times* tells you to divide. $2.5 \times 10^4 = 25{,}000$ and $5.0 \times 10^1 = 50$. The result is 500, which is 5.0×10^2.

10. **B** $\dfrac{7.2}{4.5} = \dfrac{8}{5}$ or 1.6. When dividing exponential terms with like bases, subtract the

exponents. $\dfrac{10^6}{10^{-2}} = 10^8$, and the final simplified form equals 1.6×10^8.

All of the answer choices contain 1.6, so it is not necessary to solve that value, although you do need to determine whether the result will require moving the decimal to maintain scientific notation. If you see that the result will maintain scientific notation, all you need to do is focus on the exponent.

ISEE Exponents and Roots Drill 2

1. **B** With like bases, add the exponents when the terms are multiplied. $(10^x)(10^y) = 10^{x+y}$. The product of the two numerical terms, 8.0 and 6.0 equals 48. However, 48 must be expressed as 4.8×10^1 in scientific notation. Because this requires multiplying the exponents again, add the 1 to the exponent: 10^{x+y+1}.

You can plug in values for x and y. If x and y are both set to 2, you have $800 \times 600 = 480,000$. Choice (B) matches.

2. **A** Column A: $1.5 \times 10^5 + 2.6 \times 10^{-3} = 150,000 + 0.0026 = 150,000.0026$.
Column B: $9.8 \times 10^4 + 8.7 \times 10^{-2} = 98,000 + 0.087 = 98,000.087$.

The negative exponents will have minimal effect. Raising 10 to the fifth power results in a greater value than does raising 10 to the fourth power.

3. **A** Column A: $(6.0 \times 10^2)(7.0 \times 10^2) = 42 \times 10^4 = 4.2 \times 10^5$.

Column B: $\dfrac{4.2 \times 10^9}{4.2 \times 10^5} = 1 \times 10^4$, or just 10^4.

4. **D** It is not possible to know which column is greater, because x does not have to increase when squared. It could remain the same (0 or 1) or become smaller (a fraction between 0 and 1).

 Plug in an easy number for x, such as 2. In this case, Column B is greater, which means that Column A is not *always* greater and that the two columns are not *always* equal. Eliminate (A) and (C). Now try $x = 0$. The two columns are not equal, which means Column B is not *always* greater. Eliminate (B).

5. **A** Simplify both columns, following the rules of exponents. When dividing like bases, subtract the exponents. When multiplying like bases, add the exponents. Column A equals 2^{20} and Column B equals 2^9.

6. **C** Create a common base by changing 27 to 3^3 : $(3^3)^5$. When a power is raised to a power, multiply the exponents: 3^{15}.

7. **A** A decimal gets smaller when raised to a positive power greater than 1. The greater the exponent with respect to a particular decimal, the smaller the result.

 If you are not sure what happens to decimals raised to a power, try a simple fraction (decimals and fractions are the same), such as $\dfrac{1}{2}$. As $\left(\dfrac{1}{2}\right)^2 = \dfrac{1}{4}$, and $\left(\dfrac{1}{2}\right)^3 = \dfrac{1}{8}$, you can see that the larger the exponent, the smaller the result.

8. **A** A fraction gets smaller when raised to a positive power greater than 1. The smaller the fraction with respect to a particular exponent, the smaller the result.

 If you are not sure what happens to fractions raised to a power, try simple fractions such as $\frac{1}{2}$ and $\frac{1}{3}$. As $\left(\frac{1}{2}\right)^2 = \frac{1}{4}$, and $\left(\frac{1}{3}\right)^2 = \frac{1}{9}$, you can see that the smaller the fraction, the smaller the result.

9. **A** A fraction gets larger when the square root is taken. The larger the fraction, the larger the result.

10. **B** Any number greater than 1 gets smaller when the square root is taken, including numbers greater than 1 with fractions or decimals. The smaller the number, the smaller the result.

Factors and
Multiples

SSAT Factors and Multiples Drill 1

1. Let x be an integer such that $41 < x < 60$. What is the probability that x is divisible by 3 but NOT divisible by 2?

   (A) $\dfrac{1}{6}$

   (B) $\dfrac{1}{5}$

   (C) $\dfrac{1}{4}$

   (D) $\dfrac{1}{3}$

   (E) $\dfrac{1}{2}$

   $42 - 59$
   $1\,2\,3\,4\,5$
   $45, 51, 57$
   $\dfrac{3}{18} = \dfrac{1}{6}$

2. All of the following products are equal EXCEPT

   (A) $1 \times \dfrac{1}{3}$

   (B) $2 \times \dfrac{1}{6}$

   (C) $3 \times \dfrac{1}{9}$

   (D) $4 \times \dfrac{1}{12}$

   (E) $5 \times \dfrac{1}{45}$

3. If $x + y$ is divisible by 7, which of the following is also divisible by 7?

   (A) $xy + 7$

   (B) $x + 7y$

   (C) $7x + y$

   (D) $2x + 2y$

   (E) $\dfrac{x - y}{7}$

4. How many integers between 12 and 36 are multiples of 3?

   (A) 9
   (B) 8
   (C) 7
   (D) 6
   (E) 5

5. What is the greatest common factor of 64 and 80?

   (A) 4
   (B) 6
   (C) 8
   (D) 16
   (E) 20

SSAT Factors and Multiples Drill 2

1. What is the least common multiple of 5, 6, and 7?

   (A) 210
   (B) 105
   (C) 42
   (D) 35
   (E) 30

2. A number that is a multiple of both 2 and 3 must have which of the following as one of its factors?

   (A) 4
   (B) 6
   (C) 7
   (D) 8
   (E) 12

3. Let x be an integer such that $21 < x < 43$. What is the probability that x is divisible by BOTH 2 and 3?

   (A) $\dfrac{3}{7}$

   (B) $\dfrac{8}{21}$

   (C) $\dfrac{4}{21}$

   (D) $\dfrac{1}{3}$

   (E) $\dfrac{1}{6}$

4. To simplify the expression $\dfrac{1}{2} + \dfrac{3}{4} + \dfrac{4}{7}$, each fraction must have a denominator of

   (A) 2
   (B) 4
   (C) 7
   (D) 14
   (E) 28

5. If $x + y$ is a multiple of 11, which of the following must also be a multiple of 11?

   (A) $11x + 11y$

   (B) $xy + 11$

   (C) $11x + y$

   (D) $x + 11y$

   (E) $\dfrac{x + y}{11}$

ISEE Factors and Multiples Drill 1

1. If *x* is a factor of 16 and *y* is a factor of 28, which is the least value that *xy* could be a factor of?

    (A) 448
    (B) 112
    (C) 2
    (D) 1

2. If *a* and *b* are prime numbers, what is the least common multiple of 12*a*, 15*ab*, and 6*a*^{2}?

    (A) 60*a*^{2}*b*
    (B) 60*ab*
    (C) 12*a*^{2}*b*
    (D) 12*ab*

3. If *n* is a positive integer, then the product of 14*n* and 15*n* is NOT necessarily divisible by which of the following?

    (A) 5
    (B) 10
    (C) 12
    (D) 21

4. What is the sum of the prime factors of 34?

    (A) 18
    (B) 19
    (C) 20
    (D) 21

5. What is the least common multiple of 24 and 32?

    (A) 768
    (B) 96
    (C) 64
    (D) 8

ISEE Factors and Multiples Drill 2

Directions: Using all information given in each question, compare the quantity in Column A to the quantity in Column B. All questions in Part Two have these answer choices:

(A) The quantity in Column A is greater.
(B) The quantity in Column B is greater.
(C) The two quantities are equal.
(D) The relationship cannot be determined from the information given.

	Column A		Column B
1.	The number of factors of 60	(A)	10

	Column A		Column B
4.	The least common multiple of 48 and 96	(C)	96

	Column A		Column B
2.	The number of distinct prime factors of 60	(B)	4

	Column A		Column B
5.	The number of even prime numbers	(A)	0

	Column A		Column B
3.	The greatest common factor of 48 and 96	(A)	24

Factors and
Multiples: Answers
and Explanations

ANSWER KEY

SSAT Factors and Multiples Drill 1
1. A
2. E
3. D
4. C
5. D

SSAT Factors and Multiples Drill 2
1. A
2. B
3. C
4. E
5. A

ISEE Factors and Multiples Drill 1
1. D
2. A
3. C
4. B
5. B

ISEE Factors and Multiples Drill 2
1. A
2. B
3. A
4. C
5. A

SSAT Factors and Multiples Drill 1

1. **A** List out the integers greater than 41 and less than 60. Cross out all the even integers, since all even integers are divisible by 2. Circle the remaining numbers that are divisible by 3: 45, 51, and 57. As there are three numbers that are divisible by 3 but not by 2, and there are a total of 18 numbers in the range, the probability is $\frac{3}{18} = \frac{1}{6}$.

2. **E** Solve each answer choice to determine which is different from the others. The product in each of (A), (B), (C), and (D) is $\frac{1}{3}$. The product in (E) is $\frac{1}{15}$.

3. **D** If $x + y$ is divisible by 7, then (D) must also be divisible by 7 because you can factor out a 2: $2(x + y)$. It must be the case that 2 times a number divisible by 7 is also divisible by 7.

 Plug in numbers for x and y, ideally avoiding numbers that individually are divisible by 7. A good pair would be $x = 3$ and $y = 4$. Test these numbers in the answer choices to see which will be divisible by 7. Only (D) works.

4. **C** List out the multiples between (not including) 12 and 36 that are multiples of 3: 15, 18, 21, 24, 27, 30, and 33.

5. **D** List the factors for each number in pairs: The factors of 64 are 1, 64, 2, 32, 4, 16, and 8. The factors of 80 are 1, 80, 2, 40, 4, 20, 5, 16, 8, and 10. The greatest common factor is 16.

SSAT Factors and Multiples Drill 2

1. **A** Break 6 into prime factors (5 and 7 are already prime): 2 and 3. Thus, the least common multiple must include 2, 3, 5, and 7. The result is 210.

 You can list out multiples of all three numbers, but you will quickly see that this is time consuming. You can also test the answers to see which one or ones have 5, 6, and 7 as factors. Of the two answers that are divisible by all three numbers, choice (A) is smaller.

2. **B** A number that is a multiple of 2 and 3 is also a multiple of 6. Thus, 6 must be a factor of any multiple of 6.

3. **C** List out the integers greater than 21 and less than 42. Cross out all the odd integers, since no odd integer is divisible by 2. Circle the remaining numbers that are divisible by 3: 24, 30, 36, and 42. As there are four numbers that are divisible by both 2 and 3, and there are a total of 21 numbers in the range, the probability is $\frac{4}{21}$.

4. **E** This question is asking for the least common multiple. Break 4 into prime factors (2 and 7 are already prime): 2 and 2. Thus, the least common multiple must include 2, 2, and 7. The result is 28.

 You can list out multiples of all three numbers, but you will quickly see that this is time consuming. You can also test the answers to see which one or ones have 2, 4, and 7 as factors. Only (E) does.

5. **A**   If $x + y$ is divisible by 11, then choice (A) must also be divisible by 11 because you can factor out an 11: $11(x + y)$. It must be the case that 11 times a number divisible by 11 is also divisible by 11.

  Plug in numbers for x and y, ideally avoiding numbers that individually are divisible by 11. A good pair would be $x = 5$ and $y = 6$. Test these numbers in the answer choices to see which will be divisible by 11. Only (A) works.

ISEE Factors and Multiples Drill 1

1. **D**   List out the factors for both 16 and 28, putting the factors in pairs to be sure you catch all of them. x could be 1, 16, 2, 8, or 4. y could be 1, 28, 2, 14, 4, or 7. xy could be as small as 1 and as great as 448, but the least value xy could be a factor of is 1.

2. **A**   Begin with the numbers. The least common multiple of the numerical terms is 60. Move on to a. The least common multiple of a and a^2 is a^2. Now address b. As there is only one b, the least common multiple is b. Thus, the least common multiple is $60a^2b$.

  a. If $a = 3$, the least common multiple of 3 and 9 is 9.

3. **C**   Break 14 and 15 into factors, using pairs. The factors of 14 are 1, 14, 2, and 7. The factors of 15 are 1, 15, 3, and 5. Check each answer to determine whether it can be divided by the product of any two factors. 12 does not work because there is no factor of 4 to multiply by 3 (one of the factors of 15).

  The *n* is not necessary to the solution. However, if the *n* is distracting, you can plug in. If you plug in an even number for *n*, all four answer choices will work. If you plug in an odd number for *n*, 12 will not go into your product in (C).

4. **B**   Break 34 into its prime factors, 2 and 17. Add them for a sum of 19.

5. **B**   Break 24 and 32 into prime factors. The prime factors of 24 are 2, 2, 2, and 3. The prime factors of 32 are 2, 2, 2, 2, and 2. Thus the least common multiple must include the five 2s from 32 and the 3 from 24. The result is 96.

  List out the first few multiples for the two numbers until you have a common multiple. The first four multiples of 24 are 24, 48, 72, and 96. The first three multiples of 32 are 32, 64, and 96. Thus, 96 is the least common multiple.

ISEE Factors and Multiples Drill 2

1. **A**   List the factors of 60 by pairs: 1, 60, 2, 30, 3, 20, 4, 15, 5, 12, 6, and 10. There are 12 factors of 60.

2. **B** Break 60 into its prime factors: 2, 2, 3, and 5. As distinct means different, ignore the second 2. There are three distinct prime factors.

3. **A** List out the factors for both 48 and 96 by pairs. The factors of 48 are 1, 48, 2, 24, 3, 16, 4, 12, 6, and 8. The factors of 96 are 1, 96, 2, 48, 3, 32, 4, 24, 6, 16, 8, and 12. The greatest common factor is 48.

4. **C** Break 48 and 96 into prime numbers. The prime numbers of 48 are 2, 2, 2, 2, and 3. The prime numbers of 96 are 2, 2, 2, 2, 2, and 3. Thus, the least common multiple must include all of the 2s from 96 and a 3. The result is 96.

 List out the first few multiples for the two numbers until you have a common multiple. The first two multiples of 48 are 48 and 96. The first multiple of 96 is 96. Thus, 96 is the least common multiple.

5. **A** There is one even prime number: 2.

Solving for *x*

7 min

SSAT Solving for *x* Drill 1

1. Peter has *x* marbles more than Lewis. Lewis has 9 marbles. How many marbles does Peter have?

    (A) $\dfrac{9}{x}$

    (B) $9 - x$

    (C) $\dfrac{x}{9}$

    (D) $9 + x$

    (E) $x - 9$

2. When $Y + Z = 17$ and $2X + Z = 17$, what is the value of X?

    (A) 17
    (B) 9
    (C) −9
    (D) −5
    (~~E~~) It cannot be determined from the information given.

3. The mass required to engage the sensor for a passenger-side airbag is 108 pounds. What is the smallest mass a person carrying a 5 kg backpack can be to ensure the sensor is engaged? (1 kg = 2.20 lb).

    (A) 103 lbs
    (B) 97 lbs
    (C) 54 lbs
    (D) 49 lbs
    (E) 11 lbs

4. If $27 \times P = 27$, then $27 - P =$

    (A) 26

    (B) 28

    (C) 1

    (D) $\dfrac{1}{27}$

    (E) 0

5. If $Y > 5$, then $4Y + 7$ could be

    (A) 28
    (B) 27
    (C) 26
    (D) 25
    (E) 24

6. Which of the following gives the number of seconds in *m* minutes, *h* hours, and 2 seconds?

    (A) $60m + 360h + 2$

    (B) $60m + 3,600h + 2$

    (C) $m + 60h + 2$

    (D) $\dfrac{60}{m} + \dfrac{3,600}{h} + 2$

    (E) $\dfrac{m}{60} + \dfrac{h}{3,600} + 2$

7. If $x < 0$, which of the following is greatest?

    (A) $4x + 1$

    (B) $x + 1$

    (C) $x - 1$

    (D) $\dfrac{x}{x} + 1$

    (E) $x + \dfrac{1}{x}$

8. Ruiwen plans to give a box of raisins to each of her 35 party guests. There are 8 boxes of raisins in each package. How many packages must she buy?

    (A) 3
    (B) 4
    (C) 5
    (D) 6
    (E) 9

9. There are 21 flats of pansies at a garden center that need to be delivered. If at least one but no more than six flats must go into each vehicle and no two vehicles have the same number of flats, what is the smallest number of vehicles required to deliver the 21 flats of pansies?

    (A)   21
    (B)   12
    (C)   10
    (D)   8
    (E)   6

10. Two numbers, whose difference is 7, add up to 55. Identify the smaller number.

    (A)   31
    (B)   28
    (C)   26
    (D)   24
    (E)   21

5 min

SSAT Solving for *x* Drill 2

1. When $A + B = 21$ and $3C + B = 21$, what is the value of C?

   (A) 42
   (B) 21
   (C) 7
   (D) −7
    It cannot be determined from the information given.

2. In the addition of the three-digit numbers shown, the letters W, X, Y, and Z each represent a unique single digit. Which of the following could be the sum of $W + X + Y + Z$?

   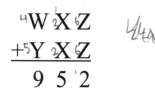
   $$\begin{array}{r} {}^4W\,{}^{2}X\,{}^6Z \\ +\,{}^5Y\,{}^2X\,{}^6Z \\ \hline 9\ 5\ 2 \end{array}$$

   (A) 23
   (B) 20
   (C) 17
   (D) 14
   (E) 11

   4 + 5 + 2 + 6

3. If $12 \div T = 1$, then $T + T =$

   (A) 1
   (B) 2
   (C) 12
   (D) 24
   (E) 48

4. Which of the following gives the number of inches in x feet, y yards, and 5 inches?

   (A) $12x + 36y + 5$

   (B) $12x + 36y + 60$

   (C) $12x + 3y + 5$

   (D) $\dfrac{12}{x} + \dfrac{36}{y} + 5$

   (E) $\dfrac{x}{12} + \dfrac{y}{36} + 60$

5. Five fans of a canceled TV series contribute a total of $30 per week to a Kickstarter campaign to fund a movie version of the TV show. How much would each person pay weekly if a sixth fan also contributed?

   (A) $1
   (B) $3
   (C) $5
   (D) $6
   (E) $7

6. If $5x = x + 24$, then $x =$

   (A) 6
   (B) 4
   (C) 3
   (D) 2
   (E) $\dfrac{1}{2}$

7. If $\dfrac{36}{x} = \dfrac{3}{4}$, then $x =$

   (A) 9
   (B) 12
   (C) 24
   (D) 48
   (E) 64

8. If $(x + 4) + y = 0$, then $x + y =$

   (A) −4
   (B) $\dfrac{-4}{3}$
   (C) 0
   (D) $\dfrac{4}{3}$
   (E) 4

9. If the sum of $a - 8$, $a - 4$, and a is 0, what is the value of a?

    (A)   12
    (B)   8
    (C)   4
    (D)   –4
    (E)   –8

10. If $\dfrac{500}{100(x+2)} = 5$, then what does x equal?

    (A)   –5
    (B)   –1
    (C)   0
    (D)   1
    (E)   3

$$\frac{500}{100x+2000} = 5$$

$$\frac{5}{x+2} = 5$$

$$5 = 5x+10$$

$$-5 = 5x$$

$$\boxed{x = -1}$$

SSAT Solving for *x* Drill 3

1. If $6z = 12 + 2z$, what is the value of $8z$?

   (A) 3
   (B) 4
   (C) 6
   (D) 16
   (E) 24

   (handwritten: $4z=12$, $8z=24$)

2. If $\dfrac{x+3}{5} = \dfrac{3}{7}$, then $x =$

   (A) $-\dfrac{7}{6}$

   (B) $-\dfrac{6}{7}$

   (C) $\dfrac{5}{7}$

   (D) 6

   (E) 12

   (handwritten: $x+3 = \dfrac{15}{7}$, $x = -\dfrac{6}{7}$)

3. If $\dfrac{4y}{3} - 2 = \dfrac{1}{5}$, then $y =$

   (A) 33

   (B) 20

   (C) 1

   (D) $\dfrac{20}{33}$

   (E) $\dfrac{33}{20}$

4. If $5x - 7 = 2x + 8$, then $x =$

   (A) $\dfrac{1}{7}$

   (B) $\dfrac{1}{3}$

   (C) $\dfrac{15}{7}$

   (D) 5

   (E) 7

5. If $\dfrac{1}{3} + \dfrac{1}{4} = \dfrac{x}{36}$, then $x =$

   (A) 21

   (B) 14

   (C) 7

   (D) $\dfrac{8}{9}$

   (E) $\dfrac{7}{12}$

6. If $\dfrac{2}{11x+6} = \dfrac{1}{21+x}$, then $x =$

   (A) 12

   (B) 4

   (C) 3

   (D) 2

   (E) $\dfrac{1}{5}$

7. If $\dfrac{\frac{x}{4}}{\frac{x}{12}} = 19 - x$, then $x =$

(A) 3
(B) 4
(C) 12
(D) 16
(E) 24

8. If $\dfrac{x}{3} + 4x = 48 - x$, then $x =$

(A) 27
(B) 15
(C) 9
(D) 4
(E) 3

9. What is the value of the least of five consecutive integers if the least minus twice the greatest equals –10?

(A) –3
(B) –2
(C) 2
(D) 6
(E) 10

10. Three less than a certain number is one-fourth of the number. What is the number?

(A) 15
(B) 12
(C) 9
(D) 6
(E) 4

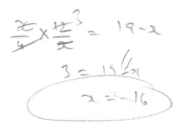

ISEE Solving for *x* Drill 1

1. If $a - b = 5$, then which expression is equal to b?

    (A) $a + 5$
    (B) $a - 5$
    (C) $-a + 5$
    (D) $-a - 5$

2. If $(3.85 + 1.15)t = t$, then what is the value of t?

    (A) 0

    (B) $\dfrac{1}{5}$

    (C) 1

    (D) 5

3. If $4a - 4 = ab - b$ and $a \neq 1$, what is the value of b?

    (A) -4
    (B) -1
    (C) 0
    (D) 4

4. For all pairs of real numbers L and N where $L = 2N + 4$, $N = ?$

    (A) $\dfrac{L + 4}{2}$

    (B) $\dfrac{L - 4}{2}$

    (C) $2L - 4$

    (D) $\dfrac{L}{2} - 4$

5. If $s = \dfrac{t(r + 1)}{7}$, then which of the following is r in terms of s and t?

    (A) $7st - 1$

    (B) $\dfrac{7s - t}{t}$

    (C) $\dfrac{7s - 1}{t}$

    (D) $\dfrac{s - 1}{7t}$

6. If $x = 3t - 5$ and $y = 7 - t$, which of the following expresses y in terms of x?

    (A) $y = \dfrac{26 - x}{3}$

    (B) $y = \dfrac{16 - x}{3}$

    (C) $y = 7 - x$

    (D) $y = 12 - 3x$

7. If x is an odd number, which of the following could be an even number?

    (A) $x + 2$
    (B) $2x + 1$
    (C) $2x - 3$
    (D) $3x + 3$

8. If $\dfrac{4}{5-p} = \dfrac{12}{2p}$, then $p = ?$

    (A) −3
    (B) −1
    (C) 1
    (D) 3

9. The square of a positive number minus the number equals 72. What is the value of the number?

    (A) 8
    (B) 9
    (C) 10
    (D) 11

10. If $-17(x-2) = 16 + x$, what is the value of x?

    (A) 1
    (B) 0
    (C) −1
    (D) −2

ISEE Solving for *x* Drill 2

1. What is the value of *x* if $3x - 24 = 3(3x - 2)$?

    (A)   9.0
    (B)   5.0
    (C)   −3.0
    (D)   −12.5

2. If $3p = 5p - 10$, then $2p - 3 = ?$

    (A)   1
    (B)   3
    (C)   5
    (D)   7

3. In the equation $4j - k + 2k - 13j = 0$, what is the value of *j* if $k = 9$?

    (A)   −2
    (B)   1
    (C)   4
    (D)   9

4. If $7 + \dfrac{x}{2} = 3x - 8$, then $x = ?$

    (A)   4
    (B)   6
    (C)   8
    (D)   10

5. If $m + 3m + 2 = 30$, then $m = ?$

    (A)   2
    (B)   4
    (C)   7
    (D)   15

6. If $x + 18 = |-9|$, then $x = ?$

    (A)   27
    (B)   9
    (C) $\dfrac{1}{2}$
    (D)   −9

    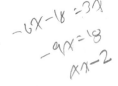
    x = 9 + 18
    x = 9

7. If $|x - 2| = x$, then what is the value of *x*?

    (A)   −2
    (B)   −1
    (C)   0
    (D)   1

    x + 2 = *x*
    0 ≠ 2

8. If $-3x - 9 = \dfrac{3x}{2}$, then $x = ?$

    (A)   6
    (B)   3
    (C)   −2
    (D)   −6

    −6x − 18 = 3x
    −9x = 18
    x = −2

x − 2 = *x* ⟹ *x* ∉

−(*x* − 2) = *x* ⟹ 2 = 2
x = 1

| −*x* − 2 |
| (*x* − 2) |

9. If $\sqrt{x + 9} = 4$, then $x = ?$

   (A)   7
   (B)   5
   (C)   −5
   (D)   −7

10. If *each of p* and *q* has a remainder of 3 when divided by 7, then which one of the following also has a remainder of 3 when divided by 7?

    (A) $p - q$
    (B) $p + 3q$
    (C) $3p + q$
    (D) $3p - 2q$

ISEE Solving for *x* Drill 3

Directions: Using all information given in each question, compare the quantity in Column A to the quantity in Column B. All questions in Part Two have these answer choices:

(A) The quantity in Column A is greater.
(B) The quantity in Column B is greater.
(C) The two quantities are equal.
(D) The relationship cannot be determined from the information given.

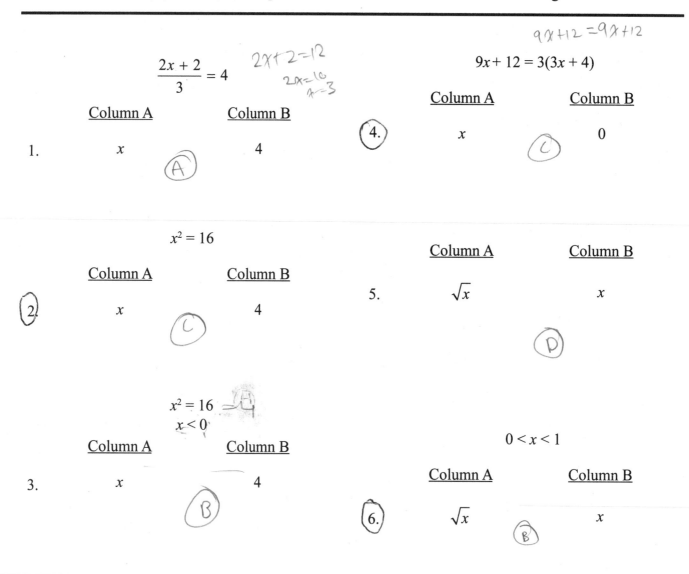

$$\frac{2x + 2}{3} = 4$$

2x+2=12
2x=10
x=5

	Column A	Column B
1.	x	4

(A)

$$x^2 = 16$$

	Column A	Column B
2.	x	4

(C)

$$x^2 = 16$$
$$x < 0$$

	Column A	Column B
3.	x	4

(B)

9x+12=9x+12

$$9x + 12 = 3(3x + 4)$$

	Column A	Column B
4.	x	0

(C)

	Column A	Column B
5.	$\sqrt{x}$	x

(D)

$$0 < x < 1$$

	Column A	Column B
6.	$\sqrt{x}$	x

(B)

$$x > 1$$

Column A	Column B

7. $\quad\sqrt{x}\qquad\qquad\qquad x$

Ⓑ

$$\sqrt{\frac{x + 2}{4}} = 1$$

Column A	Column B

8. $\quad x \qquad$ Ⓐ $\qquad 1$

$$\frac{x+2}{4} = 1$$

$$x + 2 = 4$$

$$\boxed{x = 2}$$

Column A	Column B

9. $\quad 16x - 1 \qquad$ Ⓐ $\qquad 16(x - 1)$

$$16x - 16$$

The sum of 3 consecutive integers is 33.

Column A	Column B

10. The greatest of the 3 consecutive integers $\qquad$ Ⓑ $\qquad 13$

12

$x \cdot 10, 11, \boxed{12}$

Solving for *x*:
Answers and
Explanations

ANSWER KEY

SSAT Solving for *x* **Drill 1**		**SSAT Solving for *x*** **Drill 2**		**SSAT Solving for *x*** **Drill 3**	
1.	D	1.	E	1.	E
2.	E	2.	C	2.	B
3.	B	3.	D	3.	E
4.	A	4.	A	4.	D
5.	A	5.	C	5.	A
6.	B	6.	A	6.	B
7.	D	7.	D	7.	D
8.	C	8.	A	8.	C
9.	E	9.	C	9.	C
10.	D	10.	B	10.	E

ISEE Solving for *x* **Drill 1**		**ISEE Solving for *x*** **Drill 2**		**ISEE Solving for *x*** **Drill 3**	
1.	B	1.	C	1.	A
2.	A	2.	D	2.	D
3.	D	3.	B	3.	B
4.	B	4.	B	4.	D
5.	B	5.	C	5.	D
6.	B	6.	D	6.	A
7.	D	7.	D	7.	B
8.	D	8.	C	8.	A
9.	B	9.	A	9.	A
10.	A	10.	D	10.	B

SSAT Solving for *x* Drill 1

1. **D** *More than* means addition. If Peter has *x* marbles more than Lewis has, and Lewis has 9, Peter has 9 + *x*.

 Plug in a number for *x*, such as 2. If Peter has 2 more marbles than Lewis has, Peter has 11. Only (D) will yield 11 when 2 is plugged in.

2. **E** When you have three variables, you need three equations to solve for the variables. As there are only two equations here, it is not possible to solve for *X*.

 Test the answers. For each answer, you can solve for *Z* in the second equation and then use that solution to solve for *Y* in the first equation. As all four numbers yield different *Y*s and *Z*s, the value of *X* cannot be determined.

3. **B** First, convert the kilograms to pounds, to have an apples-to-apples comparison: 5 × 2.2 = 11. As the required mass to engage is 108 pounds, the additional mass needed above the weight of the knapsack is 108 − 11 = 97.

4. **A** Solve for *P*, by dividing both sides by 27: *P* = 1. Substitute that value into the equation: 27 − 1 = 26.

5. **A** As *Y* > 5, 4*Y* + 7 > 4(5) + 7 or 27. Only (A) is greater than 27.

6. B   As there are 60 seconds in 1 minute, there are $60m$ seconds in m minutes. As there are 3,600 seconds in 1 hour (60 minutes, each 60 seconds), there are $3{,}600h$ seconds in h hours. Add these to 2 seconds for the result.

 Plug in for m and h, such as $m = 2$ and $h = 3$. As there are 60 seconds in one minute, there are 120 seconds in 2 minutes. As there are 3,600 seconds in one hour (60 minutes, each 60 seconds), there are 10,800 seconds in 3 hours. Add these to the 2 seconds to get 10,922 seconds. Only (B) matches these results when the selected numbers are tested.

7. D   No matter what value x is, (D) will be 2 because a number divided by itself is 1, and $1 + 1 = 2$. All of the other answers yield a negative number.

 Plug in a number for x, such as $x = -2$, and determine the greatest value among the answer choices. Choice (D) is greatest. To be sure the same results will occur no matter what, try a weird value for x, such as $-\dfrac{1}{2}$. Choice (D) is still largest.

8. C   Divide 35 by 8 to find out how many packages are needed. The result is 4 with a remainder of 3. Thus, 5 packages are needed.

 Test the answers, starting with (A) because you are looking for the minimum number of packages needed. Neither (A) nor (B) provides enough boxes for the guests. Choice (C) does.

9. **E**   This question requires you to work through the possibilities, based on the restrictions (maximum 6 flats, no repeated numbers of flats). Thus, the first vehicle can carry 6 flats, the second 5 (for a total of 11 flats), the third 4 (total of 15), the fourth 3 (total of 18), the fifth 2 (total of 20), and the sixth 1 (total of 21). Thus, 6 vehicles are needed.

10. **D**   Let x represent the smaller number, and let y represent the larger number. Set up two equations: $y - x = 7$, and $y + x = 55$. Place one equation over the other and combine like terms: $2y = 62$. Divide both sides by 2: $y = 31$. Substitute $y = 31$ into either equation to solve for x, which equals 24.

 Test the answers, starting with (C). If the smaller number is 26 and is 7 less than the larger number, the larger number is 33. However, $26 + 33 = 59$, which is too big. Eliminate (A), (B), and (C). Now try 24. In this case, the larger number is 31, and the sum is 55.

SSAT Solving for *x* Drill 2

1. **E**   When you have three variables, you need three equations to solve for the variables. As there are only two equations here, it is not possible to solve for C.

 Test the answers. For each answer, you can solve for B in the second equation and then use that solution to solve for A in the first equation. As all four numbers yield different As and Bs, the value of C cannot be determined.

2. **C** This question requires you to guess and check. Begin with the units digit. Z can be 1 or 6, as 1 + 1 = 2, and 6 + 6 = 12. Proceed to the tens digit. There is no number that when added to itself will yield an odd number. Thus, we need to carry a 1 from the sum of the units digit. We now know that Z is 6. Now, X can be 2 or 7, as 2 + 2 + 1 = 5, and 7 + 7 + 1 = 15. Finally go to the hundreds digit. W + Y can be any combination that adds up to 9 if X = 2. W + Y can be any combination that adds up to 8 if X = 7, and the 1 was carried. So, the two sets of numbers are (1) Z = 6, X = 2, and W + Y = 9, and (2) Z = 6, X = 7, and W + Y = 8. Thus, the two possible sums of digits are 17 and 21. Only 17 is an answer.

3. **D** Any number divided by itself is 1, so T = 12. Substitute that number in the equation: $T + T = 12 + 12 = 24$.

4. **A** There are 12 inches in 1 foot, so there are $12x$ inches in x feet. There are 36 inches in a yard (3 feet, 12 inches each), so there are $36y$ inches in y yards. Add these to 5 inches to obtain the answer.

 Plug in numbers for x and y, such as $x = 2$ and $y = 3$. As there are 12 inches in a foot, x feet is 24 inches. As there are 36 inches in a yard (3 feet, 12 inches each), there are 108 inches in 3 yards. Add these to 5 inches for a total of 135 inches. Only (A) yields the correct answer when the chosen numbers are tested.

5. **C** As six fans are splitting a $30 fee, divide 30 by 6.

6. **A** First, subtract x from both sides: $4x = 24$. Next, divide both sides by 4: $x = 6$.

 Test the answers to determine which one allows the equation to balance.

7. **D** First, cross multiply: $3x = 144$. Divide both sides by 3: $x = 48$.

 Test the answers to determine which one allows the equation to balance.

8. **A** Because the only operations are addition, the parentheses can be removed: $x + y + 4 = 0$. As the question asks for $x + y$, rather than x alone or y alone, isolate $x + y$ by subtracting 4 from both sides: $x + y = -4$.

9. **C** Write the equation: $(a - 8) + (a - 4) + a = 0$. Combine like terms: $3a - 12 = 0$. Add 12 to both sides and divide by 3: $a = 4$.

 Test the answers to determine which one allows the equation to balance.

10. **B** First, reduce the number terms in the fraction to 5. Next, multiply both sides by $(x + 2)$: $5 = 5(x + 2)$. Distribute the 5: $5 = 5x + 10$. Subtract 10 from both sides: $-5 = 5x$. Divide both sides by 5: $x = -1$.

 Test the answers to determine which one allows the equation to balance.

SSAT Solving for *x* Drill 3

1. **E**   First, subtract $2z$ from both sides: $4z = 12$. Next, you can multiply both sides by 2 to solve for $8z$: $8z = 24$. Alternatively, divide both sides by 4 to find z and then multiply both sides by 8: $z = 3$, and $8z = 24$.

2. **B**   First, cross multiply: $7x + 21 = 15$. Next, subtract 21 from both sides: $7x = -6$. Divide both sides by 7: $x = -\dfrac{6}{7}$.

     Test the answers to determine which one allows the equation to balance.

3. **E**   First, add 2 to both sides: $\dfrac{4y}{3} = 2\dfrac{1}{5}$ or $\dfrac{11}{5}$. Next, cross multiply: $20y = 33$. Finally, divide both sides by 20: $y = \dfrac{33}{20}$.

     Test the answers to determine which one allows the equation to balance.

4. **D**   First, add 7 to both sides and subtract $2x$ from both sides: $3x = 15$. Then, divide both sides by 3: $x = 5$.

     Test the answers to determine which one allows the equation to balance.

5. **A**   First, create a common denominator for the fractions: $\frac{4}{12} + \frac{3}{12} = \frac{x}{36}$. Next, add the fractions: $\frac{7}{12} = \frac{x}{36}$. Because 36 is three times 12, multiply 7 by 3 to find x: 21. Alternatively, you can cross multiply and divide by 12 to solve for x.

 Test the answers to determine which one allows the equation to balance.

6. **B**   First, cross multiply: $2(21 + x) = 11x + 6$. Next, distribute the 2: $42 + 2x = 11x + 6$. Now, subtract $2x$ and 6 from both sides: $36 = 9x$. Last, divide both sides by 9 to get $x = 4$.

 Test the answers to determine which one allows the equation to balance.

7. **D**   First, simplify the fraction by flipping the divisor and multiplying: $\dfrac{\frac{x}{4}}{\frac{x}{12}} = \left(\frac{x}{4}\right)\left(\frac{12}{x}\right) = \frac{12}{4} = 3$. So $3 = 19 - x$. Add x to both sides and subtract 3 from both sides: $x = 16$.

 Test the answers to determine which one allows the equation to balance.

8.   C   First, add $\frac{x}{3}$ $\left(\text{also known as }\frac{1}{3}x\right)$ and $4x$, to get $4\frac{1}{3}x = 48 - x$. Add x to both sides

to get $5\frac{1}{3}x = x = 48$. Last, divide both sides by $\frac{16}{3}$ (multiply by the reciprocal) to

get $x = 48 \times \frac{3}{16} = 9$.

   Test the answers to determine which one allows the equation to balance.

9.   C   First, set up the five consecutive integers, where x represents the least of the integers: x, $x + 1$, $x + 2$, $x + 3$, and $x + 4$. Write an equation for the requirement: $x - 2(x + 4) =$ -10. Distribute the -2: $x - 2x - 8 = -10$. Combine like terms and add 8 to both sides: $-x = -2$. Multiply both sides by -1: $x = 2$.

   Test the answers, starting with (C). If 2 is the least of the integers, then 6 is the greatest. Test the requirement: $2 - (2)(6) = 2 - 12 = 10$.

10.   E   Translate the English into a mathematical equation, replacing *less than* with subtrac

tion, *is* with an equal sign, and *of* with a multiplication sign: $x - 3 = \frac{1}{4}x$. Next, add

3 to both sides and subtract $\frac{1}{4}x$ from both sides: $\frac{3}{4}x = 3$. Last, divide both sides by

$\frac{3}{4}$ (multiply by the reciprocal) to get $x = 3 \times \frac{4}{3} = 4$.

Test the answers, starting with (C). Three less than 9 is 6, but that is not the same as

$\frac{1}{4}$ of $9\left(2\frac{1}{4}\right)$. It may not be clear whether (C) is too low or too high, so just proceed

until you arrive at a correct answer. Three less than 4 is 1, and that is the same as $\frac{1}{4}$

of 1.

ISEE Solving for *x* Drill 1

1. **B** First, subtract *a* from both sides: $-b = 5 - a$. Next, divide both sides by -1: $b = -5 + a$ (or $a - 5$).

 Plug in values for a and b, such that $a - b = 5$. If $a = 7$ and $b = 2$, then the correct answer will equal 2 when you plug in 7 for *a*.

2. **A** First, add the values in the parentheses: $5t = t$. There is only one value of *t* for which this can be true: 0.

 Test the answers to determine which value of *t* satisfies the equation.

3. **D** Factor common terms from the expressions on both sides of the equation: $4(a - 1) = b(a - 1)$. Next divide both sides by $(a - 1)$: $b = 4$.

 Because *a* can be anything other than 1, plug in for *a*. If $a = 2$, then $(4)(2) - 4 = 2b - b$. Thus, $4 = b$. If you are not convinced, try another value for *a*. If $a = 0$, then $(4)(0) - 4 = (0)(b) - b$. Thus, $-4 = -b$, or $4 = b$.

4. **B** First, subtract 4 from both sides: $L - 4 = 2N$. Next, divide both sides by 2: $\dfrac{L - 4}{2} = N$.

 Plug in numbers for *N* and solve for *L*. If $N = 2$, then $2(2) + 4 = L = 8$. Use 8 for *L* in each choice to find the answer whose value is 2.

5. **B**   First, multiply both sides by 7: $7s = t(r + 1)$. Next, divide both sides by t: $\dfrac{7s}{t} = r + 1$. Now, subtract 1 from both sides: $\dfrac{7s}{t} - 1 = r$. Finally, create a common denominator by multiplying 1 by $\dfrac{t}{t}$ to get $\dfrac{7s}{t} - \dfrac{t}{t} = \dfrac{7s - t}{t} = r$.

  Plug in for t and r to solve for s. If $t = 2$ and $r = 3$, then $\dfrac{2(3 + 1)}{7} = \dfrac{8}{7} = s$. Now find the expression that equals 3, using 2 for t and $\dfrac{8}{7}$ for s. If you don't like having a fraction, make $t = 7$ and keep $r = 3$. Now $s = 4$. Find the expression that equals 3, using 7 for t and 4 for s.

6. **B**   Isolate t in the second equation by adding t to both sides and subtracting y from both sides: $t = 7 - y$. Now, substitute for t in the first equation: $x = 3(7 - y) - 5$. Distribute the 3: $x = 21 - 3y - 5$. Combine the 21 and -5: $x = 16 - 3y$. Add $3y$ to both sides and subtract x from both sides: $3y = 16 - x$. Finally, divide both sides by 3: $y = \dfrac{16 - x}{3}$.

  Plug in for t and solve for x and y. If $t = 2$, then $3(2) - 5 = 6 - 5 = 1 = x$, and $7 - 2 = 5 = y$. Plug in 1 for x in the expressions in the answer choices to find $y = 5$.

7. **D**   An odd number plus or minus an even number is an odd number. Two times an odd number is an even number. An even number plus or minus an odd number is an odd number. Three times an odd number is an odd number. An odd number plus or minus an odd number is an even number.

  Plug in an odd number for x, such as $x = 3$. Only (D) yields an even number.

8. **D**   Cross multiply: $8p = 12(5 - p)$. Distribute the 12: $8p = 60 - 12p$. Add $12p$ to both sides: $20p = 60$. Divide both sides by 20: $p = 3$.

 Test the answers to determine which one makes the equation true.

9. **B**   Write the equation: $x^2 - x = 72$. Subtract 72 from both sides: $x^2 - x - 72 = 0$. Factor the left-hand side: $(x + 8)(x - 9) = 0$. Thus, $x = 9$ or -8. As the question indicated that x is a positive number, $x = 9$.

 You may not have learned how to factor a quadratic yet. Even so, this question designed for older ISEE students is solvable if you test the answers. Start with (B) or (C). If you start with 10, you get $100 - 10 = 90$, which is greater than 72. Eliminate (C) and (D). Now try 9: $81 - 9 = 72$.

10. **A**   Distribute the -17: $-17x + 34 = 16 + x$. Add $-17x$ to both sides and subtract 16: $18 = 18x$. Divide both sides by 18: and $x = 1$.

 Test the answers to determine which one makes the equation true.

ISEE Solving for *x* Drill 2

1. **C** Distribute the 3: $3x - 24 = 9x - 6$. Subtract $9x$ from both sides, and add 24 to both sides: $-6x = 18$. Divide both sides by -6: $x = -3$.

 Test the answers to determine which one makes the equation true.

2. **D** Subtract $5p$ from both sides: $-2p = -10$. Divide both sides by -2: $p = 5$. Therefore, $2p - 3 = 2(5) - 3 = 10 - 3 = 7$.

3. **B** Input the value given for k: $4j - 9 + 18 - 13j = 0$. Combine the -9 and 18 as well as the $4j$ and $-13j$: $9 - 9j = 0$. Add $9j$ to both sides: $9 = 9j$. Divide both sides by 9: $j = 1$.

4. **B** Subtract 7 from both sides: $\frac{x}{2} = 3x - 15$. Multiply both sides by 2: $x = 6x - 30$. Subtract $6x$ from both sides: $-5x = -30$. Divide both sides by -5: $x = 6$.

 Test the answers to determine which one makes the equation true.

5. **C** Combine m and $3m$: $4m + 2 = 30$. Subtract 2 from both sides: $4m = 28$. Divide both sides by 4: $m = 7$.

 Test the answers to determine which one makes the equation true.

6. **D** As the absolute value of –9 is 9, rewrite the equation: $x + 18 = 9$. Subtract 18 from both sides: $x = -9$.

 Test the answers to determine which one makes the equation true.

7. **D** The value inside the absolute value may be negative, zero, or positive, but x itself must be zero or positive because it is equal to the absolute value of a quantity. Thus, it may be that $x - 2 = x$. Subtract x from both sides: $-2 = -2x$. Divide both sides by -2: $1 = x$. This is an answer, so you may stop here. However, it may also be that $-(x - 2) = x$. Distribute the negative sign: $-x + 2 = x$. Add x to both sides: $2 = 2x$. Divide both sides by 2: $1 = x$.

 Test the answers to determine which one makes the equation true.

8. **C** Multiply all terms by 2: $-6x - 18 = 3x$. Add $6x$ to both sides: $-18 = 9x$. Divide both sides by 9: $x = -2$.

 Test the answers to determine which one makes the equation true.

9. **A** Square both sides: $x + 9 = 16$. Subtract 9 from both sides: $x = 7$.

 Test the answers to determine which one makes the equation true.

10. **D**   For a number to have a remainder of 3 when divided by 7, it must be some factor of 7 plus 3. So let each of p and $q = 7x + 3$. Substitute this expression into each answer. For (A), the result is 0, which is not equivalent to some factor of 7 plus 3. For (B), the result is $7x + 3 + 3(7x + 3)$, which is $7x + 3 + (21x + 9)$, which is $28x + 12$. When 12 is divided by 7, the remainder is 5. Choice (C) yields the same result. For (D), the result is $3(7x + 3) - 2(7x + 3)$, which is $21x + 9 - (14x + 6)$, which is $7x + 3$. This is a factor of 7 plus 3.

 If you are given a denominator of a quotient and a remainder, you can plug in for the numerator by adding the denominator and the remainder. In this case, you can set both p and q equal to 10 (7 + 3). Plug 10 into each answer (for p and q) and divide each answer by 7 to find its remainder. Only (D) yields a remainder of 3.

ISEE Solving for *x* Drill 3

1. **A**   Multiply both sides by 3: $2x + 2 = 12$. Subtract 2 from both sides: $2x = 10$. Divide both sides by 2: $x = 5$.

2. **D**   While $\sqrt{16} = 4$, when $x^2 = 16$, $x = \pm 4$. Therefore, the columns can be equal, or Column B can be greater than Column A.

3. **B**   While $\sqrt{16} = 4$, when $x^2 = 16$, $x = \pm 4$. However, in this case, we are told that $x < 0$. Thus, $x = -4$.

4. **D** Distributing the 3: $9x + 12 = 9x + 12$. As the expressions on either side are identical, all values of x will make the equation true. Therefore, the relative value of the columns cannot be determined.

5. **D** When $x > 1$, $\sqrt{x} < x$. When $x = 0$ or 1, $\sqrt{x} = x$. When $0 < x < 1$, $\sqrt{x} > x$. As x can be any non-negative number, the relative size of the columns cannot be determined.

 Plug in an easy value for x, such as $x = 4$. In this case, the value in Column B is bigger, so the value in Column A is not *always* bigger, and the values in the two columns are not *always* equal. Eliminate (A) and (C). Now plug in $x = 0$. The values in the two columns are the same, which means that the value in Column A is not *always* bigger. Eliminate (B).

6. **A** When $x > 1$, $\sqrt{x} < x$. When $x = 0$ or 1, $\sqrt{x} = x$. When $0 < x < 1$, $\sqrt{x} > x$. As we are told that $0 < x < 1$, the value in Column A is bigger.

 Plug in an acceptable value for x, such as $x = \dfrac{1}{4}$. In this case, the value in Column A is bigger, so the value in Column B is not *always* bigger, and the values in the two columns are not *always* equal. Eliminate (B) and (C). Because of the restriction, there are no other types of numbers you can plug in. Thus, the value in Column A is *always* bigger.

7. **B** When $x > 1$, $\sqrt{x} < x$. When $x = 0$ or 1, $\sqrt{x} = x$. When $0 < x < 1$, $\sqrt{x} > x$. As we are told that $0 < x < 1$, the value in Column B is bigger.

 Plug in an easy value for x, such as $x = 4$. In this case, the value in Column B is bigger, so the value in Column A is not *always* bigger, and the values in the two columns are not *always* equal. Eliminate (A) and (C). Because of the restriction, there are no other types of numbers you can plug in. Thus, the value in Column B is *always* bigger.

8. **A** Square both sides: $\dfrac{x+2}{4} = 1$. Multiply both sides by 4: $x + 2 = 4$. Subtract 2 from both sides: $x = 2$.

9. **A** Column A is simplified, but you can distribute in Column B. Doing so yields $16x - 16$. No matter the value of x, $16x - 1$ will be larger than $16x - 16$.

 Plug in for x, starting with an easy number. If $x = 2$, then the expression in Column A = $(16)(2) - 1 = 31$, and the expression in Column B = $16(2 - 1) = 16$. Because the value in Column B is not *always* greater than the value in Column A, eliminate (B). Because the two columns are not *always* equal, eliminate (C). Next, try 0: the expression in Column A = $(16)(1) - 1 = -1$, and the expression in Column B = $16(0 - 1) = (16)(-1) = -16$. The value in Column A is still greater. Now, try a negative number, such as -2: the expression in Column A = $(16)(-2) - 1 = -33$, and the expression in Column B = $16(-2 - 1) = (16)(-3) = -48$. The value in Column A is still greater. If you want to have absolute certainty, you can plug in a larger number and a fraction, but you should feel reasonably confident already that the value in Column A will *always* be greater.

10. **B** Let x be the least integer. Thus, $x + x + 1 + x + 2 = 33$, so $3x + 3 = 33$, so $3x = 30$, so $x = 10$. Therefore, the greatest of the three consecutive integers is 12.

 As Column A contains an unknown and Column B contains a known value, test the value in Column B. If the greatest of the three consecutive integers is 13, then the sum would be $11 + 12 + 13 = 36$. As the problem states that the sum is actually 33, the greatest integer must be less than 13.

Inequalities

SSAT Inequalities Drill 1

1. Which of the following could be the value of X if

    $\frac{1}{4} + X < 1$?

    $-X = \frac{2}{3}$

    (A) $\frac{9}{10}$

    (B) $\frac{6}{7}$

    (C) $\frac{5}{6}$

    (D) $\frac{4}{5}$

    (E) $\frac{2}{3}$ $\frac{3}{12} + \frac{8}{12} = \frac{11}{12}$

2. Choose the inequality represented by the statement "The sum of two times a number and five times another number is greater than or equal to twenty-one."

    (A) $2x + 5y \geq 21$
    (B) $2x + 5y \leq 21$
    (C) $2x + 5x \geq 21$
    (D) $2x \times 5y \leq 21$
    (E) $2x \times 5y \geq 21$

3. If $8x - 6 < 14 + 5x$, then

    (A) $x < 20$

    (B) $x < 13$ $8x - 5x < 14 + 6$

    (C) $x < \frac{20}{3}$ $3x < 20$

    (D) $x > \frac{20}{3}$ $x < \frac{20}{3}$

    (E) $x < \frac{8}{3}$

4. If $\frac{12 - 4y}{3} < -8$, then

    (A) $y < 9$
    (B) $y > 9$ $12 - 4y < -24$
    (C) $y < -9$ $-4y < -36$
    (D) $y < 3$
    (E) $y > 3$ $y > 9$

5. If $4x + 6 \geq 30$, then

    (A) $x \geq 24$
    (B) $x \geq 12$ $4x \geq 24$
    (C) $x \leq 6$
    (D) $x \geq 6$ $x \geq 6$
    (E) $x \geq 3$

SSAT Inequalities Drill 2

1. Which of the following could be the value of A if $\frac{1}{3} + A > 1$?

   (A) $\frac{1}{4}$

   (B) $\frac{1}{2}$

   (C) $\frac{8}{15}$

   (D) $\frac{3}{5}$

   (E) $\frac{7}{9}$ $\frac{3}{9} + \frac{7}{9} = \frac{10}{9}$

2. If $2 - 4x \leq 10$, then

   (A) $x \leq 2$ $-4x \leq 8$
   (B) $x \geq 2$
   (C) $x \leq -2$ $x \geq -2$
   (D) $x \geq -2$
   (E) $x > -2$

3. If $4x - 6 < 12 - 5x$, then

   (A) $x > 2$
   (B) $x < 2$ $9x < 18$
   (C) $x > 9$
   (D) $x < 9$ $x < 2$
   (E) $x < 18$

4. Choose the inequality represented by the statement "The product of three times a number and four times another number is less than or equal to forty eight."

   (A) $3a \times 4b \leq 48$
   (B) $3a \div 4b \leq 48$
   (C) $3a + 4b \leq 48$
   (D) $3a \times 4a \leq 48$
   (E) $3a \times 4b \geq 48$

5. Which of the following could be the value of Y if $\frac{1}{2} + Y < 0$?

   (A) $\frac{3}{4}$

   (B) $\frac{1}{2}$

   (C) $-\frac{3}{4}$

   (D) $-\frac{1}{2}$

   (E) $-\frac{1}{4}$

ISEE Inequalities Drill 1

1. What is the maximum value for y if
   $y = 3x^2 + 2$ for $-3 \le x \le 2$?

   (A) 29
   (B) 14
   (C) 7
   (D) −25

   [handwritten:] $3(-3)^2 + 2$
   $3(9) + 2$
   $3(4) + 2 \quad \frac{27+2}{29}$
   $12 + 2$

2. Which describes all values of x for which
   $|3x - 4| \ge 8$?

   (A) $x \le -\dfrac{4}{3}$ or $x \ge 4$

   (B) $x \ge \dfrac{4}{3}$ or $x \le -4$

   (C) $x \le \dfrac{4}{3}$

   (D) $x \ge 4$

   [handwritten:] $x \ge 4$
   $3x \ge 12$
   $3x - 4 \ge 8$

   $3x - 4 \ge -8$
   $3x \ge -4$
   $x \ge -\dfrac{4}{3}$

3. A solution set is graphed on the number line shown.

   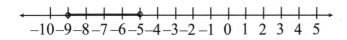

   The solution set of which inequality is shown?
   (A) $|x - 7| < 2$
   (B) $|x + 7| < 2$
   (C) $|x - 8| < 1$
   (D) $|x + 8| < 1$

4. Which of the following expressions defines the values of x if $-2x + 3 > 2x + 15$?

   (A) $x > -3$
   (B) $x > -4$
   (C) $x < -4$
   (D) $x < -3$

5. Which of the following expressions solves $2z - q < 3p + z - q$ for z?

   (A) $z < p$
   (B) $z < 3p - q$
   (C) $z < 3p$
   (D) $z < 3p + q$

ISEE Inequalities Drill 2

1. Which of the following inequalities represents the graph shown below on the real number line?

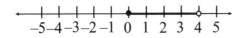

(A) $-1 < x < 4$
(B) $0 \leq x < 4$
(C) $0 < x \leq 4$
(D) $0 \geq x > 4$

Directions: Using all information given in each question, compare the quantity in Column A to the quantity in Column B. All questions in Part Two have these answer choices:

(A) The quantity in Column A is greater.
(B) The quantity in Column B is greater.
(C) The two quantities are equal.
(D) The relationship cannot be determined from the information given.

$$x + 2 > 5x$$

$-4x > -2$

$x < \frac{1}{2}$

Column A	Column B
2. $\quad x$	-1

(D)

$$5x = x$$

Column A	Column B
3. $\quad 0$	x

(C)

$$2(x + 2) \leq 6(x + 1) - 8$$

Column A	Column B
4. $\quad 1$	x

(B)

$$|x - 2| > 9$$

Column A	Column B
5. $\quad -7$	x

(D)

Inequalities:
Answers and
Explanations

ANSWER KEY

SSAT Inequalities
Drill 1
1. E
2. A
3. C
4. B
5. D

ISEE Inequalities
Drill 1
1. A
2. A
3. B
4. D
5. C

SSAT Inequalities
Drill 2
1. E
2. D
3. B
4. A
5. C

ISEE Inequalities
Drill 2
1. B
2. D
3. C
4. B
5. D

SSAT Inequalities Drill 1

1. **E** Subtract $\frac{1}{4}$ from both sides: $X < \frac{3}{4}$. As $\frac{2}{3} < \frac{3}{4}$, (E) is correct.

 You can test the answers to see which one satisfies the inequality.

2. **A** Translate the statement using x and y (as in the answers): $2x + 5y \geq 21$.

3. **C** Add 6 to both sides and subtract $5x$ from both sides: $3x < 20$. Divide both sides by 3: $x < \frac{20}{3}$.

4. **B** Multiply both sides by 3: $12 - 4y < -24$. Subtract 12 from both sides: $-4y < -36$. Divide both sides by -4 (remembering to flip the sign): $y > 9$.

5. **D** Subtract 6 from both sides: $4x \geq 24$. Divide both sides by 4: $x \geq 6$.

SSAT Inequalities Drill 2

1. **E** Subtract $\frac{1}{3}$ from both sides: $A > \frac{2}{3}$. As $\frac{7}{9} < \frac{2}{3}$, (E) is correct.

 You can test the answers to see which one satisfies the inequality.

2. **D** Subtract 2 from both sides: $-4x \leq 8$. Divide both sides by -4 (remembering to flip the sign): $x \geq -2$.

3. **B** Add 6 and $5x$ to both sides: $9x < 18$. Divide both sides by 9: $x < 2$.

4. **A** Translate the statement using a and b (as in the answers): $3a \times 4b \leq 48$.

5. **C** Subtract $\frac{1}{2}$ from both sides: $Y < -\frac{1}{2}$. As $-\frac{3}{4} < -\frac{1}{2}$, (C) is correct.

 You can test the answers to see which one satisfies the inequality.

ISEE Inequalities Drill 1

1. **A** The largest value of y is not necessarily determined by the largest value of x, so try values of x on the ends and in the middle. If $x = 2$, then $3(2)^2 + 2 = 14$. If $x = -3$, then $3(-3)^2 + 2 = 29$. If $x = 0$, then $3(0)^2 + 2 = 2$. Thus, 29 is the largest value.

2. **A** You need to solve for two cases. First, solve $3x - 4 \geq 8$. Add 4 to each side: $3x \geq 12$. Divide both sides by 3: $x \geq 4$. Now solve $3x - 4 \leq -8$. Add 4 to each side: $3x \leq -4$. Divide both sides by 3: $x \leq -\frac{4}{3}$. As the two results are not connected on the number line, the result is $x \leq -\frac{4}{3}$ or $x \geq 4$.

 With absolute value inequalities, there are always two solutions, so you can eliminate (C) and (D). If you ignore the absolute value and solve, you will get $x \geq 4$. Only one answer choice has this value.

3. **B** Test the answers to determine which one yields the indicated graph. For each answer, there are two cases. For choice (A), first solve $x - 7 < 2$. Add 7 to both sides: $x < 9$. As this is not one of the indicated end points in the graph, eliminate (A). For (B), first solve $x + 7 < 2$. Subtract 7 from both sides: $x < -5$. This is consistent with the graph. Now, solve $x + 7 > -2$. Subtract 7 from both sides: $x > -9$. This is also consistent with the graph, so (B) is correct.

4. **D** Add $-2x$ to both sides: $3 > 4x + 15$ Subtract 15 from both sides: $-12 > 4x$. Divide both sides by 4: $-3 > x$. That means that $x < -3$.

5. **C** Add q to both sides: $2z < 3p + z$. Subtract z from both sides: $z < 3p$.

ISEE Inequalities Drill 2

1. **B** The closed circle at 0 indicates that 0 is included in the range, while the open circle at 4 indicates that 4 is not included in the range. The range runs from 0 (inclusive) to 4 (not inclusive), so $0 \leq x < 4$.

2. **D** Subtract x from both sides: $2 > 4x$. Divide both sides by 4: $\frac{1}{2} > x$. This means that $x < \frac{1}{2}$. Because x can be greater than, equal to, or less than -1, the relative size of the two columns cannot be determined.

3. **C** The only way for five times a number to be equal to the number is for that number to be 0.

4. **B**   Distribute the 2 on the left and the 6 on the right: $2x + 4 \leq 6x + 6 - 8$. Combine the 6 and -8 on the right: $2x + 4 \leq 6x - 2$. Subtract $2x$ from both sides and add 2 to both sides: $6 \leq 4x$. Divide both sides by 4: $\frac{6}{4} \leq x$, which means $x \geq \frac{3}{2}$.

5. **D**   You need to solve for two cases. First, solve $x - 2 > 9$. Add 2 to both sides: $x > 11$. Now solve $x - 2 < -9$. Add 2 to both sides: $x < -7$. As x can be greater than 11 or less than -7, the relative size of the columns cannot be determined.

Triangles, Angles, and Lines

SSAT Triangles, Angles, and Lines Drill 1

1. Each side of an equilateral triangle has a length of 8. Find the perimeter of the triangle.

   (A) 8
   (B) 16
   (C) 24
   (D) 32
   (E) 64

2. The slope of the line that is perpendicular to the line $4x + 5y = 10$ is

   (A) $-\dfrac{4}{5}$

   (B) $-\dfrac{5}{4}$

   (C) $-\dfrac{1}{4}$

   (D) $\dfrac{5}{4}$

   (E) $\dfrac{4}{5}$

   handwritten: $5y = -4x + 10$
   handwritten: $y = -\frac{4}{5}x + 2$

3. In the figure, line S is parallel to line T. What is the measure of angle X?

   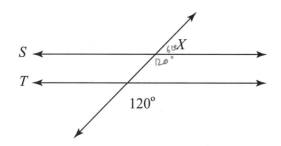

   (A) 20°
   (B) 30°
   (C) 60°
   (D) 120°
   (E) 220°

4. Seven equal pieces are cut from a piece of taffy 96 centimeters long. How long is the leftover piece of taffy?

   (A) 3 cm
   (B) 5 cm
   (C) 13 cm
   (D) 18 cm
   (E) 26 cm

   handwritten: $13 \times 7 = 91$
   handwritten: ⑤

5. In the isosceles triangle shown, find the measure of angle R.

   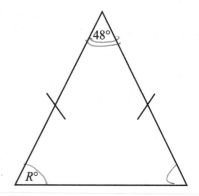

   (A) 42
   (B) 48
   (C) 60
   (D) 66
   (E) 132

   handwritten: $180 - 48 = 132$

SSAT Triangles, Angles, and Lines Drill 2

1. In the figure below, Segment *LN* is 72 inches long. How long is segment *MN*?

L   4A   M   5A   N

(A) 18
(B) 32
(C) 36
~~(D)~~ 40
(E) 45

$9A = 72$

$A = 8$

$5 \times 8 = 40$

2. If two points $(-3, 7)$ and $(2, t)$ are on a line that is perpendicular to the line given by the equation $y = 3x + 2$, what is the value of *t*?

(A) $-\dfrac{1}{3}$

(B) $-\dfrac{10}{3}$

~~(C)~~ $\dfrac{16}{3}$

(D) $\dfrac{10}{3}$

(E) 23

$y = 3x + 2$

$y = -\frac{1}{3}x +$

$\dfrac{7-t}{-3-2} = -\dfrac{1}{3}$

$21 + 3t = 5$

$-3t = -16$

$t = \frac{16}{3}$

3. Which of the following could be the lengths of the sides of a triangle?

(A) 1, 3, 4 ✗
~~(B)~~ 4, 5, 6 ✓
(C) 4, 4, 8 ✗
(D) 5, 8, 13 ✗
(E) 9, 9, 21 ✗

4. In the number line, if *k* is an integer, which of the following could be the length of segment *XY*?

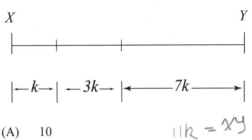

X   Y

$|{\leftarrow}k{\rightarrow}|\ {\leftarrow}3k{\rightarrow}\ |{\leftarrow}\quad 7k\quad{\rightarrow}|$

(A) 10
(B) 12
(C) 21
~~(D)~~ 33
(E) 42

$11k = XY$

5. The legs of a right triangle measure 6 and 8. If these legs are halved, what is the perimeter of the new right triangle?

(A) 5
(B) 6
(C) 10
~~(D)~~ 12
(E) 24

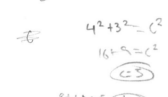

$4^2 + 3^2 = c^2$

$16 + 9 = c^2$

$c = 5$

$3 + 4 + 5 \boxed{12}$

wednesday

ISEE Triangles, Angles, and Lines Drill 1

1. Triangle ABC is similar to triangle DEF. The length of $\overline{BC}$ is 7 units, and the length of $\overline{EF}$ is 9 units. If the length of $\overline{AC}$ is 28 units, what is the length of $\overline{DF}$?

   (A) 4 units
   (B) 15 units
   (C) 36 units
   (D) 60 units

   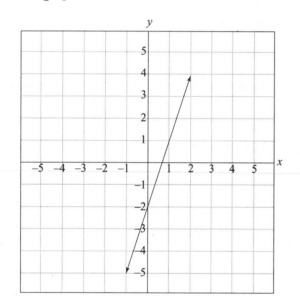

2. The graph of a line is shown.

   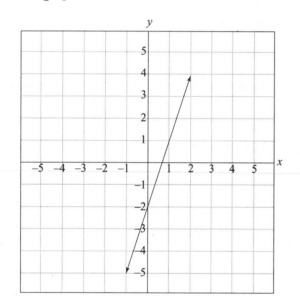

   What is the slope of the line?

   (A) −3
   (B) −2
   (C) 2
   (D) 3

3. A number line is shown.

   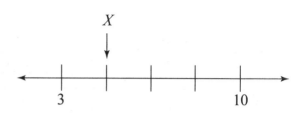

   What number does Point X represent on the number line?

   (A) $4\dfrac{3}{4}$

   (B) $5\dfrac{1}{4}$

   (C) $6\dfrac{1}{2}$

   (D) 7

4. If the length of the base of a triangle is decreased by 20 percent and the height of the triangle is increased by 20 percent, what is the percent change in the area of the triangle?

   (A) −10%
   (B) −4%
   (C) 0%
   (D) 10%

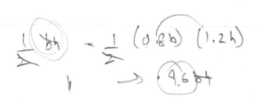

5. Triangle *HJK* is similar to triangle *LMN*.

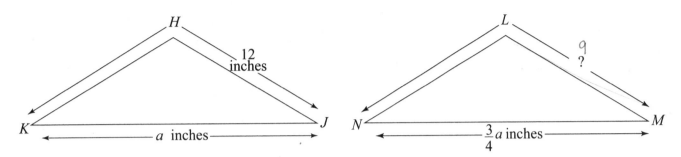

Note: Figures not drawn to scale.

What is the length of side *LM*?

(A)   9
(B)   12
(C)   9*a*
(D)   12*a*

ISEE Triangles, Angles, and Lines Drill 2

1. Which of the following is a graph of $x > -2$ and $x \leq 3$?

    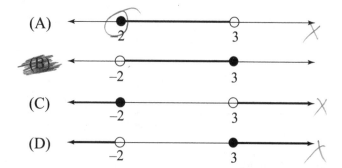

    (A)
    (B)
    (C)
    (D)

2. Mary Beth measures the height of a bush to be 4 feet and the length of its shadow to be 9 feet, as shown in the diagram.

    At the same time, the shadow of a flag pole is 27 feet in length. What is the height of the flag pole?

    (A)   8 ft
    (B)   12 ft
    (C)   15 ft
    (D)   18 ft

Directions: Using all information given in each question, compare the quantity in Column A to the quantity in Column B. All questions in Part Two have these answer choices:

(A) The quantity in Column A is greater.
(B) The quantity in Column B is greater.
(C) The two quantities are equal.
(D) The relationship cannot be determined from the information given.

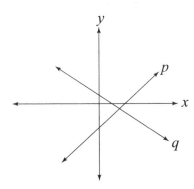

Line p is the graph of $y = 2x - 2$.
Line q is perpendicular to line p.

Column A	Column B

3. The slope of
    line q

    $\frac{1}{2}$

    Ⓑ

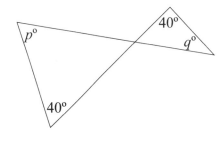

Column A	Column B

4. $p - q$ 80

    Ⓓ

Calvin's house is 30 miles due west of Meave's house, and Selena's house is 40 miles due south of Meave's house.

Column A	Column B

5. The shortest   70 miles
    distance between
    Calvin's house and
    Selena's house

Triangles, Angles,
and Lines: Answers
and Explanations

ANSWER KEY

**SSAT Triangles, Angles,
and Lines Drill 1**

1. C
2. D
3. C
4. B
5. D

**ISEE Triangles, Angles,
and Lines Drill 1**

1. C
2. D
3. A
4. B
5. A

**SSAT Triangles, Angles,
and Lines Drill 2**

1. D
2. C
3. B
4. D
5. D

**ISEE Triangles, Angles,
and Lines Drill 2**

1. B
2. B
3. B
4. B
5. B

SSAT Triangles, Angles, and Lines Drill 1

1. **C**   An equilateral triangle has 3 equal sides. $8 \times 3 = 24$.

2. **D**   Manipulate the equation into $y = mx + b$ form, by subtracting $4x$ from both sides and dividing both sides by 5: $y = -\dfrac{4}{5}x + 2$. The slope of a line perpendicular to another line is the negative reciprocal of the other line's slope. Slope is represented by m in the equation $y = mx + b$. In this case, the slope of the given line is $-\dfrac{4}{5}$. Thus, the slope of the perpendicular line is $\dfrac{5}{4}$.

3. **C**   On line T, the angles created by the transversal are supplementary, so the angle next to the 120° angle on line T is 60°. When two parallel lines are intersected by a transversal, corresponding angles are equal, so X is also 60°.

      An easy way to remember how perpendicular lines work when intersected by another line is all four little angles are the same, all four big angles are the same, and any little angle plus any big angle equals 180°. Here a big angle is 120°, so X, a little angle, is 60°.

4. **B**   Divide 96 by 7. The result is 13 with a remainder of 5.

5. **D**   In an isosceles triangle, the angles opposite the sides that are the same are also the same. As there are 180 degrees in a triangle and 48° are accounted for, the remaining two angles total 132°. Divide that in half to solve for R.

SSAT Triangles, Angles, and Lines Drill 2

1. **D** Set up an equation: $4A + 5A = 72$. Combine like terms and divide both sides by 9: $A = 8$. Multiply 8 by 5 to find MN.

2. **C** The slope of a line perpendicular to another line is the negative reciprocal of the other line's slope. Slope is represented by m in the equation $y = mx + b$. In this case, the slope of the given line is 3. Thus, the slope of perpendicular line is $-\dfrac{1}{3}$. Slope is determined by $\dfrac{rise}{run}$ or $\dfrac{y_1 - y_2}{x_1 - x_2}$. Set up a new equation: $\dfrac{7 - t}{-3 - 2} = -\dfrac{1}{3}$. Combine like terms in the denominator and cross multiply: $21 - 3t = 5$. Subtract 21 from both sides and divide both sides by -3: $t = \dfrac{16}{3}$.

 If you can sketch out the lines with reasonable accuracy, you can estimate. Doing so will allow you to guess down to two answers and possibly to know which of the two is more likely.

3. **B** For any triangle, the Third Side Rule states that the length of a side must be greater than the sum of the other two sides and less than the difference of the other two sides. Apply this rule to the answer choices to determine which one passes the test.

4. **D**   Let x be the length of the line. Write the equation: $k + 3k + 7k = x$. Combine like terms: It simplifies to $11k = x$. This indicates that the correct answer must be a multiple of 11, because k is an integer.

  Test the answers starting with (C). Here $k + 3k + 7k = 21$. Combine like terms and divide by 11: $k = \dfrac{21}{11}$. As k is an integer, eliminate (C). Try any other answer (as bigger/smaller is not at issue). If you test (D) $k + 3k + 7k = 33$. So, $11k = 33$, and $k = 3$. As that is an integer, select (D).

5. **D**   Draw a right triangle with legs of 3 and 4. Use the Pythagorean Theorem (or recognize the Pythagorean triple) to find that the hypotenuse is 5. Add the sides to find the perimeter.

ISEE Triangles, Angles, and Lines Drill 1

1. **C**   Draw the triangles to make sure the corresponding vertices of the two triangles are aligned. Set up a proportion: $\dfrac{7}{9} = \dfrac{28}{x}$.

2. **D**   Slope is determined by $\dfrac{rise}{run}$ or $\dfrac{y_1 - y_2}{x_1 - x_2}$. Find two easy points on the line. The y-intercept is $(0, -2)$. The x-intercept is not obvious, but $(1, 1)$ is. So: $\dfrac{-2 - 1}{0 - 1} = \dfrac{-3}{-1} = 3$.

3. **A** The difference between the given points is 7. There are four increases from the first tick mark to the last tick mark. Thus, each increase is $\frac{7}{4}$. Add $\frac{7}{4}$ to 3:

$3\frac{7}{4} = \frac{19}{4} = 4\frac{3}{4}$.

 Test the answers starting with (B) or (C). If X is $5\frac{1}{4}$, then each increase is $2\frac{1}{4}$. Thus, the next three tick marks would be $7\frac{1}{2}$, $9\frac{3}{4}$, and 12. As the last tick mark should be 10, (B) is too big. Choice (A) is the answer.

4. **B** Let b represent the original base, and let h represent the original height. As area of a triangle is given by $\frac{1}{2}bh$, the original area is $\frac{1}{2}bh$. As the base was decreased by 20%, the new base will be 80% of the original, or $0.8b$. As the height was increased by 20%, the new height will be 120% of the original, or $1.2b$. Thus the new area is $\frac{1}{2}(0.8b)(1.2h) = 0.48bh$, a lower area. Percent change is found by taking the difference, dividing that by the original, and then multiplying the result by 100:

$\frac{0.5bh - 0.48bh}{0.5bh} = \frac{0.02bh}{0.5bh} = \frac{0.02}{0.5} = \frac{2}{50} = 0.04 \times 100 = 4\%$. As the new area was lower than the original area, this represents a −4% change.

 As no original values were given, they do not matter, so you can plug in. Assign 10 to the original base and the original height. Thus, the original area was 50. The new base is 8 (reduced by 20% or 2, and the new height is 12 (increased by 20% or 2). Thus, the new area is 48. Because 48 is to 50 as 96 is to 100, the new area is 4% lower than the original.

5. **A**   Set up a proportion: $\dfrac{a}{12} = \dfrac{\frac{3}{4}a}{?}$. Cross multiply: $a? = 12 \times \dfrac{3}{4}a = 9a$. Divide both sides by a: $? = 9$.

 Plug in a value for a, such as 4. Now set up the proportion: $\dfrac{4}{12} = \dfrac{3}{?}$. Cross multiply and divide both sides by 4: $? = 9$.

ISEE Triangles, Angles, and Lines Drill 2

1. **B** $x > -2$ is represented by a line extending from -2 to the right, originating with an open dot. $x \le 3$ is represented by a line extending from 3 to the left, originating with a closed dot. Because these lines meet (do not extend in opposite directions), a single line between -2 and 3 is correct.

 When dealing with inequalities, *and* represents something looking like a *rubber band*, while *or* represents something looking like *oars* of a boat. Thus, in this case, *and* requires one of (A) or (B). The difference between these answers lies in the open or closed dots. The presence of "or equal to" requires a closed dot.

2. **B**   Set up a proportion: $\dfrac{4}{9} = \dfrac{x}{27}$. Cross multiply and divide by 9: $x = 12$.

3. **B**   The slope of a line perpendicular to another line is the negative reciprocal of the other line's slope. Slope is represented by m in the equation $y = mx + b$. In this case, the slope of line p is 2. Thus, the slope of line q is $-\frac{1}{2}$.

  Reading left to right, a positive slope proceeds up, and a negative slope proceeds down. Thus, the slope of line q is negative. Column B (positive) is greater.

4. **B**   Vertical angles are the same, so the unmarked angles in the triangles are the same. Call those angles x. As there are 180° in a triangle, the value of p is $180 - (40 + x)$, and the value of q is $180 - (40 + x)$. That is, p and q are the same. Thus, $p - q$ is 0. Therefore, column B is greater.

5. **B**   Plot the points, and you will see that they form a right triangle, with Meave's house located at the right angle. Thus, the shortest distance between Calvin's and Selena's house is represented by the hypotenuse. Using the Pythagorean Theorem, solve for the distance: 50.

Quadrilaterals

SSAT Quadrilaterals Drill 1

1. A rectangle has a width 7 times its length. If the area of the rectangle is 28, then what is the perimeter of the rectangle?

   (A) 2
   (B) 4
   (C) 14
   (D) 16
   (E) 32

2. A ribbon $6\frac{2}{3}$ feet long can be cut into how many

   pieces that are each 4 inches long?

   (A) 8
   (B) 20
   (C) 24
   (D) 27
   (E) 30

3. What is the measure of angle *YZW*?

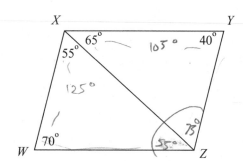

   (A) 55°
   (B) 65°
   (C) 110°
   (D) 120°
   (E) 130°

4. Mr. Riccio pays $40,000 a month for space in an office building. His office space covers a floor area that is 1,500 feet wide and 1,100 feet long. What is his approximate rental cost per square foot per month?

   (A) 2.4¢
   (B) 24¢
   (C) $2.40
   (D) $24.00
   (E) $41.25

5. A little cube has a side length of 3 centimeters. How many little cubes would be needed to make a big cube with a base perimeter of 36 centimeters?

   (A) 6
   (B) 9
   (C) 27
   (D) 36
   (E) 81

SSAT Quadrilaterals Drill 2

1. Ms. Quine bought a rectangular field 300 meters wide and 500 meters long. The cost was $3,000. What was her cost per square meter?

 (A) $ 0.02
(B) $ 0.20
(C) $ 0.50
(D) $ 1.60
(E) $ 2.00

2. How many linear feet of wallpaper are needed to trim the entire edge along the ceiling of a rectangular hallway with dimensions 18 feet by 6 feet?

(A)   108 feet
(B)   96 feet
(C)   48 feet
(D)   30 feet
(E)   24 feet

3. If *ABDE* is a rectangle, what is the area or triangle *ACE*?

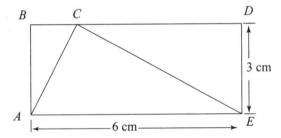

 (A)   9
(B)   12
(C)   15
(D)   18
(E)   It cannot be determined from the information given.

4. Let *m* represent the length of a rectangle. Which expression would represent the perimeter of this rectangle if the width is 9 more than the length?

(A) $m^2 + 9m$
(B) $m^2 - 9$
(C) $2m + 9$
(D) $4m - 18$
(E) $4m + 18$

5. Which of the following could be the dimensions of a rectangular box with a volume of 216 cubic inches?

(A)   4 inches by 11 inches by 9 inches
(B)   6 inches by 6 inches by 4 inches
(C)   8 inches by 8 inches by 4 inches
(D)   12 inches by 9 inches by 8 inches
(E)   18 inches by 6 inches by 2 inches

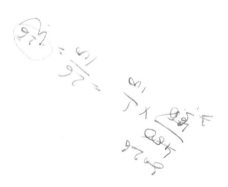

ISEE Quadrilaterals Drill 1

1. A rectangle has an area of 88 cm^2. If the base and height are measured in whole centimeters, what is the greatest possible perimeter of the rectangle?

   (A)   38 cm
   (B)   92 cm
   (C)   178 cm
   (D)   264 cm

2. The area of each grid square shown is 3 inches^2.

   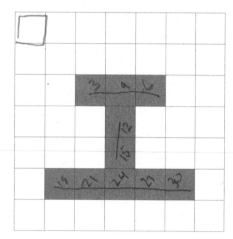

   What is the area of the shaded region?

   (A)   15 inches^2
   (B)   20 inches^2
   (C)   30 inches^2
   (D)   60 inches^2

3. The measures of three of the angles of a quadrilateral are shown below.

   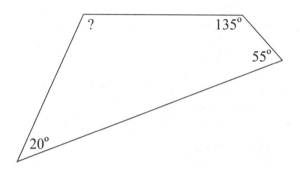

   What is the measure of the fourth angle?

   (A)   50°
   (B)   125°
   (C)   150°
   (D)   210°

4. The grid shows three vertices of a trapezoid.

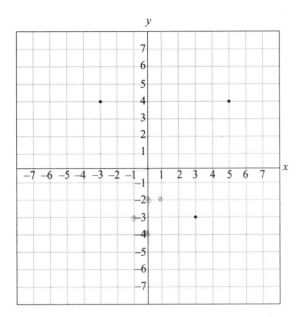

Which of the following could be the fourth vertex of the trapezoid?

(A) $(-1, -3)$
(B) $(0, -4)$
(C) $(0, -2)$
(D) $(1, -2)$

5. A rectangular parking lot was enlarged by making the width 3 times as wide and making the length $\frac{5}{4}$ as long. If the area of the parking lot was M square yards before the expansion, what is the new area, in square yards, of the parking lot, in terms of M?

(A) $\frac{5}{12} M$

(B) $\frac{12}{5} M$

(C) $\frac{15}{4} M$

(D) $\frac{15}{2} M$

ISEE Quadrilaterals Drill 2

Directions: Using all information given in each question, compare the quantity in Column A to the quantity in Column B. All questions in Part Two have these answer choices:

(A) The quantity in Column A is greater.
(B) The quantity in Column B is greater.
(C) The two quantities are equal.
(D) The relationship cannot be determined from the information given.

The area of a rectangle is 64 cm².

Column A	Column B
1. The perimeter of the rectangle	32

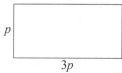

	Column A	Column B
3.	The area of a square with a side $x + 1$ cm long	$x^2 + 2x + 1$ cm²

Rectangle X

Rectangle Y

Note: Figures not drawn to scale.

The perimeter of Rectangle X is 40 m².
The area of Rectangle Y is 48 m².

Column A	Column B
2. p	q

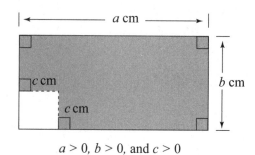

$a > 0$, $b > 0$, and $c > 0$

Note: Figure not drawn to scale.

	Column A	Column B
4.	Area of the shaded region	$ab - c^2$

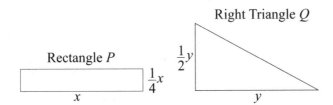

Note: Figures not drawn to scale.

Column A	Column B

5. The area of Rectangle *P*   The area of Right Triangle *Q*

Quadrilaterals:
Answers and
Explanations

ANSWER KEY

SSAT Quadrilaterals Drill 1

1. E
2. B
3. E
4. A
5. C

ISEE Quadrilaterals Drill 1

1. C
2. C
3. C
4. A
5. C

SSAT Quadrilaterals Drill 2

1. A
2. C
3. A
4. E
5. E

ISEE Quadrilaterals Drill 2

1. D
2. A
3. C
4. C
5. D

SSAT Quadrilaterals Drill 1

1. **E** Draw a rectangle and label the length x and the width $7x$. Write an equation to solve for x: $(x)(7x) = 28$. Divide both sides by 7 and take the square root of both sides: $x = 2$. Now, the length is 2, and the width is 14. Find the perimeter by adding all four sides: $2 + 2 + 14 + 14 = 32$.

2. **B** Convert feet to inches for an apples-to-apples comparison: 6 feet is 72 inches, and $\frac{2}{3}$ foot is 8 inches, for a total of 80 inches. Divide 80 by 4.

3. **E** The diagonal is a distraction; focus on the quadrilateral. As there are 360 degrees in a quadrilateral, angle $X = 360 - (70 + 55 + 65 + 40) = 360 - 230 = 130$.

4. **A** *Per* means divide, so divide the cost by the area in square feet. The cost is given. Find the area by multiplying length by width: $1{,}500 \times 1{,}100 = 1{,}650{,}000$. Divide $40,000 by this area: $0.024, which is 2.4¢.

 Rather than using long division to determine how many times $1,650,000 goes into $40,000, reduce the initial fraction in steps and stages and then estimate. Starting with $\dfrac{40{,}000}{1{,}500 \times 1{,}100}$, cancel out all the zeros, as there are four in the numerator and four in the denominator: $\dfrac{4}{15 \times 11}$. Now multiply 15 by 11: $\dfrac{4}{165}$. As $\dfrac{4}{100}$ is four cents, the bigger denominator indicates that the cost will be less than four cents.

Only (A) works.

5. **C**   To determine how many small cubes fit into a larger cube, divide the volumes of the cubes. As the smaller cube has side length of 3, its volume is 3^3 or 27. As the larger cube has a base perimeter of 36, it has side lengths of $\frac{36}{4}$ or 9, and a volume of 9^3 or 729. Divide 729 by 27: 27.

  If you are able to sketch out the scenario, you can easily count the number of little cubes.

SSAT Quadrilaterals Drill 2

1. **A**   *Per* means divide, so divide the cost by the area in square feet. The cost is given. Find the area by multiplying length by width: 300 × 500 = 150,000. Divide $3,000 by this area: $0.02.

  Rather than using long division to determine how many times $150,000 goes into $3,000, reduce the initial fraction in steps and stages and then estimate. Starting with $\frac{3,000}{500 \times 300}$, cancel out the three zeros in the numerator and three of the zeros in the denominator: $\frac{3}{5 \times 30}$. Now cancel out the threes in the numerator and denominator: $\frac{1}{5 \times 10} = \frac{1}{50} = 0.02$.

2. **C**   While square feet indicates area, linear feet indicates perimeter. Thus, find the perimeter of the room: 18 + 18 + 6 + 6 = 48.

3. **A**   The triangle and the rectangle share a base and a height, which are given. Therefore, the area of the triangle is $\frac{1}{2} \times 6 \times 3 = 9$.

4. **E**   Write an equation for perimeter, using the given side lengths: $m + m + m + 9 + m + 9 = 4m + 18$.

  Plug in a value for m such as 2. The perimeter is $2 + 2 + 11 + 11 = 26$. Only (D) yields this answer when you plug in 2 for m.

5. **E**   Test each answer by multiplying the values to determine which yields a volume of 216.

ISEE Quadrilaterals Drill 1

1. **C**   The greatest perimeter of a rectangle with a given area will have the greatest difference between the length and the width. As the area is 88 and the sides are integers, the greatest difference is created if the length is 88 and the height is 1. Thus, the perimeter is 178.

  Guess and check. If the sides are 11 and 8, the perimeter is 38. Now try another set, such as 44 and 2. Now the perimeter is 92. As you flatten the rectangle, the perimeter grows. Now try 88 and 1. This yields 178. There are no other integer values available to further flatten the rectangle.

2. **C**   Count the number of shaded squares and multiply the result by 3. There are 10 shaded squares, so the area is 30.

3. **C**   There are 360 degrees in a quadrilateral. Add up the given angles and subtract the sum from 360: 360 – (135 + 55 + 20) = 360 – 210 = 150.

4. **A**   A trapezoid has parallel bases. Draw in the trapezoid to see where the fourth vertex must be placed. The fourth vertex must be located at a y value of –3.

  Test the answers by notating each point on the grid. Only (A) creates a trapezoid, which must have two parallel bases.

5. **C**   Let the original width be x and the original length be y. As the area of a rectangle is $l \times w$, the area of the original rectangle is xy. Thus $M = xy$. The new width is $3x$, and the new length is $\frac{5}{4}y$, so the new area is $\frac{15}{4}xy$. Substitute M for xy, and the new area is $\frac{15}{4}M$.

  As no original values were given, plug in for an initial width and length, such as width = 2, and length = 4. Thus, the original area, M, was 8. The new width is 6 and the new length is 5, so the new area is 30. Only (C) yields 30 when you plug in $M = 8$.

ISEE Quadrilaterals Drill 2

1. **D** A rectangle with a given area can have several perimeters. The smallest perimeter is generated when the length and width are as close together in value as possible. In this case, all four sides can be 8, which would yield a perimeter of 32. Because the perimeter can be 32 (Column B) or larger than 32, the relative size of the columns cannot be determined.

2. **A** First, write an equation to solve for p: $p + p + 3p + 3p = 40$. Combine like terms and divide by 8: $p = 5$. Now write an equation for q: $q \times 3q = 48$. Combine like terms and divide by 3: $q^2 = 16$. Take the square root of both sides: $q = 4$.

3. **C** Solve for the area by multiplying $(x + 1)$ by $(x + 1)$: $x^2 - 2x + 1$.

    Plug in an easy number for x, such as 2. The area of the square is 9. If you plug 2 into Column B, you also get 9.

4. **C** To find the area of an irregularly shaped shaded region, find the areas of the two normal shapes and subtract the smaller from the larger. The area of a rectangle is length $\times$ width, so the area of the large rectangle is ab. The area of a square is side², so the area of the small square is c^2. Thus the area of the shaded region is $ab - c^2$.

    Plug in easy numbers for a, b, and c, such as $a = 4$, $b = 3$, and $c = 2$. To find the area of an irregularly shaped shaded region, find the areas of the two normal shapes and subtract the smaller from the larger. The area of the rectangle is 12, and the area of the square is 4, so the area of the shaded region is 8. If you plug your three values into Column B, you also get 8.

5. **D**   First, find the area of the rectangle, using length $\times$ width: $\frac{1}{4}x^2$. Now find the area of the triangle, using $\frac{1}{2}$ base $\times$ height: $\frac{1}{4}y^2$. As no information is given about the relative values of x and y, it cannot be determined which figure has a larger area.

 Plug in easy numbers for x and y, such as $x = 4$, and $y = 8$. The area of the rectangle is 4, while the area of the triangle is 16. As the value in Column A is not *always* greater than the value in Column B and the two columns do not always have the same value, eliminate (A) and (C). Now, plug in again to see if the rectangle can have a bigger area. Try switching the values: $x = 8$, and $y = 4$. Now the area of the rectangle is 16, and the area of the triangle is 4. As the value in Column B is not always greater than the value in Column B, eliminate (B).

Circles and Cylinders

SSAT Circles and Cylinders Drill

1. In the figure, the vertices of right triangle *MLN* are on the circle and *L* is the center of the circle. If the area of the region created by lines *ML*, *LN*, and arc *MN* is 9π, what is the area of the shaded region?

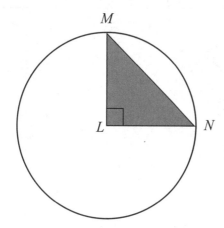

   (A) $9\pi - 6$
   (B) $9\pi - 9$
   (C)   9
   (D)   18
   (E)   36

2. Isosceles triangle *XYZ* is inscribed in Circle *O* below as shown.

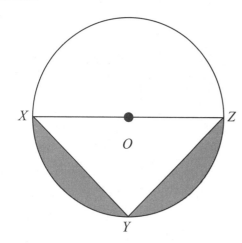

   If the radius of the circle is 10, what is the area of the shaded region?

   (A) $25\pi - 50$
   (B) $50\pi - 100$
   (C) $50\pi - 200$
   (D) $100\pi - 100$
   (E) $100\pi - 200$

3. A circle is inscribed in a square with a side length of 12. Find the area of the shaded region.

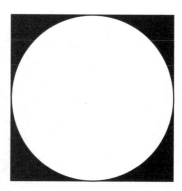

   (A)   144
   (B) 36π
   (C) 12π
   (D) $144 - 36\pi$
   (E) $36\pi - 144$

4. Cinquemani Family Pasta Sauce comes in cylindrical jars that serve 4. The jars have a base diameter of 8 cm and a height of 4 cm. They want to start selling the sauce in single-serve jars that are the same height. What will the base diameter be?

   (A)   2 cm
   (B)   4 cm
   (C)   8 cm
   (D)   16 cm
   (E)   32 cm

5. If the volume of a right circular cone is given by $V = \frac{1}{3}\pi r^2 h$, where *r* is the radius of the cone and *h* is the height of the cone, what is *h* in terms of *r* and *V*?

   (A) $\dfrac{3}{V\pi r^2}$

   (B) $\dfrac{V}{3\pi r^2}$

   (C) $\dfrac{3V}{\pi r^2}$

   (D) $\dfrac{V\pi}{3r^2}$

   (E) $\dfrac{3V\pi}{r^2}$

ISEE Circles and Cylinders Drill

1. Point $(4, -3)$ is on a circle with center $(-1, 9)$. What is the diameter of the circle?

   (A) 24
   (B) 25
   (C) 26
   (D) 27

2. A circle is inscribed in a square with side length 12 inches, as shown.

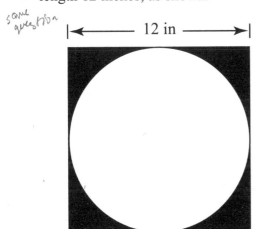

   What is the area of the shaded region?

   (A) $144 - 144\pi$ in^2
   (B) $144 - 36\pi$ in^2
   (C) $48 - 36\pi$ in^2
   (D) $48 - 24\pi$ in^2

3. The diameter of the cylinder shown is 3 times its height. The formula used to find the volume of a cylinder is $V = r^2 h\pi$, where r is the radius of the cylinder and h is the height of the cylinder.

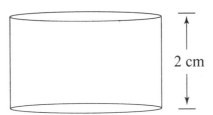

   If the height of the cylinder is 2 cm, what is its volume, in cm^3?

   (A) 12π
   (B) 18π
   (C) 24π
   (D) 72π

4. The formula for the volume of a sphere is $V = \frac{4}{3}\pi r^3$, where r is the radius of the sphere. A sphere has a volume of 36π. What is the radius of this sphere?

   (A) $\frac{3}{4}$

   (B) 3

   (C) 4

   (D) 6

5. Use the figure below to answer the question.

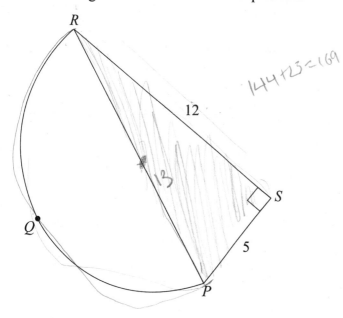

If arc *PQR* is a semicircle, what is the perimeter of *PQRS*?

(A) $17 + \left(\dfrac{13}{2}\right)\pi$

(B) $17 + \left(\dfrac{1}{2}\right)\left(\dfrac{13}{2}\right)^2 \pi$

(C) $30 + \left(\dfrac{13}{2}\right)\pi$

(D) $30 + \left(\dfrac{1}{2}\right)\left(\dfrac{13}{2}\right)^2 \pi$

Circles and Cylinders: Answers and Explanations

ANSWER KEY

SSAT Circles and Cylinders Drill

1. D
2. B
3. D
4. B
5. C

ISEE Circles and Cylinders Drill

1. C
2. B
3. B
4. B
5. A

SSAT Circles and Cylinders Drill

1. **D** Because the area of part of a circle is given, you need to determine what fraction of the circle is represented by that sector. The interior angle of the sector is 90°, which means that the area of the sector is $\frac{1}{4}$ of the area of the circle. Thus, multiply 9π by 4 to get 36π for the area of the circle. Now, solve for the radius, since the sides of the triangle are radii: $36\pi = \pi(r)^2$, so $r = 6$. The area of a triangle is $\frac{1}{2}bh = \frac{1}{2}(6)(6) = 18$.

2. **B** Questions seeking the area of a weird shaded region generally require you to subtract the area of one normal shape from the area of another normal shape. In this case, subtract the area of the triangle from the area of the semicircle. The area of a semicircle is $\frac{1}{2}\pi r^2 = \frac{1}{2}\pi(10)^2 = 50\pi$. Triangles formed by the endpoints of a diameter and part of a circle are always right triangles. Thus, the sides of the triangle are the base and height of the triangle. If you draw in a radius to split the triangle, you have formed two right triangles with sides length 10. Using the Pythagorean Theorem, you can find the side of the larger triangle: $\sqrt{10^2 + 10^2} = \sqrt{200} = \sqrt{2 \times 100} = 10\sqrt{2}$. The area of a triangle is $\frac{1}{2}bh = \frac{1}{2}\left(10\sqrt{2}\right)\left(10\sqrt{2}\right) = 100$. Choice (B) reflects the difference between the two areas.

 You can estimate that the area is a small fraction of the area of the circle ($100\pi =$ approximately 300). Choice (A) is about 25, which represents about $\frac{1}{12}$ of the circle; (B) is about 50, which represents about $\frac{1}{6}$ of the circle; (C) is negative; (D) is about 200, which represents about $\frac{2}{3}$ of the circle; and (E) is about 100, which represent about $\frac{1}{3}$ of the circle. Choices (D) and (E) are clearly too large, and (C) is impossible. You have to make your best judgment about (A) and (B); hopefully you realize that (A) is a bit too small.

3. **D**   Questions seeking the area of a weird shaded region generally require you to subtract the area of one normal shape from the area of another normal shape. In this case, subtract the area of the circle from the area of the square. The area of a square is s^2, in this case $12^2 = 144$. The area of the circle is πr^2. If you draw in a diameter, you will see that the diameter is the same length as the side of the square, so the radius is 6. Thus, the area of the circle is $\pi(6)^2 = 36\pi$. Choice (D) reflects the difference between the two areas.

  You can estimate that the area is a tiny fraction of the area of the square (144). Estimate the values of the answer choices, replacing π with 3 to keep the math simple. Choice (D) is a reasonable estimate. The other choices are too big or, in the case of (E), less than zero.

4. **B**   First, find the volume of the larger cylinder jars to determine how much sauce each one contains. The volume of a cylinder is given by $V = \pi r^2 h$, where r is the radius of the cylinder and h is its height. The radius in this case is 4, as the diameter is 8. Plug in the given values: $V = \pi(4)^2 4 = 64\pi$. Because the jars serve four people, the volume of a single-serve jar will be $\frac{1}{4}(64\pi) = 16\pi$. Now solve for the radius of the smaller jars, given the volume and height of 4: $16\pi = \pi(r)^2 4$, so $r = 2$. As the question asks for the diameter, the answer is 4.

5. **C**   To isolate h, write the equation and multiply both sides by 3: $3V = \pi r^2 h$. Next divide both sides by π and r^2: $\dfrac{3V}{\pi r^2} = h$.

  Plug in values for r and h, such as $r = 3$ and $h = 2$, and solve for V: $V = \frac{1}{3}\pi(3)^2(2) = \frac{1}{3}\pi(9)(2) = 6\pi$. Only (C) yields $h = 2$ when the values for r and V are plugged in.

ISEE Circles and Cylinders Drill

1. **C** First, find the radius by finding the distance from the center to the given point. To do so, use the distance formula, which states that $d = \sqrt{(x_1 - x_2)^2 + (y_1 - y_2)^2}$. Here, $d = \sqrt{(4 - [-1])^2 + (-3 - 9)^2} = \sqrt{5^2 + 12^2} = \sqrt{25 + 144} = \sqrt{169} = 13$. As the radius is 13, the diameter is 26.

 Sketch out the given points and connect them with a line. This line, in addition to being the radius of the circle, is the hypotenuse of a right triangle. Draw in the legs by drawing a vertical line from (4, –3) to (–1, –3) and a horizontal line from (–1, 9) to (–1, –3). Count the horizontal distance: 5. Count the vertical distance: 12. Use the Pythagorean Theorem (or recognize the Pythagorean triple) to find 13 as the radius. Thus, the diameter is 26.

2. **B** Questions seeking the area of a weird shaded region generally require you to subtract the area of one normal shape from the area of another normal shape. In this case, subtract the area of the circle from the area of the square. The area of a square is s^2, in this case $12^2 = 144$. The area of the circle is πr^2. If you draw in a diameter, you will see that the diameter is the same length as the side of the square, so the radius is 6. Thus, the area of the circle is $\pi(6)^2 = 36\pi$. Choice (B) reflects the difference between the two areas.

 You can estimate that the area is a tiny fraction of the area of the square (144). Estimate the values of the answer choices, replacing π with 3 to keep the math simple. Choice (B) is a reasonable estimate. The other choices are less than zero.

3. **B** As the formula for the volume of a cylinder and the height are given, you need to find the radius. The diameter is three times the height, $2 \times 3 = 6$. Therefore, the radius is 3. Plug $r = 3$ and $h = 2$ into the given formula: $V = \pi(3)^2(2) = 18\pi$.

4. **B** As the formula for the volume of a sphere and the sphere's volume are given, you can write an equation to solve for the radius: $36\pi = \dfrac{4}{3}\pi(r)^3$. First, divide both sides by π: $36 = \dfrac{4}{3}(r)^3$. Next, divide both sides by $\dfrac{4}{3}$, which means multiplying both sides by the reciprocal: $\dfrac{3}{4}(36) = 27 = (r)^3$. The cube root of 27 is 3.

5. **A** To find the perimeter of *PQRS*, you need the measure of the arc, which is part of the semicircle. The diameter of the semicircle is the hypotenuse of the triangle, so use the Pythagorean Theorem (or recognize the Pythagorean triple) to find that the diameter is 13. The measure of the arc is half the circumference, so write an equation with 13 as the diameter: $\dfrac{1}{2}\pi d = 13\pi = \dfrac{13}{2}\pi$. Add this to the sum of the legs of the triangle to find the perimeter: $17 + \dfrac{13}{2}\pi$.

Miscellaneous
Geometry and
Visual Perception

SSAT Miscellaneous Geometry and Visual Perception Drill

1. A fence in the shape of a regular polygon has a perimeter measuring 130 feet and each side has a length of 13 feet. How many sides does this polygon have?

   (A) 7
   (B) 9
   (C) 10
   (D) 11
   (E) 13

2. The total of the measures of all the angles of a pentagon is

   (A) 180°
   (B) 270°
   (C) 360°
   (D) 540°
   (E) 720°

   $180(n-2)$

3. An equilateral triangle has the same perimeter as a circle that has the same perimeter as a square. Which of the following lists the shapes in decreasing order of area?

   (A) triangle, square, circle
   (B) square, triangle, circle
   (C) circle, triangle, square
   (D) triangle, circle, square
   (E) circle, square, triangle

4. Donna's house is 15 kilometers from the gym and Paul's house is 8 kilometers from the same gym. In total kilometers, how far does Donna live from Paul?

   (A) 7 kilometers
   (B) 16 kilometers
   (C) 24 kilometers
   (D) 30 kilometers
   (E) It cannot be determined from the information given.

5. The perimeter of a hexagon is 15 meters. If the length of each side is increased by 3 meters, what is the new perimeter?

   (A) 18 meters
   (B) 24 meters
   (C) 30 meters
   (D) 33 meters
   (E) 45 meters

6. If the perimeters of triangle ABC and quadrilateral $BCDE$ are each 18, then $r + s =$

   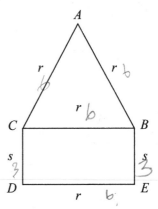

   (A) 6
   (B) 9
   (C) 12
   (D) 18
   (E) 27

7. Which of the following figures can be drawn without retracing or lifting the pencil?

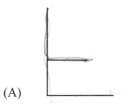

(A)

(B)

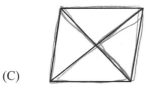

(C)

(D)

(E)

8. Below are three boxes in an L-shape. Which figure in the answers can be covered without any spaces or overlapping boxes by placing several L-shape pieces on it?

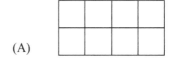

(A)

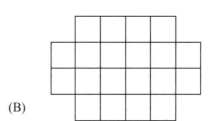

(B)

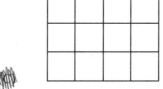

(D)

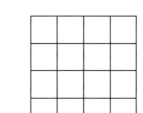

(E)

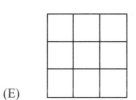

9. The region in the figure shown is divided by lines *A*, *B*, *C*, and *D*. The area between *A* and *C* is 20 square miles, between *B* and *D* is 35 square miles, and between *C* and *D* is 30 square miles. What is the area in square miles between *A* and *B*?

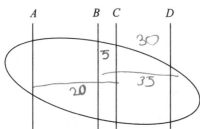

(A) 5
(B) 10
(C) 15
(D) 25
(E) 85

10. Determine the perimeter of the figure.

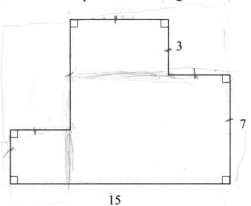

(A) 25
(B) 33
(C) 41
(D) 50
(E) It cannot be determined from the information given.

ISEE Miscellaneous Geometry and Visual Perception Drill

1. The formula for the volume of a pyramid with a square base is $\frac{1}{3}Bh$, where B represents the area of the square base of the pyramid and h represents the height of the pyramid. The volume of Pyramid A is one half the volume of Pyramid B. Which of the following statements could be true?

   (A) The height of Pyramid A is one half the height of Pyramid B, and a side of the base of Pyramid A is the two times a side of the base of Pyramid B.
   (B) The height of Pyramid A is one half the height of Pyramid B, and a side of the base of Pyramid A is the same as a side of the base of Pyramid B.
   (C) A side of the base of Pyramid A is one half a side of the base of Pyramid B, and the height of Pyramid A is the same as the height of Pyramid B.
   (D) Both a side and the height of Pyramid A are one half a side and the height of Pyramid B.

2. The surface area of a right circular cylinder is represented by $SA = 2\pi r^2 + 2\pi rh$, where r is the radius of the cylinder and h is its height. If the surface area of a right circular cylinder is 36π and its radius is 3, what is its height?

   (A) 2
   (B) 3
   (C) 4
   (D) 5

$36\pi = 2\pi \cdot 9 + 2\pi \cdot 3h$

$36\pi = 18\pi + 6\pi h$

$36\pi = 24\pi h$

$12\pi = h$

$\dfrac{36\pi - 18\pi = 6\pi h}{6\pi}$

$3 = h$

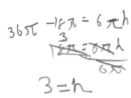

3. Triangle ABC is shown. The length of $\overline{BC}$ is 3 inches. The measure of angle ACB is 35°.

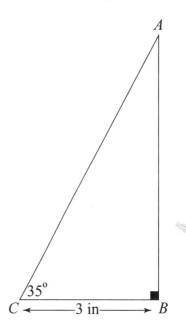

Which expression gives the value of $\overline{AB}$?

   (A) $3 \tan 35°$

   (B) $3 \cos 35°$

   (C) $\dfrac{3}{\tan 35°}$

   (D) $\dfrac{3}{\cos 35°}$

4. What gives the number of square feet of tiles needed to cover a rectangular floor that is 3 yards long by 4 yards wide?

   (A) 12 ft²
   (B) 36 ft²
   (C) 48 ft²
   (D) 108 ft²

5. Use the cube to answer the question.

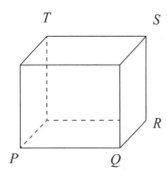

In the cube above, which corner is farthest from P?

(A) Q
(B) R
(C) S
(D) T

6. A square inscribed in a square is shown.

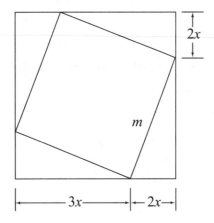

In terms of x, what is the length of line segment m?

(A) $5x^2$
(B) $13x^2$
(C) $x\sqrt{5}$
(D) $x\sqrt{13}$

7. A Venn diagram is shown.

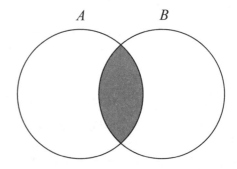

In the Venn diagram, circle A represents all multiples of 4, and circle B represents all multiples of 7. Which of the following best describes the shaded region?

(A) Multiples of 3
(B) Multiples of 11
(C) Multiples of 28
(D) Multiples of 47

8. Use the cube to answer the question.

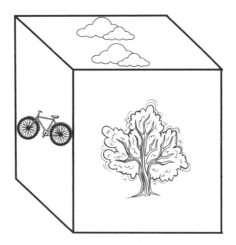

Which figure is a possible net for the cube?

(A)

(C)

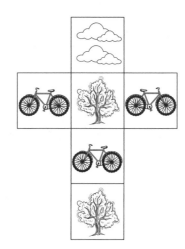

(B)

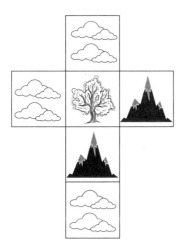

(D)

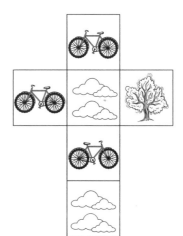

Directions: Using all information given in each question, compare the quantity in Column A to the quantity in Column B. All questions in Part Two have these answer choices:

(A) The quantity in Column A is greater.
(B) The quantity in Column B is greater.
(C) The two quantities are equal.
(D) The relationship cannot be determined from the information given.

The measure of an interior angle of a regular polygon with n sides is $\dfrac{180(n-2)}{n}$.

$V = \dfrac{4}{3}\pi r^3$

$r > 1$

	Column A	Column B		Column A	Column B
9.	The sum of the interior angles of a regular pentagon	The sum of the interior angles of a regular octagon	10.	r	$\dfrac{3V}{4\pi}$

Miscellaneous Geometry and Visual Perception: Answers and Explanations

ANSWER KEY

SSAT Miscellaneous Geometry and Visual Perception Drill

1. C
2. D
3. E
4. E
5. D
6. B
7. D
8. C
9. C
10. D

ISEE Miscellaneous Geometry and Visual Perception Drill

1. B
2. B
3. A
4. D
5. C
6. D
7. C
8. C
9. B
10. B

SSAT Miscellaneous Geometry and Visual Perception Drill

1. **C** Divide the perimeter of the polygon by the side length to determine the number of sides: $130 \div 13 = 10$.

2. **D** The sum of the degrees in a polygon of n sides is determined by $180(n - 2)$. As there are 5 sides in a pentagon, the sum of the degrees is $180(5 - 2) = 180(3) = 540$.

 Draw a pentagon and carve it into a quadrilateral and triangle. As there are 360° in a quadrilateral and 180° in a triangle, the two shapes combined will have 540°.

3. **E** Plug in a value for the common perimeter, ideally a value that is divisible by 3 and 4, such as 12. Thus, using the formulas for perimeter of a square ($4s$), triangle ($3s$), and circle ($2\pi r$), the sides of the square are 3, the sides of the triangle are 4, and the radius of the circle is $\dfrac{12}{2\pi} = \dfrac{6}{\pi}$. Now, find the area of the figures. The area of the square is 3^2, which is 9. To find the area of the triangle, first use the Pythagorean Theorem to find the height: $h^2 + \left(\dfrac{1}{2}(4)\right)^2 = 4^2$. When you distribute the exponent on the left, you find $h^2 + 4 = 16$. Thus $h^2 = 12$, and $h = \sqrt{12}$. So, area is defined as $\dfrac{1}{2}(4)(\sqrt{12}) = 2\sqrt{12} = 2\sqrt{3 \times 4} = 4\sqrt{3}$. Finally, find the area of the circle: $\pi\left(\dfrac{6}{\pi}\right)^2 = \dfrac{36}{\pi}$. Now compare the areas. As π is a bit greater than 3, the area of the circle is a bit less than 12, which is larger than the square (9). For the triangle, $\sqrt{3}$ is less than 2, so the area is less than 8.

4. E   There is not enough information about where Donna and Paul live because there is no information as to the direction from the gym in which they live. They can live 23 blocks from each other, 7 blocks from each other, or anything in between.

5. D   Adding 3 to each of 6 sides will result in an increase of 18. So, 15 + 18 = 33.

6. B   First determine the value of r: $r + r + r = 18$, so $r = 6$. Next determine the value of s: $6 + 6 + s + s = 18$, so $s + s = 6$, and $s = 3$. Add r and s: 9.

7. D   For each answer, start at one point and try to draw the figure without lifting your pencil. Keep trying from different points until you are sure the answer works or cannot work.

8. C   First, determine how many answers have a number of squares that is divisible by 3, as the shape you need to fit in has 3 squares. Eliminate (A), (B), and (D). Now work through either answer to determine if the shape you need to fit in can fill the larger grid.

9. C   Clearly label the distances on the figure. Notice that $BC + CD = BD$, so you can solve for BC: $BC + 30 - 35$, meaning $BC = 5$. Notice, as well, that $AC + BC = AC$, so you can solve for AB: $AB + 5 = 20$, meaning $AB = 15$.

10. D   Because all of the angles are right angles, the lengths of the shorter horizontal lines will add up to the length of the horizontal line on the bottom. Likewise, the lengths of the two vertical lines on the left will add up to the length of the two vertical lines on the right. Therefore, the perimeter is $15 + 15 + 7 + 3 + 7 + 3 = 50$.

ISEE Miscellaneous Geometry and Visual Perception Drill

1. **B** If Pyramid B has a base with side length s and a height of h, the volume $V_B = \frac{1}{3}s^2h$. Pyramid A, therefore, has a volume $V_A = \frac{1}{6}s^2h$. Test each answer using the given volume formula. For (A), the height is $\frac{1}{2}h$, and the side length is $2s$, making the volume $V_A = \frac{1}{3}(2s)^2\left(\frac{1}{2}h\right) = \frac{1}{3}(4s^2)\left(\frac{1}{2}h\right) = \frac{2}{3}s^2h$. Eliminate (A). For (B), the height is $\frac{1}{2}h$, and the side length is s, making the volume $V_A = \frac{1}{3}(s)^2\left(\frac{1}{2}h\right) = \frac{1}{6}s^2h$. Choice (B) is correct. If you test (C) for safety, the height is h, and the side length is $\frac{1}{2}s$, making the volume $V_A = \frac{1}{3}\left(\frac{1}{2}s\right)^2 h = \frac{1}{3}\left(\frac{1}{4}s^2\right)h = \frac{1}{12}s^2h$. Eliminate (C). If you test (D) for safety, the height is $\frac{1}{2}h$, and the side length is $\frac{1}{2}s$, making the volume $V_A = \frac{1}{3}\left(\frac{1}{2}s\right)^2\left(\frac{1}{2}h\right) = \frac{1}{3}\left(\frac{1}{4}s^2\right)\left(\frac{1}{2}h\right) = \frac{1}{24}s^2h$. Eliminate (D).

 Plug in values for the side length and height of Pyramid B, such as $s = 2$ and $h = 3$. The volume is $\frac{1}{3}(2^2)(3) = 4$. Thus, the volume of Pyramid A is 2. Only (C) yields a volume of 2 for Pyramid A when the values for s and h are plugged in.

2. **B** Using the given formula, surface area, and radius, set up an equation to solve for the height: $36\pi = 2\pi(3)^2 + 2\pi(3)(h) = 18\pi + 6\pi h$. Subtract 18π from both sides: $18\pi = 6\pi h$. Divide both sides by 6π: $h = 3$.

3. **A**   Use SohCahToa. As $\overline{AB}$ is OPPOSITE the given angle, and BC is ADJACENT TO the given angle, use tangent: $\tan 35° = \dfrac{\overline{AB}}{3}$. Multiply both sides by 3: $3 \tan 35° = \overline{AB}$.

4. **D**   There are three feet in a yard, so first convert both measurements from yards to feet: $3 \times 3 = 9$, and $3 \times 4 = 12$. To find the area in square feet, multiply the two measurements: $9 \times 12 = 108$.

5. **C**   As the diagram shows, the farthest point from any vertex of a cube is the vertex at the other end of the longest diagonal of the cube, in this case S.

6. **D**   As the outer figure is a square, each vertex is 90° and, thus, part of a right triangle. The four right triangles are identical, so set up the Pythagorean theorem to find m: $(2x)^2 + (3x)^2 = m^2$. Distribute the exponents and combine like terms: $13x^2 = m^2$. Take the square root of both sides: $m = x\sqrt{13}$.

 Plug in a value for x, such as 2. The sides of the outer square are now divided into segments of length 4 and 6. As the triangles are right triangles, use the Pythagorean Theorem to find m: $4^2 + 6^2 = m^2 = 52$. Thus $m = \sqrt{52} = \sqrt{4 \times 13} = 2\sqrt{13}$. Only (D) yields this result when you plug in x.

7. **C**   As Circle A has all multiples of 4 and Circle B has all multiples of 7, the intersection—or overlap—will be all numbers that are multiples of both 4 and 7, namely multiples of 28.

8. **C**   The net is the cube unfolded. To answer this question, you need to use your visual perception skills. Start by visually unfolding the three visible sides of the cube. The clouds will appear above the tree, and the bike will appear to the left of the tree. The bike is facing to the left. Now check the answers to find one with this configuration. Choice (C) clearly works. Check to see if any others might work depending on the orientation of the folded cube. None do.

9. **B**   Use the formula first to find the measure of an individual angle in the pentagon (call it p) and in the octagon (call it o). For the pentagon, $p = \dfrac{180(5-2)}{5} = \dfrac{180(3)}{5} = 108$. For the octagon, $o = \dfrac{180(8-2)}{8} = \dfrac{180(6)}{8} = 135$. The sum of the measures of five angles in the pentagon is $108 \times 5 = 540$. The sum the measures of the eight angles in the octagon is $135 \times 8 = 1{,}080$.

 Use logic. As the sum of the measures of the angles in a rectangle is greater than the sum of the measures of the angles in a triangle, more sides means a greater sum of the measures of the angles.

10. **B**   As Column A contains an isolated r, manipulate the given equation to isolate r. First divide both sides by $\dfrac{4}{3}$ (that is, multiply both sides by the reciprocal): $\dfrac{3}{4}V = \pi r^3$. Next, divide both sides by π: $\dfrac{3V}{4\pi} = r^3$. Finally, take the cube root of both sides: $\sqrt[3]{\dfrac{3V}{4\pi}} = r$. Because r is great than 1, the volume will be greater than r and, therefore, greater than 1. Because the value of Column B is the same as r^3, the value of Column B is greater.

 Plug in a value for r such as 3. Therefore, $V = \dfrac{4}{3}\pi(3)^3 = 36\pi$. Using the $r = 3$ value, the value of Column A is 3. Using $V = 36\pi$, the value of Column B is $\dfrac{3 \times 36\pi}{4\pi} = 27$.

Reading and Interpreting Data

SSAT Reading and Interpreting Data Drill 1

1. Josie takes 5 vocab quizzes, each worth the same amount, and scores an average of 83%. The teacher decides to delete one of her tests making her new average 86%. What was Josie's grade on the deleted quiz?

   (A) 30%
   (B) 50%
   (C) 63%
   (D) 71%
   (E) 80%

2. The graph shows the population of Neptune from 1982 through 2012. By how many people did the population increase between 2002 and 2012?

   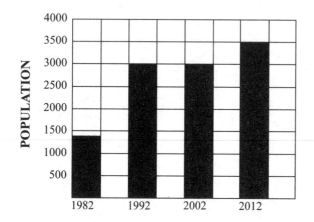

   (A) 500
   (B) 1,000
   (C) 1,500
   (D) 2,000
   (E) 2,500

3. The graph shows Jamie's monthly budget. What percentage of his budget is allocated for movies and recreation?

   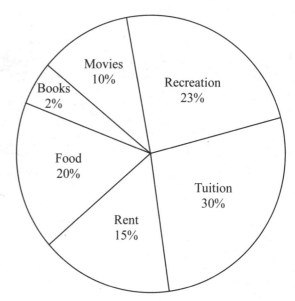

   (A) 14%
   (B) 23%
   (C) 33%
   (D) 47%
   (E) 49%

Questions 4-5 are based on the table in the figure.

College X Majors One Year After Graduation

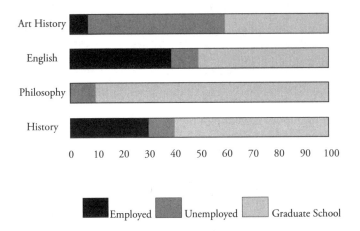

4. The fractional part of the number of art history major graduates from College X enrolled in graduate school was approximately

    (A) $\frac{1}{5}$

    (B) $\frac{1}{4}$

    (C) $\frac{1}{3}$

      $\frac{2}{5}$

    (E) $\frac{2}{3}$

5. If the number of history majors graduated from College X was 300, approximately what was the difference in the number of history majors employed and the number of history majors enrolled in graduate school?

    (A) 50
    (B) 75
    (C) 80
    (D) 85
    (E) 90

6. If the average of five consecutive whole numbers is 21, what is the greatest number?

    (A) 11
    (B) 19
    (C) 23
    (D) 26
    (E) 27

7. A coffee shop has an average of 200 customers per day. To increase sales, the owner plans to reduce the price of a large cup of coffee from $2.00 to $1.00 after 10 A.M. each day. If 50 people pay $2.00, how many people must pay $1.00 if daily sales are to remain the same as before the $1.00 reduction plan?

    (A) 250
    (B) 300
    (C) 350
    (D) 400
    (E) 450

8. The average weight of two French Bulldogs is 17.5 pounds and the average weight of four English Bulldogs is 62.5 pounds. What is the average weight, in pounds, of all six dogs?

    (A) 40
    (B) 47.5
    (C) 50
    (D) 57.5
    (E) 60

9. In a survey, each of 300 people watches TV through cable, video streaming apps, or both. If 270 of these people have cable and 90 have video streaming apps, how many people have both cable and video streaming apps?

   (A) 30
   (B) 60
   (C) 90
   (D) 180
   (E) 210

10. A runner took between 45 minutes and 1 hour to run a 10-mile loop around the lake. The average speed, in miles per hour, must have been between

   (A) 10 and $13\frac{1}{3}$

   (B) $13\frac{1}{3}$ and 17

   (C) 17 and $20\frac{2}{3}$

   (D) $20\frac{2}{3}$ and 45

   (E) 45 and 60

SSAT Reading and Interpreting Data Drill 2

Questions 1–2 refer to the graph.

How Peter Spends His Monthly Income

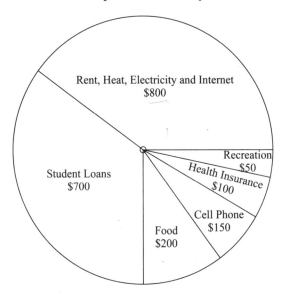

Rent, Heat, Electricity and Internet
$800

Student Loans
$700

Recreation
$50

Health Insurance
$100

Cell Phone
$150

Food
$200

1. What fraction of Peter's monthly budget is spent on student loans?

(A) $\frac{1}{10}$

(B) $\frac{3}{10}$

(C) $\frac{7}{20}$

(D) $\frac{2}{5}$

(E) $\frac{2}{3}$

2. The amount Peter spends for his cell phone is what percent of the amount he spends for food and health insurance?

(A) 20%
(B) 30%
(C) 40%
(D) 50%
(E) 60%

3. One pencil weighs 5 grams. If a box of pencils holds 250 pencils, how many kilograms does the whole box of pencils weigh?

(A) 2,500 kg
(B) 500 kg
(C) 125 kg
(D) 12.5 kg
(E) 1.25 kg

4. According to the graph in the figure, in which week was the greatest increase in the number of cookies baked compared to the week before?

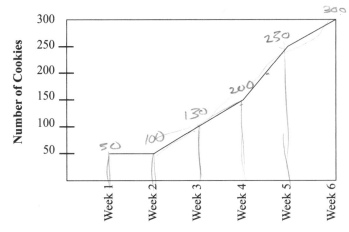

Cookies Baked Each Week for 6 Weeks

Number of Cookies

(A) Week 2
(B) Week 3
(C) Week 4
(D) Week 5
(E) Week 6

$\dfrac{F + G}{2} = 60 \Rightarrow F + G = 120$

5. Which of the following must be true if two numbers, F and G, have an average of 60 and F is less than G?

(A) $F = 60$ and $G = 60$
(B) $F - G = 60$
(C) $F + G = 60$
(D) $F = 60 + G$
(E) $F - 60 = 60 - G$

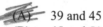

6. The heights of a basil plant and mint plant have a ratio of 5:4. If the basil plant grew 2 inches and 2 inches was cut off the top of the mint plant, the ratio of their heights would be 2:1. How much taller is the basil plant than the mint plant?

(A) 2 inches
(B) 4 inches
(C) 6 inches
(D) 8 inches
(E) 10 inches

7. If the average of five consecutive whole numbers is 30, what is the smallest number?

(A) 20
(B) 25
(C) 28
(D) 30
(E) 150

8. The average time for each section of a three-section test took Patrick 2 hours and 7 minutes. How long did it take Patrick to complete the test?

(A) 4 hours and 14 minutes
(B) 5 hours and 21 minutes
(C) 6 hours
(D) 6 hours and 21 minutes
(E) 7 hours

9. Three friends took between $3\frac{1}{2}$ and 4 hours to make a 156-mile roadtrip. The average speed, in miles per hour, must have been between

(A) 39 and 45
(B) 45 and 51
(C) 51 and 57
(D) 57 and 64
(E) 64 and 70

10. In a survey, each of 600 students was found to own either a dog, a cat, or both. If 500 of these students own a dog and 500 of these students own a cat, how many students own both a dog and a cat?

(A) 200
(B) 250
(C) 300
(D) 350
(E) 400

ISEE Reading and Interpreting Data Drill 1

1. Olivia places a package of frozen cookie
    dough in the refrigerator to defrost a week
    before she will bake cookies from the dough.
    Which graph best represents what happens
    to the temperature of the cookie dough as it
    defrosts during the week?

(A)

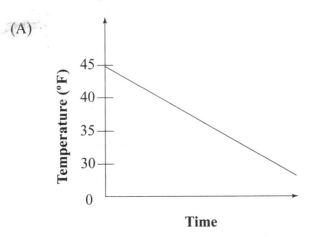

(C)

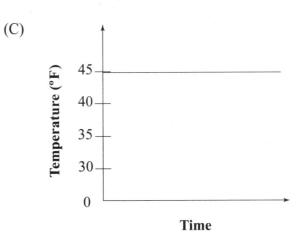

(B)

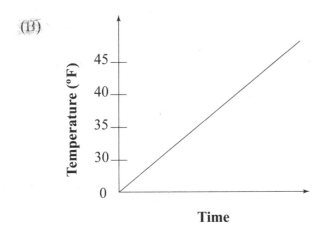

(D)

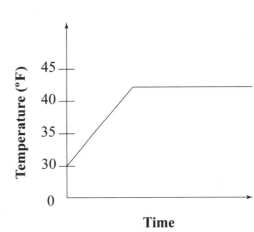

2. David was trying to determine the mean of his test scores. He did not know what he had scored on each of his final 3 tests but knew that the sum of the final 3 scores was 278. If David scored an 82 on his first test, then what was the mean of all 4 scores?

(A) 69.50
(B) 72.00
(C) 90.00
(D) 92.66

$\frac{360}{4} = 90$

3. The graph shows the distance Veronica biked from home as a function of time during a day bike ride.

VERONICA'S BIKE RIDE

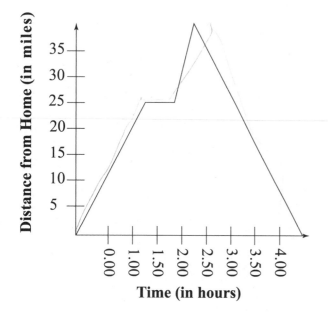

At one point in the trip, Veronica stopped for a meal. How far was Veronica from home when she stopped for a meal?

(A) 35 miles
(B) 25 miles
(C) 15 miles
(D) 5 miles

4. Mrs. Babish scored the tests of her 10 students. She then calculated the mean, median, mode, and range for the test scores. The table gives the value of each of these statistical measures.

Measure	Value
Mean	84
Median	86
Mode	81
Range	31

Mrs. Babish decided to add 7 points to each of her student's test scores, and then she recalculated the values of each statistical measure. Which measure equaled 88 after she completed her new calculations?

(A) mean
(B) median
(C) mode
(D) range

5. Sam and Ouisie are playing a game using number cubes. Each player rolls three number cubes, numbered 1 through 6, and the sum of the numbers is recorded.

- Sam receives a point if his sum is an 8.
- Ouisie receives a point if her sum is either 8 or 10.

Who has a greater probability of receiving a point?

(A) Ouisie
(B) Sam
(C) Sam and Ouisie have the same probability of receiving a point.
(D) There is not enough information given to determine the answer.

6. A cookie jar contains 4 chocolate chip cookies, 10 sugar cookies, and 13 oatmeal raisin cookies. If one cookie is chosen at random without replacement, and a second cookie is chosen at random, what is the probability that both cookies will be chocolate chip?

(A) $\dfrac{4}{27} \times \dfrac{4}{27}$

(B) $\dfrac{4}{27} \times \dfrac{3}{26}$

(C) $\dfrac{1}{4} \times \dfrac{1}{4}$

(D) $\dfrac{4}{27}$

7. The table below shows the scores of 10 different figure skaters at a skating competition.

Score	Number of Skaters with this Score
4.8	1
5.3	2
5.6	2
5.8	4
6.0	1

What is the median score?

(A) 5.3
(B) 5.6
(C) 5.7
(D) 5.8

8. Two baker's assistants bake cupcakes. Assistant A makes 3 times the number of burnt cupcakes as Assistant B. Both assistants burned a total of 12 cupcakes yesterday. How many cupcakes did Assistant B burn?

(A) 3
(B) 4
(C) 9
(D) 36

9. Buffy has taken 4 tests so far in her U.S. History class. Her scores on these tests are 72, 78, 81, and 85. The score on her final exam will be counted twice in her mean. What is the lowest score she can get on her final exam and have a mean score of no less than 80?

(A) 84
(B) 83
(C) 82
(D) 81

10. Sonya recorded the number of siblings of each student in her class in the table shown.

Number of Siblings	Number of Students with That Number of Siblings
0	2
1	4
2	7
3	6
4	3

What is the mode of the data?

(A) 2
(B) 3
(C) 6
(D) 7

ISEE Reading and Interpreting Data Drill 2

1. Sayani is trying to determine the mean number of texts students at her school send. Which sets of data will give her the least reliable information about the texting habits of students in her school?

   (A) A report showing the total number of students with phones in her school and the total number of texts sent by those phones
   (B) A survey of all the students in the school asking how many texts they send daily over the course of a month
   (C) A report showing the total number of texts sent by a random sample of students at the school
    (D) The most popular brand of phone owned by students in the school

2. The 5-member pep squad plans to send 2 of its members to the debate contest. How many combinations of 2 members are possible from the 5-member squad?

   (A) 20
   (B) 10
   (C) 5
   (D) 2

   1 2 3 4 5

   12, 13, 14, 15,
   23, 24, 25,
   34, 35, 45

3. The graph shows the number of extra-credit assignments completed by the students in Mrs. Wallace's class last semester. The numbers on the horizontal axis represent the number of extra-credit assignments completed during the semester, and the height of the bar represents the number of students who completed this number of extra-credit assignments.

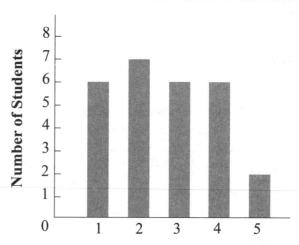

EXTRA-CREDIT ASSIGNMENTS

Number of Extra-Credit Assignments

What is the mean number of extra-credit assignments completed over the semester?

   (A) 2.67
   (B) 3.00
   (C) 3.33
   (D) 3.50

4. The box-and-whisker plot below represents the low temperature, in degrees Fahrenheit, at a particular location on the same day in February for the last 50 years.

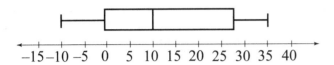

   What is the range of the data?

   (A) 65
   (B) 45
   (C) 35
   (D) 15

5. A bag contains 7 red Skittles, 6 yellow Skittles, 4 green Skittles, and 7 blue Skittles. Natalie randomly removes 1 Skittle from the bag and eats it. Ashley then randomly removes a Skittle from the bag and eats it. If the Skittle Natalie ate was red, what is the probability that Ashley ate a blue Skittle?

   (A) $\dfrac{7}{24} \times \dfrac{7}{23}$

   (B) $\dfrac{7}{24} \times \dfrac{7}{24}$

   (C) $\dfrac{7}{23}$

   (D) $\dfrac{7}{24}$

6. The stem-and-leaf plot shown represents the number of points scored by the winning team of a basketball tournament.

BASKETBALL SCORES

Stem	Leaf
4	9
5	1 1 3 9
6	2 2 4 7 7 9
7	1 4 4 4 4 5 6 7 8 9
8	2 3 3 4
9	0 8

   What is the median score in the tournament?

   (A) 74
   (B) 71
   (C) 69
   (D) 49

Directions: Using all information given in each question, compare the quantity in Column A to the quantity in Column B. All questions in Part Two have these answer choices:

    (A) The quantity in Column A is greater.
    (B) The quantity in Column B is greater.
    (C) The two quantities are equal.
    (D) The relationship cannot be determined from the information given.

A two-sided coin is tossed three times, and lands on "heads" each time. The coin is tossed a fourth time.

Column A	Column B
7. The probability that "heads" will be the result.	$\frac{1}{2}$

(C)

A drawer contains 4 hats: 1 red, 1 green, and 2 plaid. One hat is selected at random and replaced. Then a second hat is selected.

Column A	Column B
The probability that both hats selected are plaid.	The probability that the first hat selected is plaid.

8.

(B)

A 6-sided number cube, numbered 1 to 6, is rolled two times.

Column A	Column B
9. If a number greater than 3 is rolled, the probability that the next roll will be even.	If a number less than 3 is rolled, the probability that the next roll will be odd.

(C)

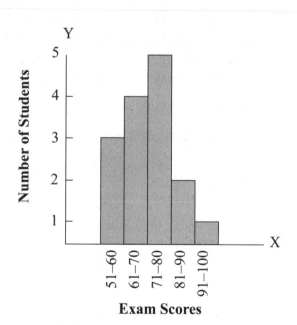

Exam Scores

10. The histogram shows exam scores of students in a history class.

Column A	Column B
The median score	The range of scores

(A)

Reading and
Interpreting Data:
Answers and
Explanations

ANSWER KEY

**SSAT Reading and Interpreting
Data Drill 1**

1. D
2. A
3. C
4. D
5. E
6. C
7. B
8. B
9. B
10. A

**SSAT Reading and Interpreting
Data Drill 2**

1. C
2. D
3. E
4. D
5. E
6. A
7. C
8. D
9. A
10. E

**ISEE Reading and Interpreting
Data Drill 1**

1. D
2. C
3. B
4. C
5. A
6. B
7. C
8. A
9. C
10. A

**ISEE Reading and Interpreting
Data Drill 2**

1. D
2. B
3. A
4. B
5. C
6. A
7. C
8. B
9. C
10. A

SSAT Reading and Interpreting Data Drill 1

1. **D** Let a, b, c, d, and e represent the individual scores, and set up the average equation $\left(\dfrac{Sum}{Number} = Average\right)$ for the five tests: $\dfrac{a + b + c + d + e}{5} = 83$. Multiply both sides by 5: $a + b + c + d + e = 415$. Now, let e represent the test that was removed, and set up the average equation for the four remaining tests: $\dfrac{a + b + c + d}{4} = 86$. Multiply both sides by 4: $a + b + c + d = 344$. Finally subtract the second equation from the first equation. On the left side, all variables will cancel out except for e. On the right side, $415 - 344 = 71$. As $e = 71$, that is the score of the removed test.

 A good way to think of average is Total = Average $\times$ Number (TAN). Here, the number of tests is 5, and the average is 80. Thus, the total score when all 5 tests are added is $83 \times 5 = 415$. The total score of the four tests after one is removed is $86 \times 4 = 344$. If you subtract the sum of the four tests from the sum of the five tests, you will have the score of the fifth test: $415 - 344 = 71$.

2. **A** The bar graph shows a 2002 population of 3,000 and 2012 population of 3,500, an increase of 500.

3. **C** The pie graph shows 10% of Jamie's budget is spent on movies and 23% on recreation, a total of 33%.

4. **D** The graph indicates that 10% of art history majors were employed, 50% were unemployed, and 40%, or $\dfrac{2}{5}$, were enrolled in graduate school.

5. **E** The graph indicates that 30% of the history majors were employed, and 60% were enrolled in graduate school. As there were 300 history majors, solve for the number of majors in each category: $\frac{30}{100} \times 300 = 90$, and $\frac{60}{100} \times 300 = 180$. Find the difference: $180 - 90 = 90$.

6. **C** Let x represent the lowest number, and set up the average equation for the five tests: $\frac{x + x + 1 + x + 2 + x + 3 + x + 4}{5} = 21$. Combine like terms in the numerator, and multiply both sides by 5: $5x + 10 = 105$. Subtract 10 from both sides, and divide both sides by 5: $x = 19$. As the question asks for the greatest number, add 4 to 19.

 The average of five consecutive numbers will be the median of the five numbers: draw five blanks for the five numbers, fill the middle spot with 21, and fill in the next two higher numbers with 22 and 23.

7. **B** Begin by determining the total sales before the price reduction by multiplying the average number of customers by the cost: $200 \times \$2 = \$400$. Next, determine the total sales received under the old price (before 10 A.M.) by multiplying the number of customers by the cost: $50 \times \$2 = \$100$. Now, subtract $100 from $400 to determine the amount of sales needed to maintain the original amount of $400: $300. Finally, divide $300 by the new price ($1) to determine the number of customers needed after 10 A.M.: 300.

8. **B**   Let *a* and *b* represent the weight of the two French Bulldogs, and set up the average equation: $\frac{a+b}{2} = 17.5$. Multiply both sides by 2: $a + b = 35$. Next, let *c, d, e,* and *f* represent the weight of the four English Bulldogs, and set up the average equation: $\frac{c+d+e+f}{4} = 62.5$. Multiply both sides by 4: $c + d + e + f = 250$. Now, set up the average equation for all six dogs and substitute the values you have determined: $\frac{a+b+c+d+e+f}{6} = \frac{35+250}{6} = \frac{285}{6} = 47.5$.

  A good way to think of average is Total = Average × Number (TAN). Here, the number of French Bulldogs is 2, and the average is 17.5. Thus, the total weight of the dogs is 17.5 × 2 = 35. Likewise, the number of English Bulldogs is 4, and the average is 62.5. Thus, the total weight of these dogs is 62.5 × 4 = 250. Finally, the total weight of all the dogs is 285, and the number of dogs is 6, so the average weight is 47.5.

9. **B**   If 270 people have cable and 90 people are video streaming, that would mean there are 360 people. However, there are only 300 people, which means 60 of those people were counted twice.

  It is useful to use the following formula in these types of questions: $G_1 + G_2 + N - B = T$. This stands for Group 1 + Group 2 + Neither − Both = Total. Here, as there is no N, the completed formula is $270 + 90 - B = 300$. Solve for B: 60.

10. **A** First convert 45 minutes to $\frac{3}{4}$ hour, as the question asks for rate in miles per hour.

Next, start with the lower range of the time and use the formula *Rate × Time = Distance*: $r \times \frac{3}{4} = 10$. Divide both sides by $\frac{3}{4}$ (multiply by the reciprocal): $r = \frac{40}{3} = 13\frac{1}{3}$. Now, repeat the process for the upper range of the time: $r \times 1 = 10$, so $r = 10$. Thus, the range of rates is between 10 and $13\frac{1}{3}$.

SSAT Reading and Interpreting Data Drill 2

1. **C** Add all of Peter's expenses to find $2,000 in monthly total expenses. Set up a fraction of the amount that he spends on student loans ($700) in the numerator and monthly budget in the denominator: $\frac{\$700}{\$2,000} = \frac{7}{20}$ of his income.

2. **D** Peter pays $150 for his cell phone and a total of $300 for food and health insurance. Set up a proportion: $\frac{x}{100} = \frac{150}{300}$. Cross-multiply and divide by 300: $x = 50$.

 Rather than set up a proportion, translate English into math. *What* means *variable* (*y*), *percent* means *over 100* $\left(\dfrac{}{100}\right)$, *of* means *times* ($\times$), and *is* means *equals* (=). So, *150 is what percent of 300* translates to $150 = \frac{y}{100} \times 300 = \frac{300y}{100} = 3y$. Divide both sides by 3: $y = 50$.

3. **E**   First, find the weight of 250 pencils in grams: $250 \times 5 = 1{,}250$ grams. Then, convert grams to kilograms, by setting up a proportion and cross-multiplying:

$$\frac{1 \text{ kg}}{1{,}000 \text{ g}} = \frac{x \text{ kg}}{1{,}250 \text{ g}} = 1.$$

4. **D**   The greatest increase from one week to the next will show the steepest slope on the graph. In Week 4, 150 cookies were baked, but in Week 5, 250 cookies were baked, an increase of 100. That is the largest of any of the weekly increases.

5. **E**   Start by writing the average equation: $\dfrac{F + G}{2} = 60$. Then multiply both sides by 2: $F + G = 120$. Check the answers. Choice (A) is wrong because $F < G$. None of answers (B), (C), and (D) match either of the equations you wrote. Choice (E) may look weird at first, but $F + G = 120$ is the same as $F + G = 60 + 60$. If you subtract G and 60 from both sides, you create (E).

  Plug in numbers for F and G, following the restrictions given, such as $F = 50$ and $G = 70$. Only (E) is valid when you plug F and G into the answer choices.

6. A   Because a ratio can be expressed in reduced form, let x be the factor by which the initial ratio must be increased to arrive at the actual heights. That is, the basil plant was $5x$ inches, and the mint plant is $4x$ inches. The basil plant grew to $5x + 2$ inches, while the mint plant was cut to $4x - 2$ inches. As these heights can be reduced to a ratio of 2:1, set up a proportion: $\dfrac{5x + 2}{4x - 2} = \dfrac{2}{1}$. Now cross multiply: $5x + 2 = 2(4x - 2)$. Distribute the 2: $5x + 2 = 8x - 4$. Subtract $5x$ from both sides and add 4 to both sides: $6 = 3x$. Divide both sides by 3: $x = 2$. Therefore, the basil plant was initially $5 \times 2 = 10$ inches, and the mint plant was initially $4 \times 2 = 8$ inches. The difference is 2.

 You can attack this problem using guess-and-check. While a ratio can be expressed in a reduced form, start by guessing that the initial height of the basil plant is 5, and the initial height of the mint plant is 4. After the change, the basil plant would be 7 and the mint plant 2, which is not a 2:1 ratio. Now try doubling the initial heights: 10 and 8, rather than 5 and 4. After the change, the basil plant would be 12 and the mint plant 6. This is a ratio of 2:1. Thus, the original difference was 2.

7. C   Let x represent the lowest number, and set up the average equation for the five tests: $\dfrac{x + x + 1 + x + 2 + x + 3 + x + 4}{5} = 30$. Combine like terms in the numerator, and multiply both sides by 5: $5x + 10 = 150$. Subtract 10 from both sides, and divide both sides by 5: $x = 28$. As the question asks for the lowest number, the answer is 28.

 The average of five consecutive numbers will be the median of the five numbers: draw five blanks for the five numbers, fill the middle spot with 30, and fill in the next two lower numbers with 29 and 28.

8. **D**   Let a, b, and c represent the times taken on each section, and set up the average equation: $\dfrac{a + b + c}{3} = 2$ hours, 7 minutes. Multiply both sides by 3: $a + b + c = 6$ hours, 21 minutes. This is the total time.

  A good way to think of average is Total = Average × Number (TAN). Here, the number of sections is 3, and the average is 2 hours, 7 minutes. Thus, the total time is 2 hours, 7 minutes × 3 = 6 hours, 21 minutes.

9. **A**   First start with the lower range of the time and use the formula *Rate × Time = Distance*: $r \times 3\dfrac{1}{2} = 156$. Divide both sides by $3\dfrac{1}{2} = \dfrac{7}{2}$ (multiply by the reciprocal): $r = \dfrac{40}{3} = 44\dfrac{4}{7}$. Now, repeat the process for the upper range of the time: $r \times 4 = 156$, so $r = 39$. Thus, the range of rates is between 39 and $44\dfrac{4}{7}$.

10. **E**   If 500 people own a dog and 500 people own a cat, that would mean there are 1,000 people. However, there are only 600 people, which means 400 of those people were counted twice.

It is useful to use the following formula in these types of questions: $G_1 + G_2 + N - B = T$. This stands for Group 1 + Group 2 + Neither − Both = Total. Here, as there is no N, the completed formula is $500 + 500 - B = 1,000$. Solve for B: 400.

ISEE Reading and Interpreting Data Drill 1

1. **D** As time passes, the temperature will increase from the temperature of the freezer and then level off at the temperature of the refrigerator. Only (D) indicates this trend.

2. **C** To calculate the mean of all 4 scores, add the scores and divide by the number of scores: 278 + 82 = 360, and 360 ÷ 4 = 90.

3. **B** When Veronica is stopped for a meal, time will continue to increase but her distance from home will stay the same. From 1.50 to 2 hours, the distance (25 miles from home) remains the same.

4. **C** Adding 7 points to each student's score will not affect the range because both the lowest and highest scores are 7 points higher, leaving the difference the same. Adding 7 points to each score will, however, affect the mean, median, and mode. The mode is easiest to address, so start there: adding 7 points to the mode scores of 81 will bring those scores to 88.

5. **A** Ouisie has a greater probability of receiving a point because there are two results that can generate a point for her and only one result that can generate a point for Sam.

6. **B** Probability is always a fraction, $\frac{\text{what you want}}{\text{what you've got}}$. In the first reach into the cookie jar, we want a chocolate chip (4) out of all the cookies (27). Therefore, the first reach is $\frac{4}{27}$. For the second reach, there is one less chocolate chip cookie and one less cookie total, so the probability of again getting a chocolate chip cookie is $\frac{3}{26}$. When you need two probabilities to occur, you multiply the fractions.

7.　**C**　　To calculate the median, list out all scores in order and find the middle number. One student scored a 4.8, 2 scored a 5.3, 2 scored a 5.6, 4 scored a 5.8, and 1 scored a 6.0. So, the list of numbers is 4.8, 5.3, 5.3, 5.6, 5.6, 5.8, 5.8, 5.8, 5.8, 6.0. When the number of terms on a list is even, the median is calculated by the average of the two numbers in the middle: $\dfrac{5.6 + 5.8}{2} = 5.7$.

8.　**A**　　Let x represent the number of cupcakes Assistant B burned. Therefore, $x + 3x = 12$. Combining like terms and dividing by 4 yields $x = 3$. Thus, Assistant B burned 3 cupcakes.

　You can test the answer choices, starting with (B) or (C). If you start with (B) that would mean that Assistant A burned 12 cupcakes, and the total would be 16 cupcakes. As this is too many cupcakes, the answer must be (A).

9.　**C**　　Mean is determined by adding the scores and dividing by the number of scores, in this case 6 (because one test is counted twice). Let x represent the unknown score: $\dfrac{72 + 78 + 81 + 85 + 2x}{6} = 80$. Combine like terms in the numerator: $\dfrac{316 + 2x}{6} = 80$.

Multiply both sides by 6, subtract 316 from both sides, and divide both sides by 2: $x = 82$.

　A good way to think of mean is Total = Average × Number (TAN). Here, the number of tests is 6, and the desired average is 80. Thus, the total score when all 6 tests are added is 480 (80 × 6). As we have four of her scores, we can subtract them from the total: $480 - 72 - 78 - 81 - 85 = 164$. Thus, 164 represents the remaining total score she needs to achieve her goal. As 164 represents the doubling of a single test score, divide it by 2. She must score 82 on her test.

10. A The mode is the number that appears the most often on the list. The table reveals that the greatest number of students (7) responded that they have 2 siblings. Therefore, the number 2 appears 7 times on the list, more than any other number.

ISEE Reading and Interpreting Data Drill 2

1. D Sayani wants to calculate the mean number of texts sent by students. Three of the choices provide data sets to help her determine this number, but the question asks for the one that is *least* reliable. The most popular phone will not tell Sayani how many texts anyone sends. On the other hand, the mean can be calculated with the total number of texts and the total number of students with phones, either by a report or by students' own admission (A) and (B). The mean can be projected with a random sample of the population (D).

2. B The number of combinations possible when r are selected from n options is given by $\dfrac{n!}{r!(n-r)!}$. Here, the number of combinations is $\dfrac{5!}{2! \times 3!} = \dfrac{5 \times 4}{2} = 10$.

 When dealing with orderings or combinations, you can set up slots for what you need and fill them with what is available. In this case we need two people, so we need two slots: ____ ____. For the first slot, 5 people are available as a possible choice, while for the second slot only 4 people are available (as one is taken for the first slot): _5_ _4_. If we wanted to know how many orderings there are, we would multiply the numbers in the slots, in this case 20. However, this would double count the number of groups because AB and BA are the same. Thus, we need to cut 20 in half.

3. **A** Calculate the mean by adding the total number of extra credit assignment and dividing it by the number of students in the graph. The graph shows that 6 students submitted 1 assignment, 7 students submitted 2, 6 students submitted 3, 6 students submitted 4, and 2 students submitted 5. The total number of assignments is (1×6) $+ (2 \times 7) + (3 \times 6) + (4 \times 6) + (5 \times 2) = 72$ total assignments. Divide by the number of students, which is 27. $\frac{72}{27} = 2\frac{2}{3}$, or approximately 2.67. The correct answer is (A).

4. **B** The vertical lines at either end of the box-and-whisker graph represent the lowest and highest data points. (The vertical line in the middle of the two boxes represents the median.) As range is calculated by subtracting the lowest value from the high value, the range here is $35 - (-10) = 45$.

5. **C** Probability is always a fraction, $\frac{\text{what you want}}{\text{what you've got}}$. The total number of Skittles to begin with is 24, but Natalie eats a red one, leaving 23 Skittles behind, 7 of which are blue. Ashley's probability of eating a blue one is therefore $\frac{7}{23}$.

6. **A** A stem-and-leaf plot shows the tens digit to the left of the vertical line and the units digits to the right of the vertical line. Thus, the first number is 49, the next is 51, the next is 51 again, the next is 53, and so on. The median is the middle number of the set of numbers arranged in order. As the numbers here are in order, you can cross out numbers at either end, one at a time, until you arrive at 74.

7. **C** No matter how many times a fair coin is tossed and no matter what the prior results were, each time the coin is tossed there is an equal chance for either heads or tails to land: $\frac{1}{2}$.

8. **B**   Probability is always a fraction, $\dfrac{\text{what you want}}{\text{what you've got}}$. The probability of obtaining one

plaid hat is 2 out of 4, or $\dfrac{1}{2}$. If the hat is replaced, the probability of selecting a plaid

hat on a second try is again 2 out of 4, or $\dfrac{1}{2}$. When you need two events to happen,

you multiply the probabilities. Thus, the probability of getting plaid hats both times

is $\dfrac{1}{2} \times \dfrac{1}{2} = \dfrac{1}{4}$.

  You can think about this question logically. If you win a prize for selecting a plaid hat, it is certainly easier to win the prize once than to win it twice!

9. **C**   The question is asking about what comes next as a probability, not about the combined probability of both rolls in each scenario. On a 6-sided number cube numbered 1 through 6, there are 3 even numbers (2, 4, and 6) and 3 odd numbers (1, 3, and 5). Therefore, the chance of rolling odd or even is the same, no matter what might have happened on the first roll.

10. **A**   The exact scores are not provided, but you can figure out the largest possible range by subtracting the smallest possible value from the largest possible value: 100 − 51 = 49. While we do not know the median, it must be greater than 51 (the lowest possible data point), so the median is greater.

Other Math Concepts

SSAT Other Math Concepts Drill

1. Mikaela earns a base hourly rate of $7 per hour baby-sitting. However, if a babysitting assignment lasts longer than 4 hours, she earns $8 per hour for each hour she babysits after the first 4 hours. How much money does Mikaela earn if she babysits 4 hours on Friday, 6 hours on Saturday, and 5 hours on Sunday?

   (A) $105
   (B) $108
   (C) $115
   (D) $120
   (E) $124

2. If one fourth of the weight of a bag of sugar is 1.25 pounds, the weight of four bags of sugar of the exact same weight can be determined by multiplying 1.25 by which of the following?

   (A) $\dfrac{1}{5}$

   (B) $\dfrac{1}{4}$

   (C) $\dfrac{5}{4}$

   (D) 4

   (E) 16

3. Combine and simplify:

   $$\left(3x^3 + 8x - 4\right) - \left(-5x^3 + 6x - 10\right)$$

   (A) $-2x^3 + 14x - 14$
   (B) $2x^3 - 2x - 6$
   (C) $8x^3 + 14x - 14$
   (D) $8x^3 - 2x + 14$
   (E) $8x^3 + 2x + 6$

4. Write the following fractions in the correct increasing sequence:

   $$\frac{4}{9}, \frac{5}{8}, \frac{6}{15}$$

   (A) $\dfrac{5}{8}, \dfrac{6}{15}, \dfrac{4}{9}$

   (B) $\dfrac{5}{8}, \dfrac{4}{9}, \dfrac{6}{15}$

   (C) $\dfrac{6}{15}, \dfrac{4}{9}, \dfrac{5}{8}$

   (D) $\dfrac{6}{15}, \dfrac{5}{8}, \dfrac{4}{9}$

   (E) $\dfrac{4}{9}, \dfrac{6}{15}, \dfrac{5}{8}$

5. Write the following fractions in the correct increasing sequence:

   $$\frac{9}{11}, \frac{5}{6}, \frac{7}{9}$$

   (A) $\dfrac{9}{11}, \dfrac{5}{6}, \dfrac{7}{9}$

   (B) $\dfrac{9}{11}, \dfrac{7}{9}, \dfrac{5}{6}$

   (C) $\dfrac{7}{9}, \dfrac{5}{6}, \dfrac{9}{11}$

   (D) $\dfrac{7}{9}, \dfrac{9}{11}, \dfrac{5}{6}$

   (E) $\dfrac{5}{6}, \dfrac{7}{9}, \dfrac{9}{11}$

6. Find the missing number in the sequence: ____, 31, 38, 45, 52

   (A) 23
   (B) 24
   (C) 25
   (D) 26
   (E) 27

7. Find the missing number in the sequence: ____, –8, 32, –128.

    (A) 2
    (B) –2
    (C) –4
    (D) 4
    (E) 8

8. Calculate the fifth term in the sequence that begins

    $$1, \frac{2}{3}, \frac{1}{3}, 0, \underline{\hspace{1cm}}$$

    (A) $-\dfrac{1}{3}$

    (B) $-\dfrac{2}{3}$

    (C) –1

    (D) $-\dfrac{3}{2}$

    (E) –2

9. Calculate the fifth term in the sequence that begins

    $$1\frac{1}{4}, \frac{3}{4}, \frac{1}{4}, -\frac{1}{4}, \underline{\hspace{1cm}}$$

    (A) $-1\dfrac{3}{4}$

    (B) $-1\dfrac{1}{2}$

    (C) $-1\dfrac{1}{4}$

    (D) –1

    (E) $-\dfrac{3}{4}$

10. Lindsay is collecting quarters. She saves one quarter on the first day, two quarters on the second day, and three quarters on the third day. If this pattern continues, how much money will Lindsay have saved at the end of 14 days?

    (A) $25.25
    (B) $26.25
    (C) $26.75
    (D) $27.25
    (E) $28.25

11. Rohan begins a weight-lifting regimen by bench-pressing 25 pounds the first week, 30 pounds the second week, and 35 pounds the third week. If he keeps increasing the weight each week by the same amount, on what week in his weight-lifting regimen will Rohan bench press 65 pounds?

    (A) Week 6
    (B) Week 7
    (C) Week 8
    (D) Week 9
    (E) Week 10

12. If Jeeves deposits $100 in a bank account that will double his money every 20 years, after how many years will his bank account be worth $1,600?

    (A) 5
    (B) 10
    (C) 50
    (D) 80
    (E) 100

13. Holly begins a weight-loss program with a goal of losing 25 pounds in no more than eight weeks. If she loses 2 pounds in the first week, how many pounds per week must she lose for the rest of the program?

    (A) Between 0.5 and 1 lb
    (B) Between 1 and 1.5 lbs
    (C) Between 1.5 and 2 lbs
    (D) Between 2.5 and 3 lbs
    (E) Between 3 and 3.5 lbs

14. Evaluate the expression: $25 \div (2 + 3) \times 4 - 10$

    (A) –30
    (B) –8.75
    (C) 10
    (D) 11.25
    (E) 30

$$\frac{71,254}{689}$$

15. The result of the calculation above is approximately which of the following?

    (A) 11
    (B) 13
    (C) 100
    (D) 1,100
    (E) 1,300

ISEE Other Math Concepts Drill

1. What type of number could result from the product of two irrational numbers?

   (A) rational or irrational
   (B) rational only
   (C) irrational only
   (D) integer only

2. Which expression is equivalent to the expression $(x - 4)(x + 5)$?

   (A) $x^2 - 20$
   (B) $x^2 + 1$
   (C) $x^2 - x - 20$
   (D) $x^2 + x - 20$

   $x^2 + x - 20$

3. If k is a positive integer, and $(x + 11)^2 = x^2 + kx + 121$, what is the value of k?

   (A) 121
   (B) 55
   (C) 22
   (D) 11

   $(x + 11)(x + 11)$

   $x^2 + 22x + 121$

4. If the sum of all integers from 1 to 400, inclusive, is x, then which expression represents the sum of all integers from 1 to 397, inclusive?

   (A) $x + 1,197$
   (B) $x + 397$
   (C) $x - 397$
   (D) $x - 1,197$

5. What is the solution set for $x^2 + 64 = 0$?

   (A) 8
   (B) $8i$
   (C) ± 8
   (D) $\pm 8i$

6. If $x^2 + y^2 = 73$, and $2xy = 48$, what is the value of $(x - y)^2$?

   (A) 5
   (B) 11
   (C) 25
   (D) 121

7. The first six terms of an arithmetic sequence of numbers are shown.

   $$-7, -4, -1, 2, 5, 8$$

   Which expression gives the value of the xth term of the sequence?

   (A) $x - 8$
   (B) $x - 6$
   (C) $3x - 10$
   (D) $3x + 7$

8. There are 1,760 yards in a mile. If Elena is walking at a speed of 4 miles per hour, which of the following expressions gives her speed in yards per second?

   (A) $\dfrac{60 \times 60 \times 4}{1,760}$

   (B) $\dfrac{60 \times 4}{1,760 \times 60}$

   (C) $\dfrac{1,760 \times 4}{60 \times 60}$

   (D) $\dfrac{60 \times 60}{1,760 \times 8}$

9. Perry and Esther are driving toward each other, each at a constant rate. Perry began his drive two hours before Esther began hers. Esther is driving at a slower speed than Perry. Which additional piece of information, if given, would allow a determination of how long Perry had been driving before he and Esther met?

    (A) the difference between Perry and Esther's speeds
    (B) the sum of Perry and Esther's speeds
    (C) Perry's speed
    (D) Esther's speed

10. What is the result of the following expression?

$$\begin{bmatrix} 3 & 5 \\ 6 & 7 \end{bmatrix} + \begin{bmatrix} 4 & 2 \\ 1 & 0 \end{bmatrix}$$

    (A) $\begin{bmatrix} 7 & 9 \\ 8 & 0 \end{bmatrix}$

    (B) $\begin{bmatrix} 6 & 9 \\ 8 & 6 \end{bmatrix}$

    (C) $\begin{bmatrix} 8 & 6 \\ 13 & 1 \end{bmatrix}$

    (D) $\begin{bmatrix} 7 & 7 \\ 7 & 7 \end{bmatrix}$

11. For what value(s) of y does $\dfrac{y^2 - 64}{(y-3)(y+7)} = 0$?

    (A) $y = 3$ and $y = -7$
    (B) $y = 7$ and $y = -3$
    (C) $y = 8$ only
    (D) $y = 8$ and $y = -8$

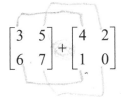

$(y-8)(y+8)$

$\dfrac{y^2 - 64}{y^2 + 4y - 21}$

$\dfrac{-64}{4y - 21}$

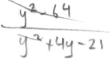

$-64 = 4y - 21$

$4y = 43$

12. For all integers x and y, let $x \updownarrow y$ be defined as $x \updownarrow y = (x+y)^2 - x - y$. For example, $2 \updownarrow 3 = 5^2 - 2 - 3 = 20$. Which one of the following is an odd number? $64 - 8 = 56$

    (A) $3 \updownarrow 4$ $(3+4)^2 - 3 - 4$
    (B) $3 \updownarrow 5$ $100 - 10 = 90 \quad 42$
    (C) $4 \updownarrow 6$
    (D) none of the above

13. In a certain city, the average height for men over 18 years old is 70 inches. All men in the city are within 5 inches of the average height. If m represents the height of a man in the city, which best describes the man's height?

    (A) $|m - 5| \le 70$ $|$specific - middle$| \le$ range
    (B) $|m - 5| \ge 70$
    (C) $|m - 70| \ge 5$
    (D) $|m - 70| \le 5$

14. The value of a varies directly as the square root of b and varies inversely as c. If b is multiplied by 4 and c is divided by 2, then by what factor does a change from its original value?

    (A) $\dfrac{1}{4}$

    (B) $\dfrac{1}{2}$

    (C) 4

    (D) 8

15. In the formula $z = \dfrac{x}{2y}$, $x > 0$, and $y > 0$. If one of the three variables does not change, which of the following is true?

    (A) as x decreases, z increases
    (B) as x increases, z decreases
    (C) as y decreases, z increases
    (D) as y increases, z increases

Directions: Using all information given in each question, compare the quantity in Column A to the quantity in Column B. All questions in Part Two have these answer choices:

(A) The quantity in Column A is greater.
(B) The quantity in Column B is greater.
(C) The two quantities are equal.
(D) The relationship cannot be determined from the information given.

Column A	Column B
16. $7 + 5 \times (2 + 3)$	32

_(C)_

Column A	Column B
17. $(a - b)(a^2 + ab + b^2)$	$a^3 - b^3$

_(C)_

$$x^2 - 7x + 12 = 0$$

Column A	Column B
18. x	4

_(D)_

A piggy bank contains $2.40 cents in nickels and pennies and contains three times as many pennies as nickels.
(Note: 1 nickel = $0.05; 1 penny = $0.01)

Column A	Column B
19. The total value of the nickels	$1.20

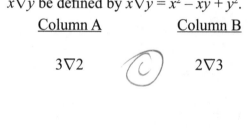

_(A)_

For all numbers x and y, let the function $x \nabla y$ be defined by $x \nabla y = x^2 - xy + y^2$.

Column A	Column B
20. $3 \nabla 2$	$2 \nabla 3$

_(C)_

Other Math
Concepts: Answers
and Explanations

ANSWER KEY

SSAT Other Math Concepts Drill		**ISEE Other Math Concepts Drill**	
1.	B	1.	A
2.	E	2.	D
3.	E	3.	C
4.	C	4.	D
5.	D	5.	D
6.	B	6.	C
7.	A	7.	C
8.	A	8.	C
9.	E	9.	B
10.	B	10.	D
11.	D	11.	D
12.	D	12.	D
13.	E	13.	D
14.	C	14.	C
15.	C	15.	C
		16.	C
		17.	C
		18.	D
		19.	A
		20.	C

SSAT Other Math Concepts Drill

1. **B** On Friday, she earns $4 \times 7 = 28$, on Saturday, she earns $(4 \times 7) + (2 \times 8) = 44$, and on Sunday, she earns $(4 \times 7) + (1 \times 8) = 36$. Add these amounts: $28 + 44 + 36 = 108$.

2. **E** Let x represent the value of a bag of sugar and set up an equation: $\frac{1}{4}x = 1.25$. Multiply both sides by 4: $x = 5$. Thus, four of these bags weigh 20 pounds. Finally, divide 20 by 1.25: to get 20, you need to multiply 1.25 by 16.

3. **E** First, distribute the negative sign: $(3x^3 + 8x - 4) + 5x^3 - 6x + 10$. Next combine like terms: $8x^3 + 2x + 6$.

4. **C** Reduce $\frac{6}{15}$ to $\frac{2}{5}$ and create a common denominator of 360 for the three fractions:

$$\frac{4 \times 40}{9 \times 40} = \frac{160}{360}, \frac{5 \times 45}{8 \times 45} = \frac{225}{360}, \text{ and } \frac{2 \times 72}{5 \times 72} = \frac{144}{360}.$$

 Work the fractions in pairs and use logic when you can. Start with $\frac{4}{9}$ and $\frac{5}{8}$. As

$\frac{4}{9} < \frac{1}{2}$ and $\frac{5}{8} > \frac{1}{2}, \frac{4}{9} < \frac{5}{8}$. Also, $\frac{6}{15} < \frac{1}{2}$, so $\frac{6}{15} < \frac{5}{8}$. Now reduce $\frac{6}{15}$ to $\frac{2}{5}$ and com-

pare $\frac{4}{9}$ and $\frac{2}{5}$. Create a common denominator of 45 for the two fractions:

$\frac{4 \times 5}{9 \times 5} = \frac{20}{45}$ and $\frac{2 \times 9}{5 \times 9} = \frac{18}{45}$. Thus, $\frac{6}{15} < \frac{4}{9} < \frac{5}{8}$.

5. **D**   Create a common denominator of 198 for the three fractions:

$$\frac{9 \times 18}{11 \times 18} = \frac{162}{198}, \frac{5 \times 33}{6 \times 33} = \frac{165}{198}, \text{ and } \frac{7 \times 22}{9 \times 22} = \frac{154}{198}.$$

   Work the fractions in pairs. Start with $\frac{9}{11}$ and $\frac{5}{6}$ by creating a common denominator of 66: $\frac{9 \times 6}{11 \times 6} = \frac{54}{66}$ and $\frac{5 \times 11}{6 \times 11} = \frac{55}{66}$, so $\frac{9}{11} < \frac{5}{6}$. Proceed to $\frac{9}{11}$ and $\frac{7}{9}$ by creating a common denominator of 99: $\frac{9 \times 9}{11 \times 9} = \frac{81}{99}$ and $\frac{7 \times 11}{9 \times 11} = \frac{77}{99}$, so $\frac{7}{9} < \frac{9}{11}$. It is unnecessary to assess the final pair, as combining the two inequalities yields $\frac{7}{9} < \frac{9}{11} < \frac{5}{6}$.

6. **B**   Each term increases by 7 from one to the next: $52 - 45 = 7$, $45 - 38 = 7$. Subtract 7 from 31, and the missing number is 24.

7. **A**   Each term is multiplied by -4: $-8 \times -4 = 32$, and $32 \times -4 = -128$. Thus, divide -8 by -4 to obtain the first term: 2.

8. **A**   Each term decreases by $\frac{1}{3}$: $1 - \frac{2}{3} = \frac{1}{3}$; $\frac{1}{3} - \frac{1}{3} = 0$. Subtract from 0, and the missing number is $-\frac{1}{3}$.

9. **E**   Each term decreases by $\frac{1}{2}$: $1\frac{1}{4} = \frac{5}{4}$; $\frac{5}{4} - \frac{3}{4} = \frac{2}{4}$, or $\frac{1}{2}$. Thus, $\left(-\frac{1}{4}\right) - \left(\frac{1}{2}\right) = -\frac{3}{4}$.

10. **B** The sum of a series of n consecutive numbers where S_1 is the first number and S_n is the last number is given by the expression $\left(\dfrac{S_1 + S_n}{2}\right)n$. Thus, Lindsey will have saved $\left(\dfrac{1 + 14}{2}\right)14 = 105$ quarters. Multiply 105 by \$0.25: \$26.25.

 You can quickly write out the number of quarters she saves and add the numbers: $1 + 2 + 3 + 4 + 5 + 6 + 7 + 8 + 9 + 10 + 11 + 12 + 13 + 14 = 105$. Multiply 105 by \$0.25: \$26.25.

11. **D** The value of the nth term, S_n of an arithmetic sequence is given by the equation $S_n = S_1 + d(n - 1)$, where S_1 is the first term of the sequence and d is the common difference between the terms. Here, the difference between terms is 5, the first term is 25, and the final term is 65. Use these numbers in an equation: $65 = 25 + 5(n - 1)$. Distribute 5: $65 = 25 + 5n - 5$. Combine like terms and divide by 5: $n = 9$.

 You can quickly write out the weights, by week, up to 65, and count the weeks: $\{25, 30, 35, 40, 45, 50, 55, 60, 65\}$ contains nine terms.

12. **D** The value of the *nth* term, S_n, of a geometric sequence is given by the equation $S_n = S_1(r^{n-1})$, where S_1 is the first term and r is the common ratio between terms. Here, the first term is $100, the final term is $1,600, and the common ratio is 2. Use these numbers in the equation: $\$1,600 = \$100(2^{n-1})$. Divide both sides by $100: $16 = 2^{n-1}$. As $16 = 2^4$, $n = 5$. This means that $1,600 is the fifth term and, therefore, there were four increases from $100. The question indicates that each increase takes place over 20 years, so multiply 4 by 20: 80.

 You can quickly write out the amounts he has, in 20-year periods, up to $1,600, and count the 20-year periods: {$100, $200, $400, $800, $1,600} contains four 20-year periods after the initial $100 deposit, which is 80 years.

13. **E** As Holly loses 2 pounds in the first week, she has 23 more pounds to lose in seven weeks. $23 \div 7 = 3.29$ pounds per week.

14. **C** Follow the order of operations (PEMDAS): $25 \div 5 \times 4 - 10 = 5 \times 4 - 10 = 20 - 10 = 10$. Remember that when ordering multiplication and division, proceed left to right rather than always performing multiplication first.

15. **C** Because the question asks for an approximation, estimate by rounding: $\dfrac{70,000}{700} = 100$. As no other answer is anywhere close to 100, you can answer the question without worrying whether you rounded too much.

ISEE Other Math Concepts Drill

1. **A**   Irrational numbers cannot be expressed as a fraction, while rational numbers can. When two irrational numbers are multiplied, the product can be rational or irrational, depending on the numbers.

     Plug in numbers to find out what can result from the product of two irrational numbers. $\sqrt{2} \times \sqrt{3} = \sqrt{6}$, which is irrational. On the other hand, $\sqrt{2} \times \sqrt{8} = \sqrt{16} = 4$, which is rational.

2. **D**   Use FOIL (First, Outside, Inside, Last) on the two factors: $(x - 4)(x + 5) = (x^2 + 5x - 4x - 20)$. Combine like terms: $x^2 + x - 20$.

     Plug in a number for x, such as $x = 5$, and solve: $(5 - 4)(5 + 5) = (1)(10) = 10$. Only (D) yields 10 when the value for x is plugged in.

3. **C**   Use FOIL (First, Outside, Inside, Last) on the two factors: $(x + 11)(x + 11) = (x^2 + 11x + 11x + 121)$. Combine like terms: $x^2 + 22x + 121$. Thus, $k = 22$.

     Plug in a number for x, such as 2, and solve both sides of the equation: $13^2 = 4 + 2k + 121$, $169 = 125 + 2k$. Combine like terms and divide by 2: $k = 22$.

4. **D** The sum of the integers from 1 to 397 will not include three numbers counted in the sum of all integers from 1 to 400, namely, 398, 399, and 400. If the sum of all integers from 1 to 400 is x, then the sum of all integers from 1 to 397 will be x minus the sum of 398, 399, and 400: $x - (398 + 399 + 400)$ or $x - 1197$.

5. **D** First subtract 64 from both sides: $x^2 = -64$. Take the square root of each side, remembering that there are two solutions for x^2: $x = \pm\sqrt{-64}$. Separate the 64 from -1: $x = \pm\sqrt{64 \times -1} = \pm 8\sqrt{-1}$. The square root of negative one is not a real number and is called the imaginary number i. Thus, $x = \pm 8i$.

6. **C** First, factor $(x - y)^2$ to $x^2 - 2xy + y^2$. Notice that two of these terms combine to $x^2 + y^2$, so substitute 73 for these terms. Also substitute 48 for $2xy$. The final result is $73 - 48 = 25$.

 Use guess and check to come up with numbers that work. As $2xy = 48$, $xy = 24$. Thus, x and y can be 1 and 24, 2 and 12, 3 and 8, or 4 and 6. If you substitute 3 and 8 into $x^2 + y^2$, you get 73. Substitute 3 and 8 in $(x - y)^2$ to arrive at 25.

7. **C** In an arithmetic sequence, the value of the xth term is given by $d(x - 1) + S_1$, where d is the difference between terms and S_1 is the value of the first term. Substitute the difference between the terms (3) and the value of the first term (-7): $3(x - 1) - 7$. This is not an answer, however, so try distributing the 3: $3x - 3 - 7$, which is $3x - 10$.

 As each term (x) yields a different value, select a term number and plug it into the answers to see which answer yields the correct value. To avoid dealing with negative numbers, pick the fourth term. In this case $x = 4$, and the expected value of the fourth term is 2. If you plug 4 into the answers, only (C) yields the expected value of 2.

8. **C**   Begin by stating the speed as a fraction with the units marked: $\frac{4m}{1h}$. Now, convert the miles into yards. As there are 1,760 yards to a mile, multiply 4 in the numerator by 1,760: $\frac{1{,}760 \times 4}{1h}$. Now, convert the hour into seconds. As there are 60 minutes per hour and 60 seconds per minute, multiply the 1 in the denominator by 60×60: $\frac{1{,}760 \times 4}{60 \times 60}$.

9. **B**   When two objects are moving in the same direction, you can subtract their rates to determine the rate of one object relative to the other. When two objects are moving in the opposite direction, as they are here, you can add the rates to determine the rate of one object relative to the other. As *rate × time = distance*, knowing the sum of their rates and the distance between them will allow you to calculate the time it will take for them to meet.

10. **D**   To add matrices, add the numbers that occupy the same position in each matrix.

That is, add the top-left numbers, the top-right numbers, and so on. So,
$$\begin{bmatrix} 3 & 5 \\ 6 & 7 \end{bmatrix} + \begin{bmatrix} 4 & 2 \\ 1 & 0 \end{bmatrix} = \begin{bmatrix} 3+4 & 5+2 \\ 6+1 & 7+0 \end{bmatrix} = \begin{bmatrix} 7 & 7 \\ 7 & 7 \end{bmatrix}.$$

11. **D**   A fraction will equal zero is the numerator equals zero. Here the numerator will equal zero if $y^2 = 64$, as $64 - 64 = 0$. There are two values of y that satisfy the equation: ±8.

  Test the answer choices. Choice (A) will create a fraction that is undefined. Choice (B) will not result in a fraction that equals 0. Choice (C) will result in a fraction that equals zero, but you need to test (D) as well in case that is a more complete answer. In fact, (D) is more complete, as both values result in a fraction that equals zero.

12. **D** A "weird symbol" defined to equal an equation is simply a different form of function notation, so plug in numbers as directed by the defined equation. Test each answer. For (A), $3 \updownarrow 4 = 7^2 - 3 - 4 = 42$. Eliminate (A). For (B), $3 \updownarrow 5 = 8^2 - 3 - 5 = 56$. Eliminate (B). For (C), $4 \updownarrow 6 = 10^2 - 4 - 6 = 90$. Eliminate (C), leaving (D).

 You can avoid testing (A) because you already know that an odd number and an even number yield an even number.

13. **D** To determine whether a specified value is within a given range around a middle or average value, subtract the middle value from the specific value, take the absolute value of that difference, and determine whether the result is less than or equal to the given range. That is $|specific - middle| \leq range$. In this case, m is the specified value, 70 is the middle value, and 5 is the given range, so $|m - 70| \leq 5$.

 Plug in a permitted value for m, such as 72. Test 72 in each answer. For (A), $|72 - 5| \leq 70$. This is true, so keep (A). For (B), $|72 - 5| \geq 70$. This is false, so eliminate (B). For (C), $|72 - 70| \geq 5$. This is false, so eliminate (C). For (D), $|72 - 70| \leq 5$. This is true, so keep (D). As two answers remain, try a value for m that is not permitted, such as 60. In this case, the equation should fail, as 60 is not permitted. For (A), $|60 - 5| \leq 70$. This is true, so eliminate (A). For (D), $|60 - 70| \leq 5$. This is false, so keep (D).

14. **C** As a varies directly as the square root of b, a will increase by a factor equal to the square root of b. As b increases by a factor of 4, a will increase by a factor of 2. As a varies inversely as c, a will decrease by a factor equal to c. Because a decreases when c increases, a will increase when c decreases. As c is decreased by one half, a will increase by a factor of 2. As a increases by a factor of 2 for both b and c, a increases by a factor of 4.

15. **C** To maintain balance when only two variables change: (1) as x increases, y must increase by the same factor or z must increase by the same factor, (2) as y increases, x must increase by the same factor or z must decrease by the same factor, or (3) as z increases, x must increase by the same factor or y must decrease by the same factor. Only (C) is consistent with these principles.

 Plug in numbers for x, y, and z, making sure the equation balances, such as $x = 12$, $y = 2$, and $z = 3$. Now test each answer choice. For (A), if x is decreased to 6, z decreases. For (B), if x is increased to 18, z increases. For (C), if y is decreased to 1, z increases. For (D), if y is increased to 4, z decreases. Thus, (A), (B), and (D) fail, and (C) passes.

16. **C** Follow the order of operations (PEMDAS): $7 + 5 \times (2 + 3) = 7 + 5 \times (5) = 7 + 25 = 32$.

17. **C** Distribute both the a and b into the second factor: $(a^3 + a^2b + ab^2 - a^2b - ab^2 - b^3)$. Combine like terms, and all of the middle terms cancel out: $a^3 - b^3$.

 Plug in values for a and b, such as $a = 5$ and $b = 2$. Both columns yield the value 117. Because the value of Column A is not *always* greater than the value of Column B, and the value of Column B is not *always* the value of Column A, eliminate (A) and (B). Now try weird values for a and b, such as 0, 1, negatives, and/or fractions. Each trial yields the same values for the two columns. Therefore, (C) is correct.

18. **D** Factor the quadratic equation to solve for x. First, create two binomials, each with x as one term within both: $(x \quad)(x \quad) = 0$. Next, consider the signs. The positive 12 means that the operations within the two binomials are the same, and the negative $7x$ means that they are both subtraction: $(x - \quad)(x - \quad) = 0$. Now list all the factors of 12, in their pairs: 1 and 12, 2 and 6, and 3 and 4. Only 3 and 4 yield a sum of 7, so they are the two second terms inside the binomials: $(x - 3)(x - 4) = 0$. Last, set each term to 0 and solve for the two values of x that satisfy the equation: $x - 3 = 0$, so $x = 3$, and $x - 4 = 0$ so $x = 4$. As one solution is equal to the value in Column B and one is less, the answer is (D).

19. **A** Let n represent the number of nickels and p represent the number of pennies. Each nickel is, therefore, worth $\$0.05n$, and each penny is worth $\$0.01p$. As the total value of the coins is \$2.40, write an equation: $\$0.05n + \$0.01p = \$2.40$. As there are three times as many pennies as nickels, $3n = p$. Substitute $3n$ for p: $\$0.05n + \$0.01(3n) = \$2.40$. Simplify: $\$0.05n + \$0.03n = \$0.08n = \$2.40$. Thus $n = 30$. The value of these 30 nickels is $30 \times 0.05 = \$1.50$.

 Test the value in (B). If the nickels are worth \$1.20, then there are 24 nickels. As there are three times as many pennies as nickels, there are 72 pennies. Add these \$0.72 to \$1.20 to get \$1.92. There should be \$2.40, so there are more than 24 nickels.

20. **C** A "weird symbol" defined to equal an equation is simply a different form of function notation, so plug in numbers as directed by the defined equation. Test each answer. For (A), $3 \nabla 2 = 3^2 - (3)(2) + 2^2 = 7$. For (B), $2 \nabla 3 = 2^2 - (2)(3) + 3^2 = 7$.

Part IV
Reading

Finding
Information

SSAT and ISEE Finding Information Drill

From the outside, the Guggenheim Museum in New York City looks like a series of white, circular ribbons spiraled on top of one another. The spiral is reflected inside too, as a grand ramp gently spirals up and around
5 from the ground floor. Works of art are displayed on the walls of this spiral and in separate rooms along the way. While today the museum is considered a masterpiece of architecture, critics were not all so kind when the museum opened. Many worried that the striking design
10 of the building would compete with the art contained in the building, defeating the purpose of a great museum. Indeed before the museum opened, twenty-one artists signed a letter of protest against the museum.

1. Which of the following is probably true of the twenty-one artists?

(A) They opposed the museum's design.
(B) They did not understand architecture.
(C) Their art could have been shown at the Guggenheim.
(D) Their fame increased after signing the letter of protest.
(E) They eventually agreed that the Guggenheim is a masterpiece.

Unlike a protest, a movement is an ongoing effort involving many people seeking significant social change. The participants are working together, and even when there are disagreements among separate groups, a
5 common goal is always shared. The Women's Rights Movement of the 1970s provides an example of a movement. The goal was to persuade American men that women were equal citizens, at home and, crucially, in the workplace. Many lawyers, a critical component of the
10 movement, used the federal court system to redefine the way in which women were treated in the workplace, by seeking to ensure that the anti-discrimination laws were applied to women as well as racial minorities.

2. According to the passage, which is true of movements?

(A) They always succeed.
(B) Various groups work together.
(C) They were most successful in the 1970s.
(D) Change cannot occur without movements.

Edgar sneered in that condescending manner. "Are you kidding me, Paul?" He followed this question with a whining voice: "But what if I can't do it? What if I make a fool of myself? What if I fail?" He said this in front
5 of everyone at Thanksgiving dinner, and several people rolled their eyes. As if that wasn't bad enough, my father chimed in, "Yes, not everyone has a sense of self. Paul does not have your confidence. I guess that's just how he is." I became angry at myself for thinking Edgar began
10 speaking to me out of candid concern. I was angry at my father, too, for taking Edgar's side.

3. Why did Paul become angry with himself?

   (A) He lacks a sense of self.
   (B) His voice was too whining.
   (C) His father took Edgar's side.
   (D) He was unsure of his abilities.
   (E) He misunderstood Edgar's real intentions.

Jason Juarez frequently claimed that his mother, Judge Erica Juarez, did not insist that he become a lawyer. Rather, she emphasized that many lawyers do not enjoy the practice of law. Her tremendous standing in both
5 the legal community and the Latino community created added pressure in his legal practice. "Her reputation as a jurist creates expectations for me as a lawyer," Juarez told a reporter after he won an important legal case. "So many people respect what Mama has accomplished."

4. It can be inferred that Juarez feels pressure because

   (A) his job is very demanding.
   (B) his mother is so well known.
   (C) he dislikes the practice of law.
   (D) he refused to take his mother's advice.

Frederick Douglass, the former slave and eloquent author, was a vocal supporter of women's right to vote, but he and the women's rights movement disagreed over the Fifteenth Amendment to the United States
5   Constitution. The proposed Amendment would grant suffrage to Black men, but women (White and Black) would still be denied the right to vote. Douglass' frequent ally, Elizabeth Cady Stanton, opposed the exclusion of women from the Fifteenth Amendment because she
10 (correctly) believed decades would pass before women would obtain the right to vote. She wanted Douglass to support an addition to the proposed Amendment including women, but he did not agree. He felt that the Fifteenth Amendment was already likely to be difficult
15 to pass and that the inclusion of women would doom the proposal to failure.

5. The author implies that Frederick Douglass believed that

   (A)   women should not be allowed to vote.
   (B)   Elizabeth Cady Stanton had the wrong priorities.
   (C)   the Fifteenth Amendment was opposed by some Americans.
   (D)   the Constitution should be amended infrequently.
   (E)   women would win the right to vote relatively soon.

On the clear days of autumn, and with Lake Michigan so close to the yard, my brothers and I used to claim that we would dive into the lake from our roof. Of course, we couldn't. Yet as the sun rose over the lake,
5   our living room sparkled with fireflies. The sun's rays bounced off the shimmering water and reflected back to dance on our white walls. Just before the effect ended, the back wall in particular was covered with so many flashing pinpoints of light that it was like fireflies at night. But
10 once we turned around and faced the lake, with the sun low on the horizon and the deep blue water reflecting the yellow and orange rays in magnificent streaks, our breath was taken away.

6. The author could enjoy the colors of the sunrise by

   (A)   diving into the lake from his roof.
   (B)   viewing the lake from his living room.
   (C)   watching the fireflies in his living room.
   (D)   dancing with his brothers on clear autumn days.

The brain has a remarkable ability to adapt and change, a phenomenon called brain plasticity. Based on changes in the environment, new connections among neurons can form. Neurons are the communication
5 network of the brain; every perception, action, reaction, and thought results from activated neurons. The results of neuronal reorganization can amaze: for example, if an area of the brain associated with a particular function is damaged, another area of the brain might form
10 connections that will allow it to take on the lost function. Brain plasticity has the potential to allow people with certain learning disabilities to compensate for, and even possibly overcome, those disabilities. Indeed, brain training exercises have shown to improve memory and
15 other cognitive functions.

7. The passage suggests that brain plasticity

   (A) is found only in humans.
   (B) is not sufficiently understood.
   (C) involves connections among neurons.
   (D) can cause changes in the environment.
   (E) provides a cure for learning disabilities.

Why do young animals play? Scientific research has yielded several theories. One theory suggests that play is related to physical development: for many animals, play is most intense when the brain and muscles are
5 at a particularly important stage of development for movement. Another theory proposes that play provides practice for important movements that will be necessary for an adult animal, such as stalking prey. Play may also have a social aspect, teaching animals about their own
10 strength and how to interact with others. Yet not all scientists are convinced of these theories. Some argue that play exists for a much less weighty purpose: just to have fun.

8. It can be inferred from the passage that "stalking prey" may be

   (A) fun for adult animals.
   (B) a skill developed through play.
   (C) a requirement for mating in the wild.
   (D) dangerous before the animal brain is fully developed.

The original *Star Wars* movie, *Episode 4: A New Hope*, introduced the unforgettable droid C3PO, an artificial being with decidedly human emotions, including fear and loyalty. Years later, the android Data was
5 introduced in *Star Trek: The Next Generation*. Much more human in appearance than C3PO, Data largely lacked human emotion, but his innate curiosity and his quest to become human reflected human needs in many ways. Today, smart phones can take commands from
10 us and even speak to us, and the field of robotics has created amazing machines that can accomplish dazzling tasks. But so far, no one has created an artificial being so relatable—so human—as C3PO or Data.

9. The passage provides information to answer which one of the following questions?

    (A) What caused C3PO to become fearful?
    (B) Did Data succeed in becoming human?
    (C) What types of tasks can robots perform?
    (D) Was C3PO's appearance more human than Data's?
    (E) When will artificial beings resemble C3PO or Data?

Is Leonardo da Vinci's *Mona Lisa* the world's most popular painting because it is the world's greatest painting? Some art historians believe so. They argue that her famous eyes, hands, and smile speak to us—all of
5 humanity. Da Vinci, these critics assert, created a figure that is unique in its ability to engage our subconscious. I am not so sure. As much as I would like to imagine that the most famous works of art have inherent worth above and beyond that of other works of art, I cannot
10 avoid thinking about the history of a work like *Mona Lisa*. Is it not possible that events and cultural forces have themselves contributed to the renown of the *Mona Lisa*? Perhaps the painting is as famous as it is in part because it is so famous.

10. In the final sentence, the author suggests that

    (A) the *Mona Lisa* is not da Vinci's best painting.
    (B) a painting's artistic merits may not fully explain its fame.
    (C) a person's subconscious may find more in the *Mona Lisa* than meets the eye.
    (D) the *Mona Lisa* would be less famous if it weren't for the eyes, hand, and smile.

Finding Information: Answers and Explanations

ANSWER KEY

SSAT and ISEE Finding
Information Drill

1. A
2. B
3. E
4. B
5. C
6. B
7. C
8. B
9. D
10. B

SSAT and ISEE Finding Information Drill

Finding information questions include phrases such as *according to the author, suggests, implies, infer, provides information, would agree, what, why,* and others seeking factual information. The answer to any such question must come from the text of the passage without reading between the lines.

1. **A** The passage states, "Many worried that the *striking design of the building* would compete with the art contained in the building, defeating the purpose of a great museum. Indeed before the museum opened, twenty-one artists signed a letter of protest against the museum."

2. **B** The passage states, "Unlike a protest, *a movement is an ongoing effort involving many people seeking significant social change. The participants are working together,* and even when there are disagreements among separate groups, a common goal is always shared."

3. **E** The passage states, "*I became angry at myself for thinking Edgar began speaking to me out of candid concern.*"

4. **B** The passage states, "Her tremendous standing in both the legal community and the Latino community *created added pressure in his legal practice. 'Her reputation as a jurist creates expectations for me as a lawyer,'* Juarez told a reporter after he won an important legal case."

5. **C** The passage states, "*He felt that the Fifteenth Amendment was already likely to be difficult to pass* and that the inclusion of women would doom the proposal to failure."

6. **B** The passage states, "Yet as the sun rose over the lake, *our living room* sparkled with fireflies. The sun's rays bounced off the shimmering water and *reflected back to dance on our white walls. Just before the effect ended, the back wall in particular was covered with so many flashing pinpoints of light that it was like fireflies at night.*"

7. **C** The passage states, "The brain has a remarkable ability to adapt and change, *a phenomenon called brain plasticity. Based on changes in the environment, new connections among neurons can form.*"

8. **B** The passage states, "Another theory proposes that *play provides practice for important movements that will be necessary for an adult animal*, such as stalking prey."

9. **D** The passage states, "*Much more human in appearance than C3PO, Data largely lacked human emotion*, but his innate curiosity and his quest to become human reflected human needs in many ways."

10. **B** The passage states, "*As much as I would like to imagine that the most famous works of art have inherent worth above and beyond that of other works of art*, I cannot avoid thinking about the history of a work like *Mona Lisa. Is it not possible that events and cultural forces have themselves contributed to the renown of the Mona Lisa? Perhaps the painting is as famous as it is in part because it is so famous.*"

Understanding
Purpose

SSAT and ISEE Understanding Purpose Drill

Unlike a protest, a movement is an ongoing effort involving many people seeking significant social change. The participants are working together, and even when there are disagreements among separate groups, a
5 common goal is always shared. The Women's Rights Movement of the 1970s provides an example of a movement. The goal was to persuade American men that women were equal citizens, at home and, crucially, in the workplace. Many lawyers, a critical component of the
10 movement, used the federal court system to redefine the way in which women were treated in the workplace, by seeking to ensure that the anti-discrimination laws were applied to women as well as racial minorities.

1. This passage is mostly about

    (A) the importance of protest. ✗
    (B) the Civil Rights Movement.
    (C) an example of a movement.
    (D) a criticism of sexist attitudes. ✗
    (E) a celebration of trial lawyers. ✗

From the outside, the Guggenheim Museum in New York City looks like a series of white, circular ribbons spiraled on top of one another. The spiral is reflected inside too, as a grand ramp gently spirals up and around
5 from the ground floor. Works of art are displayed on the walls of this spiral and in separate rooms along the way. While today the museum is considered a masterpiece of architecture, critics were not all so kind when the museum opened. Many worried that the striking design
10 of the building would compete with the art contained in the building, defeating the purpose of a great museum. Indeed before the museum opened, twenty-one artists signed a letter of protest against the museum.

2. The author most likely refers to the twenty-one artists in order to

      emphasize that the Guggenheim sparked controversy.
    (B) suggest the similarities between many artists and critics.
    (C) illustrate that artists are not qualified to judge architecture.
    (D) inform the reader why the Guggenheim is considered a masterpiece.

Edgar sneered in that condescending manner. "Are you kidding me, Paul?" He followed this question with a whining voice: "But what if I can't do it? What if I make a fool of myself? What if I fail?" He said this in front

5 of everyone at Thanksgiving dinner, and several people rolled their eyes. As if that wasn't bad enough, my father chimed in, "Yes, not everyone has a sense of self. Paul does not have your confidence. I guess that's just how he is." I became angry at myself for thinking Edgar began

10 speaking to me out of candid concern. I was angry at my father, too, for taking Edgar's side.

3. The phrase "as if that wasn't bad enough" is included to

(A) explain Paul's embarrassment over his lack of confidence.

(B) show that Edgar's insensitivity was not an isolated occurrence. ✗

(C) show Paul's father as a keen observer who can be brutally honest. ✗

(D) explain that Paul was upset over more than Edgar's treatment of him.

Jason Juarez frequently claimed that his mother, Judge Erica Juarez, did not insist that he become a lawyer. Rather, she emphasized that many lawyers do not enjoy the practice of law. Her tremendous standing in both

5 the legal community and the Latino community created added pressure in his legal practice. "Her reputation as a jurist creates expectations for me as a lawyer," Juarez told a reporter after he won an important legal case. "So many people respect what Mama has accomplished."

4. The author's primary purpose of the passage is to

(A) praise a judge.

(B) question a career. ✗

(C) criticize a parent. ✗

(D) celebrate a victory. ✗

(E) describe a concern.

Frederick Douglass, the former slave and eloquent author, was a vocal supporter of women's right to vote, but he and the women's rights movement disagreed over the Fifteenth Amendment to the United States
5 Constitution. The proposed Amendment would grant suffrage to Black men, but women (White and Black) would still be denied the right to vote. Douglass' frequent ally, Elizabeth Cady Stanton, opposed the exclusion of women from the Fifteenth Amendment because she
10 (correctly) believed decades would pass before women would obtain the right to vote. She wanted Douglass to support an addition to the proposed Amendment including women, but he did not agree. He felt that the Fifteenth Amendment was already likely to be difficult
15 to pass and that the inclusion of women would doom the proposal to failure.

5. The author likely describes Douglass as a "vocal sup-porter" of voting rights for women in order to

(A)   explain why he and Stanton were allies.
(B)   illustrate the extent of his political judgment.
(C)   expose him as inconsistent in his view on women.
(D)   provide context for his opposition to changing the Fifteenth Amendment.

On the clear days of autumn, and with Lake Michigan so close to the yard, my brothers and I used to claim that we would dive into the lake from our roof. Of course, we couldn't. Yet as the sun rose over the lake,
5 our living room sparkled with fireflies. The sun's rays bounced off the shimmering water and reflected back to dance on our white walls. Just before the effect ended, the back wall in particular was covered with so many flashing pinpoints of light that it was like fireflies at night. But
10 once we turned around and faced the lake, with the sun low on the horizon and the deep blue water reflecting the yellow and orange rays in magnificent streaks, our breath was taken away.

6. What does the author mean when he says "our living room was abuzz with fireflies"?

(A)   Many children played in the house.
(B)   The sun's light created a visual effect.
(C)   The children had lost touch with reality.
(D)   The screen doors were frequently left open.
(E)   Fireflies sought warmth inside each autumn.

The brain has a remarkable ability to adapt and change, a phenomenon called brain plasticity. Based on changes in the environment, new connections among neurons can form. Neurons are the communication
5 network of the brain; every perception, action, reaction, and thought results from activated neurons. The results of neuronal reorganization can amaze: for example, if an area of the brain associated with a particular function is damaged, another area of the brain might form
10 connections that will allow it to take on the lost function. Brain plasticity has the potential to allow people with certain learning disabilities to compensate for, and even possibly overcome, those disabilities. Indeed, brain training exercises have shown to improve memory and
15 other cognitive functions.

7. The primary purpose of the passage is to

(A) demonstrate that people with learning disabilities need only form new neural connections in order to function more effectively.

(B) suggest that the potential benefits of brain plasticity, while exciting and worthy of continued study, currently lack a scientific basis.

(C) convey the brain's remarkable ability to form new neural connections and provide possible benefits that may stem from that ability.

(D) provide an overview of brain function, particularly as it relates to sensory perception and the improvement of cognitive functions.

Why do young animals play? Scientific research has yielded several theories. One theory suggests that play is related to physical development: for many animals, play is most intense when the brain and muscles are
5 at a particularly important stage of development for movement. Another theory proposes that play provides practice for important movements that will be necessary for an adult animal, such as stalking prey. Play may also have a social aspect, teaching animals about their own
10 strength and how to interact with others. Yet not all scientists are convinced of these theories. Some argue that play exists for a much less weighty purpose: just to have fun.

8. Which of the following best states the main idea of the passage?

(A) Different theories on animal play have been proposed.

(B) It is unlikely that animal play has an important purpose.

(C) The social aspect of animal play remains a point of controversy.

(D) The purpose of play among animals is unlikely to be discovered.

(E) It is most likely that animals play as part of their physical development.

The original *Star Wars* movie, *Episode 4: A New Hope*, introduced the unforgettable droid C3PO, an artificial being with decidedly human emotions, including fear and loyalty. Years later, the android Data was
5   introduced in *Star Trek: The Next Generation*. Much more human in appearance than C3PO, Data largely lacked human emotion, but his innate curiosity and his quest to become human reflected human needs in many ways. Today, smart phones can take commands from
10 us and even speak to us, and the field of robotics has created amazing machines that can accomplish dazzling tasks. But so far, no one has created an artificial being so relatable—so human—as C3PO or Data.

9.   The author mentions smart phones in order to

(A)   illustrate human inventiveness outside of fiction.
(B)   contrast fictional androids with modern technology.
(C)   lament the slow pace of technological development.
(D)   demonstrate that fiction sometimes predicts the future.

Is Leonardo da Vinci's *Mona Lisa* the world's most popular painting because it is the world's greatest painting? Some art historians believe so. They argue that her famous eyes, hands, and smile speak to us—all of
5   humanity. Da Vinci, these critics assert, created a figure that is unique in its ability to engage our subconscious. I am not so sure. As much as I would like to imagine that the most famous works of art have inherent worth above and beyond that of other words of art, I cannot
10 avoid thinking about the history of a work like *Mona Lisa*. Is it not possible that events and cultural forces have themselves contributed to the renown of the *Mona Lisa*? Perhaps the painting is as famous it is in part because it is so famous.

10.   The main point expressed by the passage is that

(A)   the *Mona Lisa* is popular.
(B)   the *Mona Lisa* is a great painting.
(C)   the *Mona Lisa* engages the subconscious.
(D)   art historians prize the eyes, hands, and smile of the *Mona Lisa*.
(E)   more than one factor might explain the popularity of the *Mona Lisa*.

Understanding Purpose: Answers and Explanations

ANSWER KEY

SSAT and ISEE
Understanding Purpose Drill

1. C
2. A
3. D
4. E
5. D
6. B
7. C
8. A
9. B
10. E

SSAT and ISEE Understanding Purpose Drill

Understanding purpose questions include phrases such as *in order to, included to, serves to, purpose, point* and others seeking a reason for the inclusion of factual information. The answer to any such question must come from the text of the passage without reading between the lines. Take care to avoid a "finding information" answer on a purpose question.

1.   **C**   The passage states, "*The Women's Rights Movement of the 1970s provides an example of a movement.*"

2.   **A**   The passage states, "While today the museum is considered a masterpiece of architecture, *critics were not all so kind when the museum opened. Many worried that the striking design of the building would compete with the art contained in the building*, defeating the purpose of a great museum. Indeed before the museum opened, twenty-one artists signed a letter of protest against the museum."

3.   **D**   The passage states, "As if that wasn't bad enough, *my father chimed in,* 'Yes, not everyone has a sense of self. Paul does not have your confidence. I guess that's just how he is.' I became angry at myself for thinking Edgar began speaking to me out of candid concern. *I was angry at my father, too, for taking Edgar's side.*"

4.   **E**   The passage states, "*Her tremendous standing in both the legal community and the Latino community created added pressure in his legal practice. 'Her reputation as a jurist creates expectations for me as a lawyer,'* Juarez told a reporter after he won an important legal case."

5.   **D**   The passage states, "Frederick Douglass, the former slave and eloquent author, was a vocal supporter of women's right to vote, *but he and the women's rights movement disagreed over the Fifteenth Amendment to the United States Constitution.*" The part of the sentence that states that Douglass "was a vocal supporter of women's right to vote" is in the passage to juxtapose what is stated next.

6. **B**   The passage states, "Just before the effect ended, *the back wall in particular was covered with so many flashing pinpoints of light that it was like fireflies at night.*"

7. **C**   The passage states, "*The brain has a remarkable ability to adapt and change, a phenomenon called brain plasticity. Based on changes in the environment, new connections among neurons can form. ... Brain plasticity has the potential to allow people with certain learning disabilities to compensate for, and even possibly overcome, those disabilities.*"

8. **A**   The passage states, "*Why do young animals play? Scientific research has yielded several theories.*"

9. **B**   The passage states, "Today, smart phones can take commands from us and even speak to us, and the field of robotics has created amazing machines that can accomplish dazzling tasks. *But so far, no one has created an artificial being so relatable—so human—as C3PO or Data.*"

10. **E**   The passage states, "*Is it not possible that events and cultural forces have themselves contributed to the renown of the* Mona Lisa? *Perhaps the painting is as famous as it is in part because it is so famous.*"

Tone

SSAT and ISEE Tone Drill

Unlike a protest, a movement is an ongoing effort involving many people seeking significant social change. The participants are working together, and even when there are disagreements among separate groups, a
5 common goal is always shared. The Women's Rights Movement of the 1970s provides an example of a movement. The goal was to persuade American men that women were equal citizens, at home and, crucially, in the workplace. Many lawyers, a critical component of the
10 movement, used the federal court system to redefine the way in which women were treated in the workplace, by seeking to ensure that the anti-discrimination laws were applied to women as well as racial minorities.

1. In referring to lawyers, the author's tone is

   (A)   critical.
   (B)   tolerant.
   (C)   sarcastic.
   (D)   appreciative.
   (E)   unconcerned.

Frederick Douglass, the former slave and eloquent author, was a vocal supporter of women's right to vote, but he and the women's rights movement disagreed over the Fifteenth Amendment to the United States
5 Constitution. The proposed Amendment would grant suffrage to Black men, but women (White and Black) would still be denied the right to vote. Douglass' frequent ally, Elizabeth Cady Stanton, opposed the exclusion of women from the Fifteenth Amendment because she
10 (correctly) believed decades would pass before women would obtain the right to vote. She wanted Douglass to support an addition to the proposed Amendment including women, but he did not agree. He felt that the Fifteenth Amendment was already likely to be difficult
15 to pass and that the inclusion of women would doom the proposal to failure.

2. The author's tone can best be described as

   (A)   critical.
   (B)   indifferent.
   (C)   informative.
   (D)   unpersuaded.

On the clear days of autumn, and with Lake Michigan so close to the yard, my brothers and I used to claim that we would dive into the lake from our roof. Of course, we couldn't. Yet as the sun rose over the lake,
5 our living room sparkled with fireflies. The sun's rays bounced off the shimmering water and reflected back to dance on our white walls. Just before the effect ended, the back wall in particular was covered with so many flashing pinpoints of light that it was like fireflies at night. But
10 once we turned around and faced the lake, with the sun low on the horizon and the deep blue water reflecting the yellow and orange rays in magnificent streaks, our breath was taken away.

3. The writer's reaction when looking out at the lake is one of

   (A)　wonder.
   (B)　amusement.
   (C)　melancholy.
   (D)　understanding.
   (E)　unresponsiveness.

The original *Star Wars* movie, *Episode 4: A New Hope*, introduced the unforgettable droid C3PO, an artificial being with decidedly human emotions, including fear and loyalty. Years later, the android Data was
5 introduced in *Star Trek: The Next Generation*. Much more human in appearance than C3PO, Data largely lacked human emotion, but his innate curiosity and his quest to become human reflected human needs in many ways. Today, smart phones can take commands from
10 us and even speak to us, and the field of robotics has created amazing machines that can accomplish dazzling tasks. But so far, no one has created an artificial being so relatable—so human—as C3PO or Data.

4. When describing C3PO and Data, the author's tone is best described as

   (A)　fearful.
   (B)　humorous.
   (C)　conflicted.
   (D)　admiring.

Is Leonardo da Vinci's *Mona Lisa* the world's most popular painting because it is the world's greatest painting? Some art historians believe so. They argue that her famous eyes, hands, and smile speak to us—all of
5   humanity. Da Vinci, these critics assert, created a figure that is unique in its ability to engage our subconscious. I am not so sure. As much as I would like to imagine that the most famous works of art have inherent worth above and beyond that of other words of art, I cannot
10   avoid thinking about the history of a work like *Mona Lisa*. Is it not possible that events and cultural forces have themselves contributed to the renown of the *Mona Lisa*? Perhaps the painting is as famous it is in part because it is so famous.

5.   The author's attitude toward the art historians' explanation for the fame of the *Mona Lisa* can best be described as

(A)   skepticism.
(B)   amusement.
(C)   aggravation.
(D)   profound disbelief.
(E)   complete agreement.

Tone: Answers and Explanations

ANSWER KEY

SSAT and ISEE
Tone Drill
1. D
2. C
3. A
4. D
5. A

SSAT and ISEE Tone Drill

Tone questions include phrases such as *tone*, *attitude*, *views as*, *reaction to*, and others seeking assessment of how the author feels about something. An author can have a positive view, a negative view, or a neutral view. A neutral view does not imply a lack of interest, but rather a decision not to show how the author feels. Take care to avoid answers that are too strong.

1. **D** The author states, "Many lawyers, a critical component of the movement…", meaning that the lawyers are important to the movement. Therefore, the best answer is (D).

2. **C** The author does not praise or criticize Douglass for his opposition to including women in the Fifteenth Amendment. The passage simply describes Douglass's position in a neutral way.

3. **A** The author's "breath was taken away," which is an expression of wonder.

4. **D** The author has a positive view of the complexity of C3P0 and Data.

5. **A** While the author proposes an alternative explanation for the fame of the *Mona Lisa*, the tone is more questioning than defiant, with phrases such as "perhaps" and "is it not possible." The author is skeptical.

Vocab in Context

SSAT and ISEE Vocab in Context Drill

From the outside, the Guggenheim Museum in New York City looks like a series of white, circular ribbons spiraled on top of one another. The spiral is reflected inside too, as a grand ramp gently spirals up and around
5 from the ground floor. Works of art are displayed on the walls of this spiral and in separate rooms along the way. While today the museum is considered a masterpiece of architecture, critics were not all so kind when the museum opened. Many worried that the striking design
10 of the building would compete with the art contained in the building, defeating the purpose of a great museum. Indeed before the museum opened, twenty-one artists signed a letter of protest against the museum.

1. The word "striking" most closely corresponds to

   (A) clear.
   (B) thumping.
   (C) arranging.
   (D) eye-catching.
   (E) work-stopping.

Edgar sneered in that condescending manner. "Are you kidding me, Paul?" He followed this question with a whining voice: "But what if I can't do it? What if I make a fool of myself? What if I fail?" He said this in front
5 of everyone at Thanksgiving dinner, and several people rolled their eyes. As if that wasn't bad enough, my father chimed in, "Yes, not everyone has a sense of self. Paul does not have your confidence. I guess that's just how he is." I became angry at myself for thinking Edgar began
10 speaking to me out of candid concern. I was angry at my father, too, for taking Edgar's side.

2. The word "candid" most nearly means

   (A) fake.
   (B) sincere.
   (C) peculiar.
   (D) apologetic.

The brain has a remarkable ability to adapt and change, a phenomenon called brain plasticity. Based on changes in the environment, new connections among neurons can form. Neurons are the communication

5 network of the brain; every perception, action, reaction, and thought results from activated neurons. The results of neuronal reorganization can amaze: for example, if an area of the brain associated with a particular function is damaged, another area of the brain might form

10 connections that will allow it to take on the lost function. Brain plasticity has the potential to allow people with certain learning disabilities to compensate for, and even possibly overcome, those disabilities. Indeed, brain training exercises have shown to improve memory and

15 other cognitive functions.

3. The word "cognitive" most likely means

(A)   mental.
(B)   athletic.
(C)   practical.
(D)   systematic.
(E)   spectacular.

The original *Star Wars* movie, *Episode 4: A New Hope*, introduced the unforgettable droid C3PO, an artificial being with decidedly human emotions, including fear and loyalty. Years later, the android Data was

5 introduced in *Star Trek: The Next Generation*. Much more human in appearance than C3PO, Data largely lacked human emotion, but his innate curiosity and his quest to become human reflected human needs in many ways. Today, smart phones can take commands from

10 us and even speak to us, and the field of robotics has created amazing machines that can accomplish dazzling tasks. But so far, no one has created an artificial being so relatable—so human—as C3PO or Data.

4. In context, the word "dazzling" most likely means

(A)   blazing.
(B)   glittering.
(C)   confusing.
(D)   astounding.
(E)   overwhelming.

Is Leonardo da Vinci's *Mona Lisa* the world's
most popular painting because it is the world's greatest
painting? Some art historians believe so. They argue that
her famous eyes, hands, and smile speak to us—all of
5   humanity. Da Vinci, these critics assert, created a figure
that is unique in its ability to engage our subconscious.
I am not so sure. As much as I would like to imagine
that the most famous works of art have inherent worth
above and beyond that of other words of art, I cannot
10   avoid thinking about the history of a work like *Mona
Lisa*. Is it not possible that events and cultural forces have
themselves contributed to the renown of the *Mona Lisa*?
Perhaps the painting is as famous as it is in part because it
is so famous.

5.   The word "renown" most nearly means

(A)   fame.
(B)   beauty.
(C)   controversy.
(D)   interpretation.

Vocab in Context:
Answers and
Explanations

ANSWER KEY

SSAT and ISEE
Vocab in Context Drill

1. D
2. B
3. A
4. D
5. A

SSAT and ISEE Vocab-in-Context Drill

Vocab-in-context questions include phrases such as *most likely means, most nearly means, most closely corresponds to* and others seeking the meaning of a word in the particular context of its use. Whether you recognize the word or not, determine how the author is using the word based on its context.

1. **D** The author describes the building as a *masterpiece of architecture,* so striking must mean something similar to "amazing." The closest choice to "amazing" is *eye-catching.* The correct answer is (D).

2. **B** A good substitute for the word in context is *real.* The closest choice to "real" is *sincere.* The correct answer is (B).

3. **A** The clues in the passage are *memory* and *brain training,* so the word must mean something similar. *Mental* is the closest match to *brain training.* The correct answer is (A).

4. **D** The author uses the word *amazing* earlier in the sentence. The closest match to *amazing* is *astounding.* The correct answer is (D).

5. **A** The passage states *Perhaps the painting is as famous as it is in part because it is so famous.* Therefore, the word must mean something similar to fame. Choice (A) is a direct match. The correct answer is (A).

Miscellaneous Reading

SSAT and ISEE Miscellaneous Drill

From the outside, the Guggenheim Museum in New York City looks like a series of white, circular ribbons spiraled on top of one another. The spiral is reflected inside too, as a grand ramp gently spirals up and around
5 from the ground floor. Works of art are displayed on the walls of this spiral and in separate rooms along the way. While today the museum is considered a masterpiece of architecture, critics were not all so kind when the museum opened. Many worried that the striking design
10 of the building would compete with the art contained in the building, defeating the purpose of a great museum. Indeed before the museum opened, twenty-one artists signed a letter of protest against the museum.

1. This passage is probably taken from

(A) a textbook.
(B) a critic's review.
(C) an autobiography.
(D) a historical novel.
(E) a letter to the editor.

Jason Juarez frequently claimed that his mother, Judge Erica Juarez, did not insist that he become a lawyer. Rather, she emphasized that many lawyers do not enjoy the practice of law. Her tremendous standing in both
5 the legal community and the Latino community created added pressure in his legal practice. "Her reputation as a jurist creates expectations for me as a lawyer," Juarez told a reporter after he won an important legal case. "So many people respect what Mama has accomplished."

 2. The passage describes the viewpoint of a

(A) judge.
(B) lawyer.
(C) reporter.
(D) law student.
(E) community organizer.

The brain has a remarkable ability to adapt and change, a phenomenon called brain plasticity. Based on changes in the environment, new connections among neurons can form. Neurons are the communication
5   network of the brain; every perception, action, reaction, and thought results from activated neurons. The results of neuronal reorganization can amaze: for example, if an area of the brain associated with a particular function is damaged, another area of the brain might form
10 connections that will allow it to take on the lost function. Brain plasticity has the potential to allow people with certain learning disabilities to compensate for, and even possibly overcome, those disabilities. Indeed, brain training exercises have shown to improve memory and
15 other cognitive functions.

3. The author of the passage does all of the following EXCEPT

   (A)   define a term.
   (B)   cite an authority.
   (C)   describe a function.
   (D)   provide an example.

Why do young animals play? Scientific research has yielded several theories. One theory suggests that play is related to physical development: for many animals, play is most intense when the brain and muscles are
5   at a particularly important stage of development for movement. Another theory proposes that play provides practice for important movements that will be necessary for an adult animal, such as stalking prey. Play may also have a social aspect, teaching animals about their own
10 strength and how to interact with others. Yet not all scientists are convinced of these theories. Some argue that play exists for a much less weighty purpose: just to have fun.

4. Which best describes the organization of the paragraph?

   (A)   A controversy is evaluated and then settled.
   (B)   An opinion is offered and supported with facts.
   (C)   The history of research on animal play is summarized.
   (D)   Several theories relating to a scientific question are presented.

Is Leonardo da Vinci's *Mona Lisa* the world's most popular painting because it is the world's greatest painting? Some art historians believe so. They argue that her famous eyes, hands, and smile speak to us—all of

5 humanity. Da Vinci, these critics assert, created a figure that is unique in its ability to engage our subconscious. I am not so sure. As much as I would like to imagine that the most famous works of art have inherent worth above and beyond that of other words of art, I cannot

10 avoid thinking about the history of a work like *Mona Lisa*. Is it not possible that events and cultural forces have themselves contributed to the renown of the *Mona Lisa*? Perhaps the painting is as famous it is in part because it is so famous.

5. Which of the following is the author of the passage most likely to discuss next?

(A)   da Vinci's works in addition to his paintings
(B)   da Vinci's intention when painting the *Mona Lisa*
(C)   how art historians evaluate the quality of paintings
(D)   museum visitors who choose not to view the *Mona Lisa*
(E)   events that may have contributed to the fame of the *Mona Lisa*

Miscellaneous
Reading: Answers
and Explanations

ANSWER KEY

SSAT and ISEE
Miscellaneous Reading Drill

1. A
2. B
3. B
4. D
5. E

SSAT and ISEE Miscellaneous Reading Drill

Some questions ask for particular tasks, such as EXCEPT questions (both tests), identifying the organization of a passage (typically ISEE), determining what source a passage might be taken from (typically SSAT), and predicting what the author will discuss next (typically SSAT). On EXCEPT questions, be sure to eliminate answers that appear in the passage. On organization questions, use process of elimination to match the answer to the passage. On source and "discuss next" questions, use common sense.

1. **A**   This passage is an overview of the Guggenheim Museum and gives some basic information. Keep (A) since informational text could be in a textbook. Eliminate (B) because a review would contain an opinion, and this text is objective. It is not a first-person account of themselves, so eliminate (C). Eliminate (D) because it is not fictional. Finally, eliminate (E) because it is not addressing anyone. The correct answer is (A).

2. **B**   The passage states "*Her reputation as a jurist creates expectations for me as a lawyer.*" This is from the perspective of Juarez, who is a lawyer. The correct answer is (B).

3. **B**   Choice (A) is supported: "The brain has a remarkable ability to adapt and change, a phenomenon called brain plasticity." Choice (C) is supported: "every perception, action, reaction, and thought results from activated neurons." Choice (D) is supported: "for example, if an area of the brain associated with a particular function is damaged, another area of the brain might form connections that will allow it to take on the lost function." No authority is cited.

4. **D**   Even if the theories concerning animal play constitute a "controversy," the author does not settle it, so eliminate (A). The author presents several opinions, not just one, and the opinions are not supported with facts, so eliminate (B). No mention of research is mentioned, so eliminate (C). Several theories on a scientific question (why animals play) are presented.

5. E   As the author offers the opinion that "events and cultural forces have themselves contributed to the renown of the *Mona Lisa*," the author likely will provide examples of such events and cultural forces next.

Full Passages

SSAT Full Passages Drill

C-4, also known as Composition C-4, is a generic version of the plastic explosive, Composition C. It is composed of explosives, plastic binder, plasticizer, and usually some variety of chemical marker like 2, 3-dimethyl-2, 3-dinitrobutane (DMNDB). When these ingredients are combined, the final product is off-white in color and is like modeling clay in consistency. This quality directly impacts the utility of C-4, as it can be pressed into small crevices where other explosives might not fit.

C-4 was widely used during the Vietnam War because it burns when ignited by a flame instead of being detonated. Unfortunately, burning C-4 creates noxious fumes, so its utility as a heat source is limited. Additionally, during the Vietnam War, soldiers would occasionally ingest a small amount of C-4 to make themselves temporarily sick, which would earn them medical leave so they could go home.

1. It can be inferred that C-4

    (A) is economical
    (B) requires a fuse to ignite
    (C) produces an unpleasant aroma before being detonated
    (D) is malleable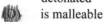
    (E) is an ideal heat source

2. Which of the following titles best summarizes the main idea of the passage?

    (A) The Use of C-4 in Vietnam
    (B) Pros & Cons of C-4 Use
    (C) Heat Sources for Soldiers at War
    (D) C-4 & DMNDB
    (E) An Overview of C-4

3. The author implies that C-4

    (A) is nauseating
    (B) is not unique
    (C) hardens quickly
    (D) can be used to fill cracks
    (E) is advantageous on the battlefield

4. The author uses the phrase "directly impacts the utility of C-4" to show that C-4 is

    (A) comparatively useful
    (B) extremely combustible
    (C) not moldable
    (D) highly noxious
    (E) inedible

5. According to the passage, C-4

    (A) has a short lifetime
    (B) exists in nature
    (C) is only beneficial during times of war
    (D) is composed of several ingredients
    (E) is an effective means of getting out of work

6. The author's attitude can best be described as

    (A) cautionary
    (B) didactic
    (C) sarcastic
    (D) wry
    (E) encouraging

7. The author suggests that C-4

    (A) generates heat quickly
    (B) is fatal if ingested
    (C) does not always have a chemical marker
    (D) contains DMNDB
    (E) is unique

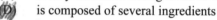

> As a decrepit father takes delight
> To see his active child do deeds of youth,
> So I, made lame by fortune's dearest spite,
> Take all my comfort of thy worth and truth.
> For whether beauty, birth, or wealth, or wit,
> Or any of these all, or all, or more,
> Entitled in thy parts do crowned sit,
> I make my love engrafted to this store:
> So then I am not lame, poor, nor despised,
> Whilst that this shadow doth such substance give
> That I in thy abundance am sufficed
> And by a part of all thy glory live.
> Look, what is best, that best I wish in thee:
> This wish I have; then ten times happy me!

8. As it is used in line 3, the word "lame" most nearly means

   (A) dull
   (B) impoverished
   (C) disabled
   (D) crippled
   (E) uninteresting

9. According to the passage, the speaker is "ten times happy" because

   (A) he is a decrepit father
   (B) he has become lame
   (C) the youth has what is best
   (D) he has earned wealth and beauty
   (E) he can watch someone he loves live well

10. Which is true about the speaker?

    (A) He is satisfied to appreciate someone else's life.
    (B) He has lost all of his money.
    (C) He believes in God.
    (D) He thinks the youth has significant faults.
    (E) He is arrogant about his own capacities.

11. The speaker suggests that "abundance" is most likely

    (A) his own self-worth
    (B) physical opulence
    (C) 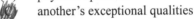 another's exceptional qualities
    (D) another's desires
    (E) his own material wealth

12. The first four lines of the poem provide an example of which of the following literary devices?

    (A) Personification
    (B) Metaphor
    (C) Oxymoron
    (D) Simile
    (E) Hyperbole

ISEE Full Passages Drill

Questions 1–6

The following passage describes an incident from Thomas Edison's early days in New York City.

Line

1   Opportunity, well overdue, came just three
2 weeks after arriving in New York. Seventeen
3 months as a telegrapher in Boston found me
4 deeply in debt, despite having acquired several
5 patents. Thirty-five dollars, borrowed from
6 a friend, bought a steamer ticket to the more
7 'commercially oriented' city farther south.
8   Upon arriving in the Big Apple, I took up
9 residency in the basement of a building in the
10 Financial District, as I had nowhere else to live.
11 I spent my days meandering through buildings
12 in the area, watching, listening, and waiting in
13 solitude, wondering when opportunity might
14 present itself.
15   On the particular morning in question, I
16 found myself wandering through a brokerage
17 firm, bedraggled and sipping a cup of tea I
18 had begged from a vendor. Suddenly, I heard
19 quite the commotion. It would seem that one
20 of the stock-tickers had malfunctioned, and the
21 manager was in quite a tizzy.
22   Luckily, I had been sleeping in the
23 basement of this very building for three weeks
24 and had walked through this very office
25 before, so I had observed this very machine in
26 operation before.
27   Seeing that no one else's attempts had
28 proven successful, I made my way through the
29 crowd of onlookers to have a go at it.
30   After taking a few minutes to better
31 acquaint myself with the workings of the beast,
32 I maneuvered an errant spring back into its
33 rightful place. To the others' astonishment, the
34 machine settled itself back into work. What
35 boggled my mind, however, was the manager's
36 response: an offer of a position as repairman for
37 all machines in the company, for the ridiculous
38 sum of $300 per month. And thus, I was
39 suddenly delivered from abject poverty and into
40 prosperity.

1. The primary purpose of the passage is to

   (A) show how heroic Edison's actions were.
   (B) describe a turning point in Edison's life.
   (C) explain why Edison was so deeply in debt.
   (D) chastise managers who can't repair their own equipment.

2. The tone of the second paragraph can best be described as

   (A) friendly optimism.
   (B) solitary trepidation.
   (C) lonely anticipation.
   (D) peaceful nostalgia.

3. It can be inferred that Edison's patents

   (A) were one-of-a-kind.
   (B) were popular on the open market.
   (C) paid for his steamer ticket.
   (D) were insufficiently profitable.

4. The phrase "commercially oriented" (line 7) refers to Edison's belief that in New York City, he could

   (A) get out of debt.
   (B) sell real estate.
   (C) live in a basement apartment.
   (D) get a job repairing equipment.

5. The phrase "boggled my mind" is included in order to

   (A) show Edison's shock at being able to fix the machine.
   (B) show Edison's surprise that he was in the right place at the right time.
   (C) show the others' disbelief at Edison's ability to fix the machine.
   (D) show Edison's amazement at the job offer that resulted from fixing the machine.

6. In line 39, "delivered" most nearly means

   (A) saved.
   (B) carried.
   (C) produced.
   (D) detached.

Questions 7–12

Line

1   Matryoshka dolls, also known as Russian
2   nesting dolls, are hallmarks of Russian
3   traditional folk art. There are traditionally at
4   least five nested dolls, each of which detaches
5   top from bottom to uncover a smaller figure of
6   the same style inside. Each hand-crafted set is
7   unique, and individual sets are often designed to
8   follow a specific theme.
9   The classic Matryoshka doll portrays a
10 cheerful Russian lady with a sarafan covering
11 her head. Inside, the figures may be male or
12 female, and the smallest, innermost doll is
13 usually designed to look like a baby. The real
14 artwork is displayed in the painting of the dolls,
15 which can depict anything from peasant girls
16 in traditional attire to fairy-tale characters and
17 leaders.
18   These dolls were originally modeled after
19 a doll from Honshu, Japan, and were adapted
20 to represent Russian culture. Today they are
21 known around the world and have served as
22 inspiration for many other types of 'object-in-
23 object'—or layering schemes—in all types of
24 artwork ranging from clothing to furniture.

7. Which best expresses the main idea of the passage?

(A) The popularity of Matryoshka dolls is declining.
(B) Matryoshka dolls are no longer artistically significant.
(C) Each Matryoshka doll set is unique.
(D) Matryoshka dolls are classic forms of Russian art.

8. The author suggests that Matryoshka dolls were

(A) used as inspiration for other art forms.
(B) traditionally designed to represent Russian leaders.
(C) intended to be used for clothing designs.
(D) designed to portray unhappy Russian people.

9. Which best describes the organization of lines 18-24?

(A) A procedure is described sequentially.
(B) A claim is made and examples supporting that claim are presented.
(C) The inspiration for an art form and its effects are given.
(D) The future of an art form is discussed.

10. According to the passage, which is true of Matryoshka dolls?

    (A) They are no longer popular outside of Russia.
    (B) They are a style of art unique to Russia.
    (C) They have several dolls in a single set.
    (D) They represent one gender in each set.

11. The author of the passage appears to care most deeply about the fact that

    (A) Matryoshka dolls are trademarks of Russian art.
    (B) the innermost doll represents a baby.
    (C) Matryoshka dolls are artistically valuable because of the way they are painted.
    (D) some Matryoshka dolls take months to make.

12. According to the passage, the Matryoshka dolls were originally inspired by

    (A) Russia leaders.
    (B) Japanese dolls.
    (C) traditional fairy tale characters.
    (D) the desire to create a uniquely Russian art form.

Full Passages:
Answers and
Explanations

ANSWER KEY

SSAT Full Passages Drill

1. D
2. E
3. D
4. A
5. D
6. A
7. C
8. D
9. E
10. A
11. C
12. D

ISEE Full Passages Drill

1. B
2. C
3. D
4. A
5. D
6. A
7. D
8. A
9. C
10. C
11. C
12. B

SSAT Full Passages Drill

When you arrive at a longer new passage, read it quickly if you are a faster reader, or read the first sentence of each paragraph if you are a slower reader. If it is a one-paragraph or very short two-paragraph passage, read through it as quickly as you can. For each detail question, read about 10 lines of text and try to predict what you believe will answer the question. Evaluate the answers against your prediction and make sure that the answer you selected is fully supported by the text.

1. **D** The passage states, "When these ingredients are combined, the final product is off-white in color and *is like modeling clay in consistency.* This quality directly impacts the utility of C-4, as *it can be pressed into small crevices* where other explosives might not fit.

2. **E** The passage provides an overview of C-4, including what it is made from and one of its well-known uses.

3. **D** The passage states, "This quality directly impacts the utility of C-4, as *it can be pressed into small crevices* where other explosives might not fit."

4. **A** The passages states "the final product is off-white in color *and is like modeling clay in consistency.* This quality directly impacts the utility of C-4, as *it can be pressed into small crevices where other explosives might not fit.*"

5. **D** The passage states that "*It is composed of explosives, plastic binder, plasticizer, and usually some variety of chemical marker like 2, 3-dimethyl-2, 3-dinitrobutane (DMNDB).*"

6. **A** The author, while earlier describing the benefits of C-4, devotes the second paragraph to a warning about the problems associated with C-4.

7. **C**   The passage states, "It is composed of explosives, plastic binder, plasticizer, and *usually* some variety of chemical marker like 2,3-dimethul-2,3-dinitrobutane (DMNDB)." The word *usually* indicates that a chemical marker is not always present.

8. **D**   The speaker in the poem is comparing himself to a *decrepit father*. In the speaker's case, he has been *made lame by fortune's dearest spite*. *Lame* must mean something like *decrepit* (or broken-down). Knowing what *decrepit* means helps to eliminate (A), (B), and (E). *Lame* refers to a specific disability, so (C) is too general. Since *lame* means unable to walk normally, the correct answer is (D).

9. **E**   In lines 9–12, the speaker states that *So then I am not lame, poor, nor despised,/Whilst that this shadow doth such substance give/That I in thy abundance am sufficed/And by a part of all thy glory live.* He has a wish for this person who gives him substance and whose abundance satisfies him to have all the best (lines 13–14). Bearing witness to this person's glorious life can bring the speaker happiness, so keep (E). The speaker compares himself to a *decrepit father* and claims that *fortune's dearest spite* has made him lame. In both cases, those references to weakness have not brought him happiness; it's the person to whom he is speaking that has. Eliminate (A) and (B). The speaker wishes his addressee *what is best* but doesn't say that that person already has it. Eliminate (C). The speaker mentions wealth and beauty in lines 5–7 but is talking about the other person *(Entitled in thy parts do crowned sit),* so eliminate (D). The correct answer is (E).

10. **A**   The correct answers to questions 9 and 11 as well as lines 11–12 support (A), so keep it. The speaker never states that he lost his money. Eliminate (B). There is no reference to God or a higher power in this poem, so eliminate (C). The speaker never shares his opinion of the child mentioned in line 2, nor does he state that his addressee is a youth. Furthermore, the speaker never refers to his addressee in a critical tone. Eliminate (D). There is no evidence in the poem to support (E). The correct answer is (A).

11. **C**   The word *abundance* is preceded by *thy*, which refers to the speaker's addressee. Since the speaker is not talking about himself, eliminate (A) and (E). Abundance is not specifically referring to any physical grandeur about the addressee. It could be, but abundance could also be a reference to status, wealth, intelligence, etc. (Note lines 5–7: *For whether beauty, birth, or wealth, or wit,/Or any of these all, or all, or more,/Entitled in thy parts do crowned sit.*) Eliminate (B). Lines 5–7 do support (C), so keep it. Abundance is something the addressee possesses, not desires, so eliminate (D). The correct answer is (C).

12. **D** The poem begins with a comparison (notice the *As...So...* construction in lines 1 and 3). The speaker is comparing a *decrepit father* who *takes delight/To see his active child do deeds of youth* to how he views himself (*made lame by fortune's dearest spite,/Take all my comfort of thy worth and truth*). A simile is a comparison of two unlike using the words like or as. The correct answer is (D).

ISEE Full Passages Drill

 When you arrive at a new passage, read it quickly if you are a faster reader, or read the first sentence of each paragraph if you are a slower reader. For each detail question, read about 10 lines of text and try to predict what you believe will answer the question. Evaluate the answers against your prediction and make sure that the answer you selected is fully supported by the text.

1. **B** The passage is a story leading up to a well-paying and important job Edison obtained.

2. **C** The author describes himself as "waiting in solitude, wondering when opportunity might present itself."

3. **D** The author states "Seventeen months as a telegrapher in *Boston found me deeply in debt, despite having acquired several patents.*"

4. **A** The author states "*Seventeen months as a telegrapher in Boston found me deeply in debt,* despite having acquired several patents. Thirty-five dollars, borrowed from a friend, bought a steamer ticket to the more 'commercially oriented' city farther south."

5. **D** The author states "To the others' astonishment, the machine settled itself back into work. *What boggled my mind, however, was the manager's response: an offer of a position as repairman* for all machines in the company, for the ridiculous sum of $300 per month.

6. **A** The unexpected job saved the author from poverty.

7. **D** The passage provides general information about Russian Matryoshka dolls, "hallmarks" of Russian folk art.

8. **A** The passage states, "Today they are known around the *world and have served as inspiration for many other types of 'object-in-object'—or layering schemes—in all types of artwork* ranging from clothing to furniture."

9. **C** This paragraph explains the inspiration for Matryoshka dolls and the art that has been inspired by those dolls.

10. **C** The passage states, "There are traditionally *at least five nested dolls.*"

11. **C** The part of the passage where the author's tone is most apparent states "*The real artwork is displayed in the painting of the dolls*, which can depict anything from peasant girls in traditional attire to fairy-tale characters and leaders."

12. **B** The passage states, "These dolls were originally modeled after a doll from Honshu, Japan."

Part V
Writing

- Writing

Writing

SSAT Writing Drill 1

<u>Writing Sample</u>

Schools would like to get to know you better through a story you tell using one of the ideas below. Please choose the idea you find most interesting and write a story using the idea as your first sentence. Please fill in the circle next to the one you choose.

> (A) Name three historical figures you would spend a day with and explain why.

> (B) He swallowed nervously as he opened the box.

SSAT Writing Drill 2

<u>Writing Sample</u>

Schools would like to get to know you better through a story you tell using one of the ideas below. Please choose the idea you find most interesting and write a story using the idea as your first sentence. Please fill in the circle next to the one you choose.

Ⓐ   If you could change anything about your school, what change would you make and why?

Ⓑ   Looking down the road, I could not believe what I saw.

Essay

You will have 30 minutes to plan and write an essay on the topic printed on the other side of this page. **Do not write on another topic. An essay on another topic is not acceptable.**

The essay is designed to give you an opportunity to show how well you can write. You should try to express your thoughts clearly. How well you write is much more important than how much you write, but you need to say enough for a reader to understand what you mean.

You will probably want to write more than a short paragraph. You should also be aware that a copy of your essay will be sent to each school that will be receiving your test results. You are to write only in the appropriate section of the answer sheet. Please write or print so that your writing may be read by someone who is not familiar with your handwriting.

You may make notes and plan your essay on the reverse side of the page. Allow enough time to copy the final form on to your answer sheet. You must copy the essay topic onto your answer sheet, on page 3, in the box provided.

Please remember to write only the final draft of the essay on pages 3 and 4 of your answer sheet and to write it in blue or black pen. Again, you may use cursive writing or you may print. Only pages 3 and 4 will be sent to the schools.

Directions continue on next page.

ISEE Writing Drill 1

REMINDER: Please write this essay topic on the first few lines of page 3 of your answer sheet.

Essay Topic

Imagine you can do any type of community service, even if it is not practical where you live. Describe the type of community service you would choose and why you would make that choice.

- Only write on this essay question
- Only pages 3 and 4 will be sent to the schools
- Only write in blue or black pen

NOTES

ISEE Writing Drill 2

REMINDER: Please write this essay topic on the first few lines of page 3 of your answer sheet.

Essay Topic

There are many ways to define success in an adult. How would you define success in an adult and why?

- Only write on this essay question
- Only pages 3 and 4 will be sent to the schools
- Only write in blue or black pen

NOTES

_____

_____

_____

_____

_____

_____

_____

_____

_____

_____

_____

_____

_____

_____

_____

_____

_____

INSTRUCTIONS FOR REVIEW OF WRITING

Give each essay to a parent or teacher, along with the prompt. Your reviewer should comment on whether someone working in an admissions office would think that you are nice, thoughtful, funny, or any other positive quality. Your reviewer should also focus on organization, grammar, spelling, and other aspects of good writing, but he or she should not hold you to the standard required of a well-polished essay. While glaring problems should be identified, very few people will write a perfect first draft in a timed setting.

Part VI
Practice Tests

SSAT Practice Test

Writing Sample

Time - 25 Minutes
1 Topic

<u>Writing Sample</u>

Schools would like to get to know you better through a story you will tell using one of the ideas below. Please choose the idea you find most interesting and write a story using the idea in your first sentence. Please fill in the circle next to the one you choose.

Ⓐ   Describe what you believe is the world's most important invention and why.

Ⓑ   If only I could reach the water's edge.

Section 1
Time - 30 Minutes
25 Questions

Following each problem in this section, there are five suggested answers. Work each problem in your head or in the blank space provided at the right of the page. Then look at the five suggested answers and decide which one is best.

Note: Figures that accompany problems in this section are drawn as accurately as possible EXCEPT when it is stated in a specific problem that its figure is not drawn to scale.

Sample Problem:

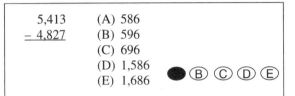

5,413	(A) 586
− 4,827	(B) 596
	(C) 696
	(D) 1,586
	(E) 1,686

●Ⓑ Ⓒ Ⓓ Ⓔ

---

1. If $12 \times B = 24$, then $24 - B =$

 (A) 0

 (B) $\dfrac{1}{24}$

 (C) 2

 (D) 12

  (E) 22

---

2. When 7,497 is divided by 198, the result is closest to which one of the following?

 (A) 25
 (B) 30
 (C) 40
 (D) 45
 (E) 450

GO ON TO THE NEXT PAGE.

3. Based on the figure provided, approximately how much snow accumulated during the 7 hours?

USE THIS SPACE FOR FIGURING.

1

Hour	inches of snow
1	2.3
2	3.5
3	5.4
4	6.0
5	3.9
6	1.2
7	0.8

(A) 6 in
(B) 11 in
(C) 20 in
(D) 23 in
(E) 24 in

---

4. $0.025 \times 30 =$

(A) 0.0075
(B) 0.075
(C) 0.075
(D) 0.75
(E) 7.5

---

5. If $Z > 3$, then $5Z + 7$ could be

(A) 19
(B) 20
(C) 21
(D) 22
(E) 23

---

6. $\left(-\dfrac{3}{2}\right)^3 =$

$-\dfrac{27}{8}$

(A) $\dfrac{9}{6}$

(B) $\dfrac{27}{8}$

(C) $-\dfrac{9}{6}$

(D) $-\dfrac{9}{8}$

(E) $-\dfrac{27}{8}$

GO ON TO THE NEXT PAGE.

7. A large square box is made up of smaller square boxes. Each of these smaller boxes has a side length of 4 inches. How many of these smaller boxes are used to create the larger box if the larger box's base has a perimeter of 32 inches?

USE THIS SPACE FOR FIGURING.

(A) 4
(B) 8
(C) 16
(D) 64
(E) 124

8. Evaluate: $(-15) + (-19) + 39$

(A) −73
(B) −5
(C) 0
(D) 5
(E) 73

9. What is the value of the greatest of four consecutive integers if the greatest is three less than one-third of the least?

(A) −9
(B) −6
(C) 0
(D) 6
(E) 9

10. The perimeter of a hexagon is 42 units. If the length of each side is reduced by 3 units, what is the perimeter of the new figure?

(A) 20
(B) 24
(C) 30
(D) 36
(E) 39

GO ON TO THE NEXT PAGE.

USE THIS SPACE FOR FIGURING.

1

11. What fraction of the people chose Documentary?

(A) $\dfrac{3}{8}$

(B) $\dfrac{1}{4}$

(C) $\dfrac{1}{5}$

(D) $\dfrac{3}{20}$

(E) $\dfrac{1}{8}$

FAVORITE MOVIE GENRE

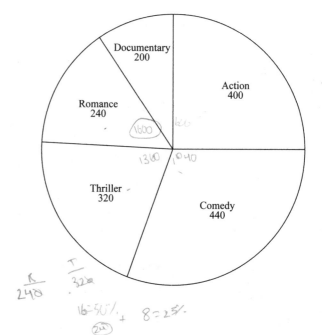

12. The number of people who chose Romance is what percent of the number of people who chose Thriller?

(A) 25%
(B) 50%
(C) 67%
(D) 75%
(E) 90%

13. A particular entrance is 84 inches tall. Kyle is planning a costume party and wants to enter the room through this doorway. If Kyle is 1.5 meters tall, the tallest hat he can place on his head and still be able to walk through the doorway without his hat touching the frame of the entrance must be less than which of the following?
(1 m = 39 in)

(A) 24 in
(B) 25 in
(C) 25.5 in
(D) 39 in
(E) 58.5 in

GO ON TO THE NEXT PAGE.

14. Carol works 60 yards from the coffee shop, and Mike works 80 yards from the same coffee shop. What is the distance, in yards, from Carol's place of work to Mike's place of work?

(A) 10 yards
(B) 20 yards
(C) 100 yards
(D) 140 yards
(E) It cannot be determined from the information given.

USE THIS SPACE FOR FIGURING.

1

15. $\dfrac{3^{-2} a^2 b^{-4}}{9 c^3 d^{-6}} =$

$\dfrac{a^2 d^6}{b^4 c^3 \, 81}$

(A) $\dfrac{a^2 c^3}{81 b^{-4} d^{-6}}$

(B) $\dfrac{a^2}{3 b^{-4} c^3 d^{-6}}$

(C) $\dfrac{a^2 d^6}{81 c^3 b^4}$

(D) $\dfrac{a^2 d^6}{18 c^3 b^4}$

(E) $\dfrac{a^2 d^6}{c^3 b^4}$

16. $5\overline{)855} =$

(A) $\dfrac{8}{5} + \dfrac{5}{5} + \dfrac{5}{5}$

(B) $\dfrac{80}{5} + \dfrac{55}{5}$

(C) $\dfrac{850}{5} + 5$

(D) $\dfrac{800}{5} + \dfrac{50}{5} + \dfrac{5}{5}$

(E) $\dfrac{800}{5} \times \dfrac{50}{5} \times \dfrac{5}{5}$

GO ON TO THE NEXT PAGE.

17. For a certain number, 40% of that number is 240. What is 60% of that number?

(A) 60
(B) 100
(C) 260
(D) 360
(E) 2,400

18. The length of a rectangle is four times its width. If the perimeter of the rectangle is 50, what is the area of the rectangle?

(A) 5
(B) 10
(C) 20
(D) 50
(E) 100

19. In the figure, P is the center of the circle, and triangle QPR is a right triangle with vertices Q and P on the circle. If the circumference of the circle is 12π, what is the area of the shaded region?

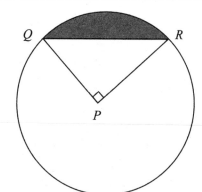

(A) $36 - 18\pi$
(B) $18\pi - 36$
(C) $9\pi - 18$
(D) $18 - 9\pi$
(E) It cannot be determined from the information given.

20. Which of the following gives the value, in cents, of a dimes, b quarters, and 6 pennies?

(A) $\dfrac{10}{a} + \dfrac{25}{b} + 1$

(B) $\dfrac{10}{a} + \dfrac{25}{b} + 6$

(C) $10a + 10b + 6$

(D) $10a + 25b + 1$

(E) $10a + 25b + 6$

GO ON TO THE NEXT PAGE.

| For more free content, visit PrincetonReview.com

21. If 70% of $3k$ is 12, what is 35% of $6k$?

(A) 2
(B) 6
(C) 12
(D) 24
(E) 28

USE THIS SPACE FOR FIGURING.

$$\boxed{1}$$

22. What is the fifth term of the following sequence?

$$1, \frac{1}{4}, -\frac{1}{2}, -\frac{5}{4}, \underline{\hspace{1cm}}$$

(A) $-\frac{5}{2}$

(B) $-\frac{7}{4}$

(C) -2

(D) $-\frac{9}{4}$

(E) $-\frac{9}{2}$

23. A survey found that each of 400 people has a smart phone, a tablet, or both. If 350 of these people have smart phones, and 150 have tablets, how many people have both a smart phone and a tablet?

(A) 50
(B) 100
(C) 150
(D) 200
(E) 250

GO ON TO THE NEXT PAGE.

24. If y is an integer greater than 1, which of the following is greatest?

   (A) $y + 2$

   (B) $2y + 2$

   (C) $2y - 2$

   (D) $y + \dfrac{1}{y}$

   (E) $\dfrac{y + 1}{y}$

---

25. What is the sum of the exterior angles of an equilateral triangle?

   (A) $60°$
   (B) $90°$
   (C) $120°$
   (D) $240°$
   (E) $360°$

STOP

IF YOU FINISH BEFORE TIME IS CALLED,
YOU MAY CHECK YOUR WORK ON THIS SECTION ONLY.
DO NOT TURN TO ANY OTHER SECTION IN THE TEST.

Upper Level SSAT
Section 2
Time - 40 Minutes
40 Questions

2

Read each passage carefully and then answer the questions about it. For each question, decide on the basis of the passage which one of the choices best answers the question.

The reading passages in this test are brief excerpts or adaptations of excerpts from published material. To make the text suitable for testing purposes, we may have, in some cases, altered the style, contents, or point of view of the original.

Since the early 1900s, the temperature of the air and sea at Earth's surface has increased approximately 0.8°C (1.8°F), and roughly 66% of that increase has taken place in the last 30 years. Scientists are nearly certain that this increase, commonly known as 'global warming,' is caused primarily by rising concentrations of greenhouse gases, which are produced by human activities such as fossil fuel combustion and deforestation. The long-term effects of global warming will differ around the world and will likely include an increase in sea levels, more frequent extreme weather occurrences, and the extinction of species due to changes in temperature. Most countries are part of the United Nations Framework Convention on Climate Change and have agreed that major cuts in emissions are required to stem the tide of global warming.

1. This passage was likely an excerpt from

   (A) a romance novel
   (B) a dictionary
   (C) a political advertisement
   (D) a poem
   (E) a newspaper article

2. According to the passage, global warming

   (A) has escalated in the last 30 years
   (B) began well before the nineteenth century
   (C) is caused entirely by humans
   (D) will have negligible long-term effects
   (E) is tapering off

3. This passage is mostly about

   (A) deforestation
   (B) fossil fuel combustion
   (C) need for reduced emissions
   (D) warming of the air and sea
   (E) possible causes and effects of climate change

4. This passage gives evidence to answer which of the following questions?

   (A) When did global warming begin?
   (B) How will global warming be slowed?
   (C) Which countries are taking steps to cut emissions?
   (D) How much has the global temperature increased in the last 30 years?
   (E) What will the lasting consequences of global warming be?

GO ON TO THE NEXT PAGE.

Born to a teenage mother, choreographer Alvin Ailey grew up in Texas in the 1940s, when racial segregation was rampant. After moving to Los Angeles during his preteen years, Ailey began dancing during high school. A friend introduced him to the Horton Dance Company, where Lester Horton became a significant influence
5 on his dance style. When the opportunity to perform on Broadway came along, Ailey moved to New York and sought a new dance studio. Unable to find one like the Horton Dance Company, he started his own group, and the Alvin Ailey American Dance Theater was born.

The Alvin Ailey American Dance Theater has since become one of the most
10 revolutionary dance companies in the world. The company debuted a unique experience for the audience, combining multiple dance influences with theatrical elements. Ailey was particularly proud that his company was multiracial and that hiring decisions were always made based solely on a dancer's talent—not his race.

The company's overseas travel began in 1962, when the US State Department
15 sponsored its first overseas tour. In the five decades since then, the Alvin Ailey American Dance Theater has performed for an estimated 25 million people in theaters in 48 states in the US and in 71 countries on six continents—and that doesn't include the millions who have watched the company perform through television broadcasts. This organization, which started out of one man's vision of enriching American
20 dance customs and preserving the distinctiveness of the African-American cultural experience, was designated "a vital American cultural ambassador to the world" in a 2008 US Congressional resolution.

5. The author's primary purpose is to

(A) explain how one dance company has impacted others
(B) describe the evolution of one dance company
(C) compare the philosophies of several dance companies
(D) promote multiracial dance companies
(E) discuss one dancer's influences

6. Without changing the author's intent, "elements" (line 12) could be replaced by

(A) items
(B) particles
(C) aspects
(D) hints
(E) roots

7. The author's attitude toward the Alvin Ailey American Dance Theater can most accurately be described as

(A) guarded skepticism
(B) appreciative enthusiasm
(C) puzzled uncertainty
(D) restrained adoration
(E) sullen resentment

8. The author implies which of the following about the Horton Dance Company?

(A) It was founded in the 1940s.
(B) It had a style that appealed to Alvin Ailey.
(C) It was comprised entirely of African American dancers.
(D) Its dancers traveled internationally.
(E) It became well known for its diversity.

9. Ailey's attitude toward the use of race in making hiring decisions was

(A) critical
(B) ambivalent
(C) supportive
(D) subjective
(E) sarcastic

GO ON TO THE NEXT PAGE.

On the 18th of August, 1920, I walked into the Tennessee state legislature, gripping my mother's letter and wearing my anti-suffrage red rose boutonniere. On this day, 35 other states had already ratified the 19th Amendment to the US Constitution. Only one more state's vote was necessary to finally grant suffrage to women. The measure had already passed through the State Senate, but progress stalled when the vote came up before the House of Representatives. We had lobbied for weeks, firmly against the idea of allowing women to vote, with still others in the opposite corner. Pro- and anti-suffragists had descended upon Nashville in swarms, and it seemed that, even after a motion to table the vote was defeated in a tie, today's vote would not allow the amendment to pass its last barrier en route to adoption. As the proceedings began, words from my mother's letter rang in my head: "Hurrah, and vote for suffrage! Don't keep them in doubt." When asked for my vote on the matter, my response was so quick, the looks of surprise on my fellow legislators' faces could not be disguised. With that single utterance, a half-century of activism by the likes of Susan B. Anthony and Alice Paul came to an end. The next day, I shared: "I know that a mother's advice is always safest for her boy to follow."

10. Which of the following events occurred in August 1920?

(A) Women began campaigning for equal rights.
(B) Women were granted equal employment opportunities.
(C) Pro- and anti-suffragists traveled to Nashville.
(D) Susan B. Anthony was born.
(E) The 19th Amendment was defeated.

11. In the context of the passage, suffrage most likely means

(A) right to work
(B) right to bear arms
(C) right to vote
(D) right to life, liberty, and the pursuit of happiness
(E) right to free speech

12. You can tell that the author had previously voted against women's suffrage because

(A) his mother's letter said "don't keep them in doubt"
(B) he knew a mother's advice is always best to follow
(C) the Senate had voted against the bill
(D) his colleagues were surprised by his affirmative vote
(E) he was wearing a yellow rose

13. According to the passage, the red rose was a symbol of

(A) anti-suffrage beliefs
(B) the author's love for his mother
(C) Nashville
(D) Susan B. Anthony
(E) nothing

14. The author's main purpose in writing this passage was most likely to

(A) tell a fictional story
(B) explain the challenges of the women's suffrage movement
(C) recount a significant event in his life
(D) criticize anti-suffrage beliefs
(E) compare women's suffrage to equal rights

GO ON TO THE NEXT PAGE.

Florence Nightingale was born into a rich, well-connected British family, and if her parents had had their way, she would have married a rich gentleman and settled into a conventional upper-class woman's life. Alas, at 17 she had several encounters that she felt were calls from God, compelling her to serve others; by 24 she renounced her parents' wishes and undertook the task of educating herself to become a nurse.

During the Crimean War, Florence Nightingale and a team of 38 volunteer nurses—whom she had trained herself—were sent to the Ottoman Empire, near modern day Istanbul. When they arrived, they found soldiers receiving poor care from overworked doctors, living in squalor, and developing infections as a result of neglected hygiene. Nutrition was paltry and supplies were extremely limited, which Nightingale believed profoundly influenced the death rate. Ultimately, her experience in Crimea led her to advocate for sanitary living conditions, which reduced peacetime deaths in the army and influenced how future hospitals were designed. After two years in Crimea, Nightingale returned to England and established the Nightingale Training School for nurses at St. Thomas' Hospital. After nurse training, nurses were sent all over Britain to work in hospitals using the Nightingale model. Florence Nightingale's theories, particularly regarding sanitation, military health, and hospital planning, still influence the medical field today.

15. It can be inferred that Nightingale's parents believed that

(A) maintaining sanitary conditions was a necessary component of overall good health
(B) Nightingale should not have gone to the Ottoman Empire
(C) nursing was an inappropriate vocation for an upper-class woman
(D) Nightingale was too young to decide her own career
(E) Nightingale should have become a nun

16. The author implies that Nightingale believed soldiers were dying especially from

(A) unsanitary conditions
(B) poor medical care from overworked doctors
(C) fetid living conditions
(D) inadequate nutrition
(E) infections

17. According to the author, upper-class women of Nightingale's generation

(A) pursued a variety of interests
(B) had few vocational options
(C) typically got married
(D) went to college
(E) followed callings from God

18. According to the passage, upon her return to England, Nightingale

(A) found soldiers receiving poor care
(B) got married
(C) advocated for sanitary conditions
(D) influenced hospital planning
(E) established a nursing school

19. It can be inferred that Nightingale believed in

(A) fulfilling her parents' aspirations
(B) God
(C) the Crimean War
(D) conforming to conventions
(E) St. Thomas

20. The author refers to modern-day Istanbul as

(A) the Ottoman Empire
(B) the location of St. Thomas' hospital
(C) Nightingale's first nursing assignment
(D) an area near which Nightingale worked
(E) Nightingale's birthplace

GO ON TO THE NEXT PAGE.

More than fifty years ago, Jane Goodall arrived in Tanganyika (now Tanzania), East Africa, where she planned to study chimpanzees in what would become Gombe Stream National Park. At that time, there was not much known about chimpanzees, and scientists hoped that studying these animals would lead to insights about human evolution.

At first, the chimpanzees fled from Jane, but she persisted, climbing peaks to watch them through binoculars, and hiding behind palm fronds when she came near them during her hikes.

Jane made a major discovery just a few months after she first arrived in Gombe, when she observed a chimp feeding on a baby pig. Until then, scientists had believed that chimpanzees were vegetarians; further studies showed the chimps frequently hunting smaller animals.

An even more significant discovery occurred just weeks after she first saw chimps eating meat: she watched two chimps strip the leaves off twigs in order to fashion tools they used to dig termites out of a termite mound. This was revolutionary because up until this time anthropologists considered tool-making a distinctly human characteristic. The research Jane was conducting was beginning to blur the lines distinguishing humans from apes.

2

21. The passage is primarily about

(A) how chimpanzees accepted Goodall's presence
(B) discovering similarities between chimpanzees and humans
(C) creating a national park
(D) teaching chimps to make tools
(E) learning about chimpanzee mating rituals

22. According to the passage, studying chimpanzees is helpful because

(A) their hunting habits can be replicated by humans
(B) they are an endangered species
(C) anthropologists may learn more about human evolution
(D) they are hunted by larger animals
(E) their population is on the rebound

23. The passage implies that scientists

(A) have completed learning about chimpanzees in the last fifty years
(B) thought making tools was common among many species
(C) had believed chimpanzees did not eat meat
(D) had never studied chimpanzees more than fifty years ago
(E) believed chimpanzees were very similar to humans

24. It can be inferred from the passage that Gombe Stream National Park was

(A) Tanganyika's first national park
(B) the best place to study chimpanzees
(C) not a national park when Jane first arrived
(D) the first place Jane ever studied chimpanzees
(E) was a hard place to study chimpanzees

25. The author indicates the line between humans and chimps was blurring because

(A) the chimpanzees' dietary needs are very similar to that of humans
(B) the chimpanzees look very much like humans
(C) the evolution of chimpanzees and humans is very comparable
(D) the chimpanzees could do something that only humans were thought to do
(E) chimpanzees and humans are both shy and do not like to be watched

GO ON TO THE NEXT PAGE.

On July 13, 1863, New York City saw the most destructive civil disturbance in
its history, a direct response to the U.S. government's attempt to enforce the draft.
Only recently had the U.S. Congress passed a law that required all men between the
ages of 20 and 45 to register to be drafted into military service. The idea of serving in
5   the war wasn't the problem. Instead, the devil was in the details: conscription could
be avoided with a simple payment of only three hundred dollars.

In the middle of the Civil War, inflation was sky-high, competition for jobs was
immense, and racial tension and prejudice were monumental. A vast majority of those
affected by the law were incredibly poor, and thus could never dream of paying the
10   three hundred dollar sum. This combination of economic hardship, political struggle,
and ethnic strife came to a head in the New York Draft Riots. Government buildings
were burned, and on July 15, 1863, rioters fought with troops who had been sent in
to restore order. By the time all was said and done, 119 people perished—most of
them rioters, but some were black New Yorkers who fell prey to racists who used
15   them as scapegoats for perceived injustices.

26. Which of the following is the main idea of the passage?

(A) The New York Draft Riots were the worst civil
     disturbance in New York City history.
(B) Racism caused the New York Draft Riots.
(C) Poor men didn't want to serve in the Civil War.
(D) The New York Draft Riots occurred because of a
     variety of factors.
(E) The New York Draft Riots could have been
     avoided.

27. It can be inferred that

(A) all rioters were between the ages of 20 and 45
(B) no rioters were black New Yorkers
(C) more than 100 people died in the riots
(D) July 1863 was the first time the U.S. government
     attempted to enforce the draft
(E) black New Yorkers took jobs from white New
     Yorkers

28. According to the author, some rioters

(A) took their frustrations out on innocent people
(B) were not poor
(C) were black
(D) paid 300 dollars
(E) disapproved of the Civil War

29. Which of the following is probably true?

(A) The New York Draft Riots lasted only a few days.
(B) All of the rioters were white.
(C) The U.S. government wanted to incite riots.
(D) The U.S. government hoped to raise money
     through the draft avoidance payment.
(E) Men under the age of 20 could not be drafted.

30. In the context of the passage, the word strife (line 11)
    most nearly means

(A) conflict
(B) heritage
(C) identity
(D) understanding
(E) neighborhood

GO ON TO THE NEXT PAGE.

While with reverence and resignation we contemplate the dispensations of Divine Providence in the alarming and destructive pestilence with which several of our cities and towns have been visited, there is cause for gratitude and mutual congratulations that the malady has disappeared and that we are again permitted to assemble in safety

5 at the seat of Government for the discharge of our important duties. But when we reflect that this fatal disorder has within a few years made repeated ravages in some of our principal sea ports, and with increased malignancy, and when we consider the magnitude of the evils arising from the interruption of public and private business, whereby the national interests are deeply affected, I think it my duty to invite the

10 Legislature of the Union to examine the expediency of establishing suitable regulations in aid of the health laws of the respective States; for these being formed on the idea that contagious sickness may be communicated through the channels of commerce, there seems to be a necessity that Congress, who alone can regulate trade, should frame a system which, while it may tend to preserve the general health, may be

15 compatible with the interests of commerce and the safety of the revenue.

31. What best summarizes the main point of the passage?

(A) Congress has the power to regulate trade.
(B) Congress should enact laws related to public health.
(C) An absence of order is inconsistent with a free society.
(D) Good manners are as important in government as in private business.
(E) Religion must remain a part of public and private life.

32. The author expresses gratitude that

(A) a disease has vanished and Congress may without worry meet
(B) Congress has the ability to enact laws to protect health
(C) sea ports were unaffected by a recent health problem
(D) commerce and revenue continue to grow
(E) public and private business have been cleansed of evil

33. The "ravages in some of our principal sea ports" (lines 6-7) refers to

(A) losses during a battle
(B) damage from a hurricane
(C) spoilage of food to be shipped
(D) disease affecting people in business
(E) work stoppages relating to a bitter strike

34. It can be inferred from the passage that Congress

(A) has failed in its duties
(B) has power to regulate commerce
(C) is revered by the people
(D) previously passed health laws
(E) raised insufficient revenues

35. The word "visited" (line 3) most closely corresponds to

(A) called upon
(B) joined in
(C) traveled
(D) remained
(E) afflicted

GO ON TO THE NEXT PAGE.

By eight o'clock everything was ready, and we were on the other side of the river. We jumped into the stage, the driver cracked his whip, and we bowled away and left "the States" behind us. It was a superb summer morning, and all the landscape was brilliant with sunshine. There was a freshness and breeziness, too, and an exhilarating sense of emancipation from all sorts of cares and responsibilities, that almost made us feel that the years we had spent in the close, hot city, toiling and slaving, had been wasted and thrown away. We were spinning along through Kansas, and in the course of an hour and a half we were fairly abroad on the great Plains. Just here the land was rolling—a grand sweep of regular elevations and depressions as far as the eye could reach—like the stately heave and swell of the ocean's bosom after a storm. And everywhere were cornfields, accenting with squares of deeper green, this limitless expanse of grassy land. But presently this sea upon dry ground was to lose its "rolling" character and stretch away for seven hundred miles as level as a floor!

We changed horses every ten miles, all day long, and fairly flew over the hard, level road. We jumped out and stretched our legs every time the coach stopped, and so the night found us still vivacious and unfatigued.

36. The passage focuses on the

(A) variety of landscapes throughout Kansas
(B) lives of people in a foreign country
(C) enjoyment of a journey away from a city
(D) importance of taking proper care of horses
(E) fellowship of men with a common goal

37. The passage is written from the point of view of which of the following?

(A) the driver
(B) an outlaw
(C) a Kansas resident
(D) a passenger
(E) an observer

38. The sensory image most important to this passage is the

(A) sound of the crack of the whip
(B) sensation of brilliant sunshine
(C) smell of horses
(D) sound of the ocean
(E) view of the terrain

39. The narrator of the passage is

(A) in a stagecoach, leaving an old life behind
(B) aboard a ship sailing from the United States
(C) on a train heading to work in a city
(D) riding a horse through cornfields
(E) aboard a boat sailing down a river

40. The mood of the author and his companions is

(A) disconcerted
(B) excited
(C) brooding
(D) concerned
(E) calm

STOP

IF YOU FINISH BEFORE TIME IS CALLED,
YOU MAY CHECK YOUR WORK ON THIS SECTION ONLY.
DO NOT TURN TO ANY OTHER SECTION IN THE TEST.

Section 3
Time - 30 Minutes
60 Questions

3

This section consists of two different types of questions. There are directions and a sample question for each type.

Each of the following questions consists of one word followed by five words or phrases. You are to select the one word or phrase whose meaning is closest to the word in capital letters.

Sample Question:

CHILLY:
(A) lazy
(B) nice
(C) dry
(D) cold
(E) sunny   (A) (B) (C) ● (E)

---

1. HABITUAL:
   (A) routine
   (B) moral
   (C) probable
   (D) primary
   (E) conditional

2. INVESTIGATE:
   (A) wonder
   (B) study
   (C) destroy
   (D) shred
   (E) energize

3. CONSIDER:
   (A) pretend
   (B) delight
   (C) ponder
   (D) create
   (E) shatter

4. MEANDER:
   (A) flabbergast
   (B) trade
   (C) forget
   (D) roam
   (E) try

5. ANSWER:
   (A) flee from
   (B) delight over
   (C) reply to
   (D) look upon
   (E) forget about

6. STUMBLE:
   (A) pray
   (B) remind
   (C) clarify
   (D) test
   (E) trip

7. SINGULAR:
   (A) unusual
   (B) indifferent
   (C) creative
   (D) unappealing
   (E) sincere

8. ARTICULATE:
   (A) evenhanded
   (B) cross-sectional
   (C) self-evident
   (D) all-inclusive
   (E) well-spoken

9. CUMBERSOME:
   (A) infrequent
   (B) bulky
   (C) abnormal
   (D) attractive
   (E) secretive

GO ON TO THE NEXT PAGE.

10. GLEAN:
    (A) pester
    (B) clinch
    (C) enrage
    (D) garner
    (E) adorn

11. PATRIOTIC:
    (A) devoted
    (B) careful
    (C) armed
    (D) objective
    (E) obnoxious

12. TEDIOUS:
    (A) amusing
    (B) clever
    (C) savage
    (D) awkward
    (E) boring

13. LOGICAL:
    (A) rational
    (B) selective
    (C) sensory
    (D) apparent
    (E) muscular

14. GRATITUDE:
    (A) confidence
    (B) understanding
    (C) appreciation
    (D) talent
    (E) devotion

15. FOOLHARDY:
    (A) unbelievable
    (B) intolerant
    (C) ambiguous
    (D) impatient
    (E) unwise

16. DEVIOUS:
    (A) stormy
    (B) tricky
    (C) degraded
    (D) challenged
    (E) particular

17. CAPITULATE:
    (A) give up
    (B) step in
    (C) act for
    (D) move on
    (E) fade out

18. CORRODE:
    (A) crumble
    (B) drive
    (C) write
    (D) charge
    (E) speed

19. CONSUME:
    (A) pant
    (B) spy
    (C) clap
    (D) dent
    (E) eat

20. MNEMONIC:
    (A) style
    (B) joyfulness
    (C) reminder
    (D) warning
    (E) favoritism

21. PEDESTRIAN:
    (A) athletic
    (B) ordinary
    (C) intelligent
    (D) studious
    (E) muddled

22. FURTIVE:
    (A) secret
    (B) satisfied
    (C) cherished
    (D) protected
    (E) shocking

23. COPIOUS:
    (A) skilled
    (B) illustrative
    (C) energized
    (D) plentiful
    (E) pompous

24. AVARICE:
    (A) assortment
    (B) fortune
    (C) sorrow
    (D) benefit
    (E) greed

GO ON TO THE NEXT PAGE.

25. MISGIVING:
   (A) selfishness
   (B) threat
   (C) error
   (D) doubt
   (E) generosity

26. TEMPERATE:
   (A) restrained
   (B) irritated
   (C) frenzied
   (D) passionate
   (E) weakened

27. STOIC:
   (A) sinister
   (B) marvelous
   (C) impassive
   (D) tortured
   (E) believable

28. ACRID:
   (A) disgust
   (B) convincing
   (C) dry
   (D) sharp
   (E) flip

29. OBSTINATE:
   (A) pregnant
   (B) moderate
   (C) judgmental
   (D) indecent
   (E) stubborn

30. TEMPEST:
   (A) storm
   (B) nuisance
   (C) quickness
   (D) phlegm
   (E) destiny

3

GO ON TO THE NEXT PAGE.

The following questions ask you to find relationships between words. For each question, select the answer choice that best completes the meaning of the sentence.

Sample Question:

Kitten is to cat as
(A) fawn is to colt
(B) puppy is to dog
(C) cow is to bull
(D) wolf is to bear
(E) hen is to rooster

Choice (B) is the best answer because a kitten is a young cat, just as a puppy is a young dog. Of all the answer choices, (B) states a relationship that is most like the relationship between <u>kitten</u> and <u>cat</u>.

---

31. Sweet is to flavor as
    (A) warm is to blanket
    (B) cacophony is to sound
    (C) pretty is to sight
    (D) robust is to effort
    (E) excited is to anticipation

32. Wheat is to bread as
    (A) oil is to gasoline
    (B) earring is to jewelry
    (C) syrup is to pancakes
    (D) fruit is to basket
    (E) hospital is to wing

33. Pen is to writing as
    (A) table is to reading
    (B) trumpet is to marching
    (C) pillow is to sleeping
    (D) knife is to framing
    (E) mop is to cleaning

34. Insistent is to tenacious as concerned is to
    (A) arrogant
    (B) worried
    (C) eager
    (D) serene
    (E) established

35. Mohair is to goat as
    (A) thread is to cap
    (B) wool is to sweater
    (C) down is to pillow
    (D) angora is to rabbit
    (E) cage is to mouse

36. Miner is to jeweler as
    (A) fisher is to chef
    (B) nurse is to doctor
    (C) carpenter is to painter
    (D) engineer is to conductor
    (E) designer is to photographer

37. Table is to delay as
    (A) yell is to whisper
    (B) cover is to prevent
    (C) grow is to shift
    (D) color is to distort
    (E) improve is to escalate

38. Acumen is to shrewdness as flamboyance is to
    (A) friendliness
    (B) generosity
    (C) sorrow
    (D) cruelty
    (E) showiness

39. Scale is to weight as
    (A) speedometer is to sound
    (B) protractor is to angle
    (C) pipette is to area
    (D) tachometer is to direction
    (E) thermometer is to energy

40. Precocious is to developed as
    (A) insolent is to impolite
    (B) lengthy is to round
    (C) scared is to terrified
    (D) teary is to sad
    (E) happy is to joyful

GO ON TO THE NEXT PAGE.

41. Car is to transportation as
(A) table is to chair
(B) faucet is to water
(C) oven is to cooking
(D) sofa is to cushion
(E) sheet is to pillow

42. Display is to artwork as
(A) brandish is to sword
(B) pretend is to scene
(C) dazzle is to brooch
(D) entertain is to dinner
(E) locate is to map

43. Camera is to filmmaker as ladle is to
(A) waiter
(B) dishwasher
(C) diner
(D) writer
(E) cook

44. Problem is to fiasco as
(A) mistake is to error
(B) puzzle is to question
(C) complaint is to lamentation
(D) correction is to improvement
(E) amalgamation is to collection

45. Rules is to parents as
(A) arguments is to fights
(B) laws is to governments
(C) schools is to children
(D) obligations is to promises
(E) instructions is to systems

46. Immature is to callow as
(A) smart is to skilled
(B) movie is to set
(C) fresh is to salad
(D) hurried is to rushed
(E) prepared is to careful

47. Talkative is to loquacious as
(A) implicating is to congratulating
(B) articulate is to understandable
(C) socialized is to mesmerized
(D) presumptive is to possible
(E) interesting is to fascinating

48. Buckle is to belt as
(A) lace is to shoe
(B) scarf is to coat
(C) collar is to shirt
(D) code is to alarm
(E) cuff is to wrist

49. Wolf is to pack as
(A) lawyer is to courtroom
(B) flower is to garden
(C) puddle is to ocean
(D) school is to fish
(E) division is to country

50. Talented is to actor as
(A) loud is to teacher
(B) unusual is to physician
(C) happy is to detective
(D) strong is to weight lifter
(E) gracious is to salesperson

51. Agony is to pleasure as interference is to
(A) restraint
(B) listening
(C) cooperation
(D) beauty
(E) charm

52. Connive is to scheme as
(A) suspend is to satisfy
(B) grow is to flourish
(C) prevent is to remove
(D) question is to answer
(E) promise is to engage

53. Page is to website as
(A) violin is to string
(B) scenery is to drama
(C) photograph is to portfolio
(D) elegy is to song
(E) dog is to kennel

54. Dubious is to doubtful as
(A) idiosyncratic is to peculiar
(B) lovely is to polished
(C) quick is to serious
(D) honest is to kind
(E) fearful is to annoyed

GO ON TO THE NEXT PAGE.

55. Qualm is to conviction as
    (A) yank is to pull
    (B) box is to carton
    (C) manager is to owner
    (D) joy is to pleasure
    (E) compliment is to criticism

56. Breeze is to hurricane as
    (A) warmth is to coldness
    (B) whirlpool is to maelstrom
    (C) day is to week
    (D) downpour is to drizzle
    (E) gold is to silver

57. Debilitate is to strengthen as
    (A) eradicate is to destroy
    (B) neglect is to cultivate
    (C) bend is to snap
    (D) decorate is to adorn
    (E) simulate is to pretend

58. Glare is to yell as
    (A) pucker is to kiss
    (B) sneer is to bow
    (C) laugh is to sneeze
    (D) sob is to weep
    (E) stand is to deliver

59. Dishonest is to speaking as
    (A) noxious is to gas
    (B) muggy is to summer
    (C) furry is to cat
    (D) cloudy is to mountain
    (E) healthy is to look

60. Subtle is to obvious as
    (A) false is to affected
    (B) wonderful is to terrific
    (C) assumed is to understood
    (D) clean is to classy
    (E) possible is to guaranteed

3

STOP

IF YOU FINISH BEFORE TIME IS CALLED,
YOU MAY CHECK YOUR WORK ON THIS SECTION ONLY.
DO NOT TURN TO ANY OTHER SECTION IN THE TEST.

Section 4
Time - 30 Minutes
25 Questions

4

Following each problem in this section, there are five suggested answers. Work each problem in your head or in the blank space provided at the right of the page. Then look at the five suggested answers and decide which one is best.

Note: Figures that accompany problems in this section are drawn as accurately as possible EXCEPT when it is stated in a specific problem that its figure is not drawn to scale.

Sample Problem:

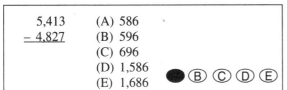

5,413	(A) 586
− 4,827	(B) 596
	(C) 696
	(D) 1,586
	(E) 1,686 ● Ⓑ Ⓒ Ⓓ Ⓔ

USE THIS SPACE FOR FIGURING.

1. Alexandra plans to give a stapler to each of her 17 new employees. Four staplers come in a box. How many boxes of staplers must she buy?

 (A) 3
 (B) 4
 (C) 5
 (D) 6
 (E) 13

5

2. $100 - 39\frac{3}{4} =$

 (A) $59\frac{3}{4}$

 (B) $60\frac{1}{4}$

 (C) $60\frac{1}{2}$

 (D) $60\frac{3}{4}$

 (E) $61\frac{1}{4}$

GO ON TO THE NEXT PAGE.

4

3. A wire that is $8\frac{2}{3}$ yards long can be cut into how many

    2 foot long pieces?

    (A) 4
    (B) 5
    (C) 13
    (D) 16
    (E) 26

4. Calculate $10a + b^2$ when $a = 4$ and $b = 5$.

    (A) 40
    (B) 45
    (C) 65
    (D) 66
    (E) 95

5. Sarah receives a standard rate of $12 for every flower
    bouquet she assembles. When she makes more than
    15 bouquets in a week, Sarah makes $16 per bouquet
    for every bouquet after the 15th one she assembles.
    How much will Sarah make during a week in which
    she assembles 19 flower bouquets?

    (A) $228
    (B) $244
    (C) $260
    (D) $266
    (E) $304

6. $4\frac{3}{4} + 3\frac{1}{4} + 4\frac{3}{4} =$

    (A) 11.75
    (B) 12.25
    (C) 12.50
    (D) 12.75
    (E) 13.25

7. The average length of two female hamsters is 4.1 inches,
    and the average length of six male hamsters is 5.3
    inches. What is the average length, in inches, of all eight
    hamsters?

    (A) 1.175
    (B) 2.93
    (C) 4.7
    (D) 5
    (E) 6

GO ON TO THE NEXT PAGE.

8. On the number line to the right, $-\dfrac{15}{4}$ falls between which of the following two numbers?

   (A) 0 and –1
   (B) –1 and –2
   (C) –2 and –3
   (D) –3 and –4
   (E) –4 and –5

Questions 9 and 10 are based on the accompanying table.

9. Among those who rated dalmatians their favorite, what is the approximate fractional part from suburban areas?

   (A) $\dfrac{3}{20}$

   (B) $\dfrac{6}{10}$

   (C) $\dfrac{1}{2}$

   (D) $\dfrac{13}{20}$

   (E) $\dfrac{7}{10}$

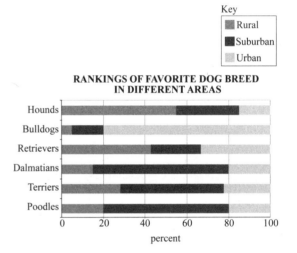

RANKINGS OF FAVORITE DOG BREED
IN DIFFERENT AREAS

10. If 20,000 people selected bulldogs as their favorite breed of dog, approximately how many more suburban people than rural people chose that breed?

   (A) 2,000
   (B) 4,000
   (C) 6,500
   (D) 13,000
   (E) 15,000

GO ON TO THE NEXT PAGE.

11. Kelsey is participating in a walk-a-thon to raise money for a charity. Her parents are going to contribute twenty cents for the first mile, forty cents for the second mile, and sixty cents for the third mile. If her parents continue to donate money in this manner, how much money will Kelsey's parents contribute to her charity if Kelsey walks 26 miles?

    (A) $68.00
    (B) $68.20
    (C) $70.00
    (D) $70.20
    (E) $71.20

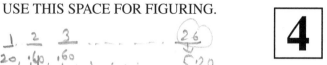

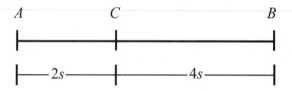

12. Select the inequality represented by the statement "The sum of five times a number and two times a different number is less than or equal to 44."

    (A) $5x + 2x \leq 44$
    (B) $5x \times 2y \leq 44$
    (C) $5x + 2y \leq 44$
    (D) $5x \times 2y \geq 44$
    (E) $5x + 2y \geq 44$

13. If the line segment AB is 24 meters long, based on the figure, how long is line segment CB?

    (A) 6 m
    (B) 8 m
    (C) 12 m
    (D) 16 m
    (E) 18 m

14. $-2(-5)^2 =$

    (A) -100
    (B) -50
    (C) -20
    (D) 50
    (E) 100

GO ON TO THE NEXT PAGE.

15. Approximately what percent of the figure is shaded?

(A) 15%
(B) 33%
(C) 50%
(D) 66%
(E) 75%

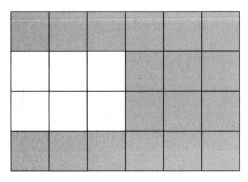

16. If two numbers, P and Q, have an average of 80, and $P - Q \neq 0$, which of the following must be true?

(A) $P + Q = 80$
(B) $P - Q = 40$
(C) $P = 30$ and $Q = 50$
(D) $80 - P = Q - 80$
(E) $80 + P = Q + 80$

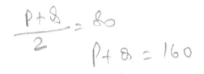

17. At the beginning of March, Alice gave Luke 40% of her baseball card collection. At the end of that month, she decides to give Luke 40% of the remaining cards in her baseball card collection. What percent of her original collection does Alice still have?

(A) 20%
(B) 24%
(C) 36%
(D) 60%
(E) 80%

18. Amy is selling a concert ticket for 55% of the price. If Amy paid $72.75, including tax, for the ticket, which amount is the closest to how much Amy is charging to sell the ticket?

(A) $32.00
(B) $33.00
(C) $36.00
(D) $36.50
(E) $40.00

GO ON TO THE NEXT PAGE.

19. Combine and simplify:

$(6x^5 - 2x^3 + 8) - (4x^5 - x^4 + 3x^2 + 12)$

(A) $2x^5 - x^4 - x^3 + 20$
(B) $2x^5 - x^4 + x^3 - 4$
(C) $2x^5 + x^4 - 2x^3 + 3x^2 - 4$
(D) $2x^5 + x^4 - 5x^3 + 20$
(E) $2x^5 + x^4 - 2x^3 - 3x^2 - 4$

20. Let b represent the base of a rectangle. If the height of the rectangle is 4 less than the base, which expression would represent the perimeter of the rectangle?

(A) $2b - 4$
(B) $2b - 8$
(C) $4b - 4$
(D) $4b - 8$
(E) $b^2 - 4$

21. Simplify the variable expression: $\dfrac{12k^3s^2u^4}{30ks^2u^3}$

(A) $\dfrac{k^2u}{3}$

(B) $\dfrac{2u}{5k}$

(C) $\dfrac{2k^2s^2u}{5}$

(D) $\dfrac{2k^2u}{5}$

(E) $\dfrac{3k^3s^2u^4}{5ks^2u^3}$

GO ON TO THE NEXT PAGE.

22. If the dots shown below are connected by starting at J and then going to K, for which answer choice is it necessary to retrace a line or lift the pencil in order to draw it?

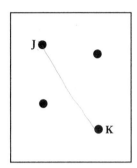

(A)
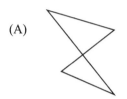

(B)
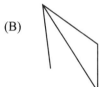

(C)

(D)
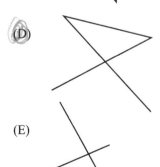

(E)

GO ON TO THE NEXT PAGE.

23. The average of five consecutive even integers is 12. What is the greatest of these integers?

= 60

(A) 8
(B) 10
(C) 13
(D) 14
(E) 16

24. If $p + q$ is divisible by 13, which of the following is also divisible by 13?

(A) $(p \times 3) + (q \times 3)$

(B) $\dfrac{(p \times q)}{13}$

(C) $(p \times 13) + q$

(D) $p + (q \times 13)$

(E) $(p \times q) - 13$

25. What could be the sum of M, N, P, and Q if each letter represents a different digit?

$$\begin{array}{r} M\,N\,Q \\ +\,P\,N\,Q \\ \hline 6\;\;7\;\;0 \end{array}$$

(A) 18
(B) 17
(C) 16
(D) 13
(E) 10

STOP

IF YOU FINISH BEFORE TIME IS CALLED,
YOU MAY CHECK YOUR WORK ON THIS SECTION ONLY.
DO NOT TURN TO ANY OTHER SECTION IN THE TEST.

SSAT Practice Test: Answers and Explanations

ANSWER KEY

Section 1		**Section 2**		**Section 3**				**Section 4**	
1.	E	1.	E	1.	A	31.	C	1.	C
2.	C	2.	A	2.	B	32.	A	2.	B
3.	D	3.	E	3.	C	33.	E	3.	C
4.	D	4.	D	4.	D	34.	B	4.	C
5.	E	5.	B	5.	C	35.	D	5.	B
6.	E	6.	C	6.	E	36.	A	6.	D
7.	B	7.	B	7.	A	37.	D	7.	D
8.	D	8.	B	8.	E	38.	E	8.	D
9.	B	9.	A	9.	B	39.	B	9.	D
10.	B	10.	C	10.	D	40.	A	10.	A
11.	E	11.	C	11.	A	41.	C	11.	D
12.	D	12.	D	12.	E	42.	A	12.	C
13.	C	13.	A	13.	A	43.	E	13.	D
14.	E	14.	C	14.	C	44.	C	14.	B
15.	C	15.	C	15.	E	45.	B	15.	E
16.	D	16.	D	16.	B	46.	D	16.	D
17.	D	17.	C	17.	A	47.	E	17.	C
18.	E	18.	E	18.	A	48.	A	18.	E
19.	C	19.	B	19.	E	49.	B	19.	E
20.	E	20.	D	20.	C	50.	D	20.	D
21.	C	21.	B	21.	B	51.	C	21.	D
22.	C	22.	C	22.	A	52.	B	22.	D
23.	B	23.	C	23.	D	53.	C	23.	E
24.	B	24.	C	24.	E	54.	A	24.	A
25.	E	25.	D	25.	D	55.	E	25.	A
		26.	D	26.	A	56.	B		
		27.	C	27.	C	57.	B		
		28.	A	28.	D	58.	A		
		29.	E	29.	E	59.	A		
		30.	A	30.	A	60.	E		
		31.	B						
		32.	A						
		33.	D						
		34.	B						
		35.	E						
		36.	C						
		37.	D						
		38.	E						
		39.	A						
		40.	B						

Writing Sample

Give your essay to a parent or teacher, along with the prompt. Your reviewer should comment on whether someone working in an admissions office would think that you are nice, thoughtful, funny, or any other positive quality. Your reviewer should also focus on organization, grammar, spelling, and other aspects of good writing, but he or she should not hold you to the standard required of a well-polished essay. While glaring problems should be identified, very few people will write a perfect first draft in a timed setting.

Section 1

1. **E** Solve for B by dividing both sides by 12: $B = 2$. Subtract 2 from 24: 22.

2. **C** Because the question asks for an approximation, estimate by rounding: $\frac{7,500}{200} = \frac{75}{2} = 37.5$. The closest answer is 40.

3. **D** Add the values in the chart.

     Because the question asks for an approximation, you can round each value to the nearest whole number before adding. However, there is some risk here because some of the answers are fairly close together.

4. **D** Carefully proceed through the multiplication to obtain 0.75.

     Because all of the answers contain the same digits, all you need to do is determine the decimal value. Multiplying 0.025 by 30 (a factor of 10) will move the decimal one place to the right.

5. E   As $Z > 3$, $5Z + 7 > 5(3) + 7$ or 22. Only (E) is greater than 27. Only (E) is greater than 22.

6. E   Distribute the exponent to the numerator and the denominator, and maintain the negative sign as cubing a negative number generates a negative number.

7. B   To determine how many small boxes fit into the larger box, divide the volumes of the boxes. As the smaller cube has a side length of 4, its volume is 4^3 or 64. As the larger cube has a base perimeter of 32, it has side lengths of $\frac{32}{4}$ or 8, and a volume of 8^3 or 512. Divide 512 by 64: 8.

8. D   Because there are not separate operations inside the parentheses, the parentheses do not matter. Under PEMDAS, addition and subtraction are co-equal, and you solve left to right.

9. B   First, set up the four consecutive integers, where x represents the least of the integers: x, $x + 1$, $x + 2$, and $x + 3$. Write an equation for the requirement: $(x + 3) = \frac{1}{3}x - 3$. Add 3 to both sides and multiply both sides by 3: $3x + 18 = x$. Subtract x and 18 from both sides: $2x = -18$. Divide both sides by 2: $x = -9$. As the question asks for the greatest of the integers, add 3 to -9.

  Test the answers, starting with (C). If 0 is the greatest of the integers, then -3 is the least. Test the requirement: $0 \neq \frac{1}{3}(-3) - 3$. It may not be obvious whether you need a larger or smaller number, so pick a direction. When you test (B), the requirement will be satisfied: $-6 = \frac{1}{3}(-9) - 3 = -6$.

10. **B** As there are six sides to a hexagon and each side is reduced by 3, the total reduction will be 18. 42 – 18 = 24.

 You can plug in for each of the 6 sides, making sure that the sides add up to 42. To keep things simple, pick the same number: 7. If each side is reduced by 3, the new sides will be 4, resulting in a perimeter of 24.

11. **E** Add the numbers together for the denominator: 1,600. Of those 1,600, 200 chose Documentary: $\frac{200}{1,600} = \frac{1}{8}$.

12. **D** Set up a proportion: $\frac{x}{100} = \frac{240}{320}$. Cross multiply and divide both sides by 320: $x = 75$.

 Translate English into Math, using a variable (y) for *what*, multiplication ($\times$) for *of*, and equals (=) for *is*: $240 = \frac{y}{100} \times 320$. Multiply both sides by 100 and divide both sides by 320: $x = 75$.

13. **C** First, convert meters to inches to obtain an apples-to-apples comparison: 1.5 × 39 = 58.5. Subtract 58.5 from 84: 25.5.

14. **E** There is not enough information about where Carol and Mike work because there is no information about the direction from the coffee shop in which they work. They can work 20 blocks from each other, 140 blocks from each other, or anything in between.

15. **C** Deal with one term at a time, starting with the coefficients. A negative exponent is the reciprocal of a positive exponent. Thus, 3^{-2} is the same as $\frac{1}{3^2} = \frac{1}{9}$. As the denominator already contains 9, the simplified denominator must contain 81. As a appears only in the numerator and has a positive exponent, nothing needs to be changed. As b has a negative exponent, the term becomes $\frac{1}{b^4}$. As c appears only in the denominator and has a positive exponent, nothing needs to be changed. As d has a negative exponent, the term becomes $\frac{1}{\frac{1}{d^6}} = d^6$.

16. **D** The 8 represents 800, the first 5 represents 50, and the second 5 represents 5. These three values are added together ($800 + 50 + 5 = 855$). When the original number is divided by 5, each of the three values is divided by 5.

17. **D** First, set up a proportion to find the number: $\frac{40}{100} = \frac{240}{x}$. Cross multiply and divide both sides by 40: $x = 600$. Now, set up a proportion to find the requested value: $\frac{60}{100} = \frac{y}{600}$. Cross multiply and divide by 100: $y = 360$

 You can use logic. If 40% of a number is 240, 60% of the number will be greater than 240 but not by a factor of 10. Eliminate (A), (B), and (E). An increase from 40% of 240 to 60% of 240 is certainly going to add more than 20. Eliminate (C).

18. **E** Let x represent the width of the rectangle, and write an equation to solve for x based on the given perimeter: $x + x + 4x + 4x = 50$. Combine like terms and divide both sides by 10: $x = 5$. Thus, the width is 5, and the length is 20. The area is 100.

19.　C　 Questions seeking the area of a weird shaded region generally require you to subtract the area of one normal shape from the area of another normal shape. In this case, subtract the area of the triangle from the area of the quarter circle. The area of a quarter circle is $\frac{1}{4}\pi r^2$, but we need to find the radius from the circumference. As $C = 2\pi r = 12\pi$, the radius is 6. Now find the area of the quarter circle: $\frac{1}{4}\pi(6)^2 = 9\pi$. As the triangle is a right triangle, the radii are also the base and height. The area of a triangle is $\frac{1}{2}bh = \frac{1}{2}(6)(6) = 18$. Choice (C) reflects the difference between the two areas.

 You can estimate that the area is a small fraction of the area of the circle. Using the circumference, find that the radius is 6. So, the area is 36π = approximately 108. (100π = approximately 300.) Choices (A) and (D) are negative, so you can eliminate them. Choice (B) is about 18, while (C) is about 9. Given that one quarter of the circle is about 27, (B) is too large.

20.　E　 As there are 10 cents in one dime, there are $10a$ cents in a dimes. As there are 25 cents in one quarter, there are $25b$ cents in b quarters. There are 6 cents in six pennies.

 Plug in for a and b such as $a = 2$ and $b = 3$. As there are 10 cents in one dime, there are 20 cents in two dimes. As there are 25 cents in one quarter, there are 75 cents in three quarters. Add these, along with 6 cents for the six pennies, for 101 cents. Only (E) matches these results when the selected numbers are tested.

21. **C**   Set up a proportion to solve for *3k*, cross multiply, and divide by 210: $\dfrac{70}{100} = \dfrac{12}{3k}$,

1,200 = 210*k*, and $k = \dfrac{1,200}{210}$ or $\dfrac{40}{7}$. The next proportion calls for *6k*, which is $\dfrac{240}{7}$.

Follow the same procedure: $\dfrac{35}{100} = \dfrac{x}{\frac{240}{7}}$, 1,200 = 100*x*, and *x* = 12.

  If you cut a percent in half and double the number, the result will be the same.

22. **C**   Each term decreases by $\dfrac{3}{4}$: $1 - \dfrac{3}{4} = \dfrac{1}{4}$; $\dfrac{1}{4} - \dfrac{3}{4} = -\dfrac{1}{2}$. Subtract $\dfrac{3}{4}$ from $-\dfrac{5}{4}$, and

the missing number is –2.

23. **B**   If 350 people have smart phones and 150 people have tablets, that would mean there are 500 people. However, there are only 400 people, which means 100 of those people were counted twice.

  It is useful to use the following formula in these types of questions: $G_1 + G_2 + N - B = T$. This stands for Group 1 + Group 2 + Neither – Both = Total. Here, as there is no N, the completed formula is 350 + 150 – B = 400. Solve for B: 100.

24. **B** Plug in a value for *y*, such as *y* = 2. Test each answer. Choice (B) is largest when *y* = 2. In (A), 2 + 2 = 4. In (B), 2(2) + 2 = 6, which is greater than (A), so eliminate (A). In (C), 2(2) − 2 = 2, so eliminate this choice as well since it is less than 6. In (D), $2 + \frac{1}{2}$ is still less than 6, so eliminate (D). Finally, $\frac{2+1}{2} = \frac{3}{2}$, which is less than 6. Choice (B) is the greatest and therefore it is the correct answer.

25. **E** The sum of the external angles of any triangle, including an equilateral triangle, is always 360°.

 Draw an equilateral triangle and write in 60° at each vertex. Extend a line at each vertex to create an exterior angle. As there are 180° in a line, each exterior angle is 120°. Therefore, the sum is 360°.

Section 2

 When you arrive at a longer new passage, read it quickly if you are a faster reader, or read the first sentence of each paragraph if you are a slower reader. If it is a one-paragraph or very short two-paragraph passage, read through it as quickly as you can. For each detail question, read about 10 lines of text and try to predict what you believe will answer the question. Evaluate the answers against your prediction and make sure that the answer you selected is fully supported by the text.

1. **E** The author uses an objective, neutral tone in presenting information. It is not a romance novel, which would have characters in it; eliminate (A). A dictionary would give the meaning of a word, so eliminate (B) as well. Nothing is politicized in the information, so eliminate (C). The text is not in prose, so eliminate (D). The best answer is in a newspaper article, relaying facts to the reader. The correct is (E).

2. **A** The passage states, "Since the early 1900s, the temperature of the air and sea at Earth's surface has increased approximately 0.8°C (1.8°F), *and roughly 66% of that increase has taken place in the last 30 years.*"

3. **E** The passage is about global warming and its possible causes and effects.

4. **D** The passage states, "Since the early 1900s, the temperate of the air and sea at Earth's surface has increased approximately 0.8°C (1.8°F), *and roughly 66% of that increase has taken place in the last 30 years.*"

5. **B** The passage provides a brief introduction to the history of the Alvin Ailey American Dance Theater.

6. **C** "Influences" earlier in the sentence leads to "aspects" as the answer.

7. **B** The author has a positive attitude toward the topic.

8. **B** The passage states, "When the opportunity to perform on Broadway came along, Ailey moved to New York and sought a new dance studio. *Unable to find one like the Horton Dance Company*, he started his own group, and the Alvin Ailey American Dance Theater was born."

9. **A** The passage states, "Ailey was particularly proud that his company was multiracial, *and that hiring decisions were always made based solely on a dancer's talent—not his race.*" Since the question asks about the *use* of race in the hiring process, the passage states that Ailey was against doing so. Therefore, he was critical. The correct answer is (A).

10. **C** The passage states, *Pro- and anti-suffragists had descended upon Nashville in swarms.*

11. **C** The passage states, *the idea of allowing women to vote.*

12. **D** The passages states "As the proceedings began, words from my mother's letter rang in my head: 'Hurrah, and vote for suffrage! Don't keep them in doubt.' *When asked for my vote on the matter, my response was so quick, the looks of surprise on my fellow legislators' faces could not be disguised.* With that single utterance, a half-century of activism by the likes of Susan B. Anthony and Alice Paul came to an end. The next day, I shared: "I know that a mother's advice is always safest for her boy to follow."

13. **A** The passage states, "I walked into the Tennessee state legislature, gripping my mother's letter and *wearing my anti-suffrage red rose boutonniere.*"

14. **C** The passage tells the story of the day the narrator changed his vote from opposing the 19th Amendment to favoring it.

15. **C** The passage states, "*Florence Nightingale was born into a rich, well-connected British family, **and if her parents had had their way, she would have married a rich gentleman** and settled into a conventional upper-class woman's life. Alas, at 17 she had several encounters that she felt were calls from God, compelling her to serve others; **by 24 she renounced her parents' wishes and undertook the task of educating herself to become a nurse.***"

16. **D** The passage states, "*Nutrition was paltry and supplies were extremely limited, which Nightingale believed profoundly influenced the death rate.*"

17. **C** The passage states, "Florence Nightingale was born into a rich, well-connected British family, and if her parents had had their way, *she would have married a rich gentleman and settled into a conventional upper-class woman's life.*"

18. **E** The passage states, "After two years in Crimea, *Nightingale returned to England and established the Nightingale Training School for nurses* at St. Thomas' Hospital."

19. **B** The passage states, "Alas, at 17 *she had several encounters that she felt were calls from God,* compelling her to serve others; by 24 she renounced her parents' wishes and undertook the task of educating herself to become a nurse."

20. **D** The passage states, "During the Crimean War, Florence Nightingale and a team of 38 volunteer nurses—whom she had trained herself—*were sent to the Ottoman Empire, near modern day Istanbul.*"

21. **B** The passage focuses primarily on discoveries of chimpanzee behaviors that were similar to behaviors of humans.

22. **C** The passage states, "At that time, there was not much known about chimpanzees, and *scientists hoped that studying these animals would lead to insights about human evolution.*"

23. **C** The passage states, "Jane made a major discovery just a few months after she first arrived in Gombe, when she observed a chimp feeding on a baby pig. *Until then, scientists had believed that chimpanzees were vegetarians*; further studies showed the chimps frequently hunting smaller animals."

24. **C** The passage states, "More than fifty years ago, Jane Goodall arrived in Tanganyika (now Tanzania), East Africa, where she planned to study chimpanzees *in what would become Gombe Stream National Park.*"

25. **D** The passage states, "An even more significant discovery occurred just weeks after she first saw chimps eating meat: *she watched two chimps strip the leaves off twigs in order to fashion tools* they used to dig termites out of a termite mound. *This was revolutionary because up until this time anthropologists considered tool-making a distinctly human characteristic.*"

26. **D** The passage primarily focuses on the various causes of the Draft Riots.

27. **C** The passage states, "*By the time all was said and done, 119 people perished*—most of them rioters, but some were black New Yorkers who fell prey to racists who used them as scapegoats for perceived injustices."

28. **A** The passage states, "By the time all was said and done, *119 people perished*—most of them rioters, *but some were black New Yorkers who fell prey to racists who used them as scapegoats for perceived injustices.*"

29. **E** The passage states, "Only recently had the U.S. Congress passed a law that *required all men between the ages of 20 and 45 to register to be drafted* into military service."

30. **A** As the passage later mentioned acts of violence against black people, "conflict" is the answer.

31. **B** The passage is about the president's call for public health laws, following a devastating disease that affected commerce.

32. **A** The passage states, "While with reverence and resignation we contemplate the dispensations of Divine Providence in *the alarming and destructive pestilence* with which several of our cities and towns have been visited, there is cause for gratitude and mutual congratulations that *the malady has disappeared and that we are again permitted to assemble in safety at the seat of Government for the discharge of our important duties.*"

33. **D** The passage states, "But when we reflect that *this fatal disorder has within a few years made repeated ravages in some of our principal sea ports*, and with increased malignancy, and when we consider the magnitude of the evils arising from *the interruption of public and private business*, whereby the national interests are deeply affected, *I think it my duty to invite the Legislature of the Union to examine the expediency of establishing suitable regulations in aid of the health laws of the respective States.*"

34. **B** The passage states, "[T]here seems to be a necessity that *Congress, who alone can regulate trade, should frame a system which, while it may tend to preserve the general health, may be compatible with the interests of commerce and the safety of the revenue.*"

35. **E** As the passage focuses on a devastating disease, "afflicted" is the answer.

36. **C** The passage describes part of a journey and the excitement shared by the author and his friends.

37. **D** The author is one of the passengers in the stagecoach and provides a first-person point of view.

38. **E** Most of the imagery relates to the terrain: "Just here the land was rolling—a grand sweep of regular elevations and depressions as far as the eye could reach—like the stately heave and swell of the ocean's bosom after a storm. And everywhere were cornfields, accenting with squares of deeper green, this limitless expanse of grassy land. But presently this sea upon dry ground was to lose its 'rolling' character and stretch away for seven hundred miles as level as a floor!"

39. **A** The passage states, *We jumped into the stage, the driver cracked his whip, and we bowled away and left the States behind us…. There was a freshness and breeziness, too, and an exhilarating sense of emancipation from all sorts of cares and responsibilities, that almost made us feel that the years we had spent in the close, hot city, toiling and slaving, had been wasted and thrown away…. We jumped out and stretched our legs every time the coach stopped, and so the night found us still vivacious and unfatigued.*

40. **B** The tone is positive and expressive of excitement for the journey.

Section 3

1. **A** *Habitual* means *routine*.

2. **B** To *investigate* is to *study* something.

3. **C** To *consider* is to *ponder* something.

4. **D** To *meander* is to *wander* or *roam* about.

5. **C** To *answer* is to *reply to* someone.

6. **E** To *stumble* is to *trip*.

7. **A** *Singular* means *unusual* or *out of the ordinary*.

 Some words have less commonly known definitions, called secondary definitions. *Unusual* is a secondary definition of *singular*.

8. **E** *Articulate* means *well-spoken*.

9. **B** *Cumbersome* means *bulky* or *hard to carry*.

10. **D** To *glean* is to *collect* or *garner*.

11. **A** To be *patriotic* is to be *devoted*.

12. **E** *Tedious* means *boring*.

13. **A** To be *logical* is to be *rational*.

14. **C** *Gratitude* means *appreciation*.

15. **E** *Foolhardy* means *unwise*.

16. **B** *Devious* means *tricky*.

17. **A** To *capitulate* is to *give up*.

18. **A** To *corrode* is to *crumble*.

19. **E**  To *consume* is to *eat*.

20. **C**  A *mnemonic* is a type of *reminder*.

21. **B**  *Pedestrian* means *ordinary*.

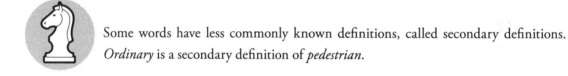 Some words have less commonly known definitions, called secondary definitions. *Ordinary* is a secondary definition of *pedestrian*.

22. **A**  *Furtive* means *secret*.

23. **D** *Copious* means *plentiful*.

24. **E** *Avarice* means *greed*.

25. **D** *Misgiving* means *doubt*.

26. **A** *Temperate* means calm or *restrained*.

27. **C** *Stoic* means *impassive*, especially in the face of pain or misfortune.

28. **D** *Acrid* means *sharp*, especially as in an odor.

29. **E** *Obstinate* means *stubborn*.

30. **A** A *tempest* is a *storm*.

 You may have heard the phrase *a tempest in a teapot*, which refers to a small problem that has been exaggerated. After all, how bad can a storm in a teapot really be?

31. **C** *Sweet* is a pleasant *flavor*. *Pretty* is a *pleasant* sight.

32. **A** *Bread* is made from *wheat*. *Gasoline* is made from *oil*.

33. **E** A *pen* is used for *writing*. A *mop* is used for *cleaning*.

34. **B** To be *insistent* is to be *tenacious*. To be *concerned* is to be *worried*.

 If you don't know the meaning of *tenacious*, work backward. *Concerned* is not by definition related to any word except *worried*. Select (B).

35. **D**   *Mohair* is a fiber that comes from a *goat*. *Angora* is a fiber that comes from a *rabbit*.

 If you don't know the meaning of *mohair*, work backward. *Thread* and *cap*, *wool* and *sweater*, and *down* (type of feather) and *pillow*, and *cage* and *mouse* are not by definition related, so you can select (D).

36. **A**   A *miner* provides raw materials for a *jeweler*. A *fisher* provides raw materials for a *chef*.

37. **D**   To *table* is to *delay*. To *color* is to *distort*.

 The answers indicate that *table* is being used as a verb. If you don't know the secondary meaning of *table*, work backward. *Yell* and *whisper* are opposites. Could a word mean the opposite of *delay*? Sure, so keep (A). *Cover* and *prevent*, *grow* and *shift*, and *improve* and *escalate* are not by definition related, so you can eliminate (B), (C), and (E). You may not know that the secondary meaning of *color* means *distort*, in which case you might eliminate (D) and select (A). If you think that *color* might mean *distort*, could a word mean the same as *delay*? Of course, so keep (D) as well. You should always guess when you are down to two.

38. **E**   *Acumen* means *shrewdness*. *Flamboyance* means showiness.

 If you don't know the meaning of *flamboyance*, you need to leave this question blank. If you don't know the meaning of *acumen* or *shrewdness* or both but do know the word *flamboyance*, work backward. *Flamboyance* is not by definition related to any word except *showiness*. Select (E).

39. **B** A *scale* measures *weight*. A *protractor* measures *angles*.

 If you don't know what a protractor is, use process of elimination. The easier answers to eliminate are (A) and (E) because a *speedometer* does not measure *sound* and a *thermometer* does not measure *energy*. If you know that a *pipette* measures *volume* or a *tachometer* measures *rotation* (or both), you can also eliminate (B) or (C) or both. Always guess when you are down to two.

40. **A** To be *precocious* is to be quite *developed*. To be *insolent* is to be quite *impolite*.

 If you don't know the meaning of *precocious*, work backward. If you know that *insolent* means to be quite *impolite*, keep (A) because a word can mean quite developed. If you don't know the word *insolent*, keep (A) because you should never eliminate a word you don't know. Neither *lengthy* and *round* nor *teary* and *sad* are by definition related, so you can eliminate (B) and (D). *Scared* is a lesser version of *terrified*. Could there be a word that is a lesser version of *developed*? Sure, so keep (C). *Happy* is a lesser version of *joyful*. While there could be a word that is a lesser version of *developed*, (C) and (E) have the same defining sentence and therefore cancel themselves out. Eliminate both answers and select (A).

41. **C** A *car* is used for *transportation*. An *oven* is used for *cooking*.

42. **A** To *display* artwork is to show it off. To *brandish* a sword is to show it off.

 If you don't know the meaning of *brandish*, use process of elimination. None of the pairs in (B), (C), (D), and (E) are by definition related, so select (A).

43. **E** A *camera* is used by a *filmmaker*. A *ladle* is used by a *cook*.

44. **C** A *fiasco* is a big *problem*. A *lamentation* is a big *complaint*.

 If you don't know the meaning of *fiasco*, work backward. *Mistake* and *error* are the same, and something can be the same as a *problem*, so keep (A). *Puzzle* and *question* are not by definition related, so eliminate (B). If you know *lamentation*, keep (C) because a *lamentation* is a big *complaint*, and something can be a big *problem*. If you don't know *lamentation*, keep (C) because you should never eliminate words you don't know. Arguably, a *correction* is used for *improvement*. Can something be used for a *problem* in the same manner? Probably not, so eliminate (D). An *amalgamation* is a *collection*. If you know *amalgamation*, you can eliminate (A) and (E), as they share a defining sentence and cancel each other out. This leaves (C). If you do not know *amalgamation*, keep (E) because you should never eliminate a word you don't know.

45. **B** *Rules* are set by *parents*. *Laws* are set by *governments*.

46. **D** *Callow* means *immature*. *Rushed* means *hurried*.

 If you don't know the meaning of *callow*, work backward. None of the pairs in (A), (B), (C), and (E) are by definition related. Select (D).

47. **E** *Loquacious* is very *talkative*. *Fascinating* is very *interesting*.

 If you don't know the meaning of *loquacious*, work backward. Neither *implicating* (*accusing*) and *congratulating* nor *socialized* and *mesmerized* are by definition related, so you can eliminate (A) and (C). If you don't know implicating, though, keep (A) because you should never eliminate a word you don't know. To be *articulate* (*clear*) is to be *understandable*. Could *loquacious* mean *talkative*? Sure, so keep (B). *Presumptive* means highly *probable*. Can *talkative* mean highly *loquacious*? Possibly, so keep (D). *Fascinating* is very *interesting*. Can *loquacious* mean very *talkative*? Sure, so keep (E). Depending on how many words you don't know, you may need to skip this question.

48. **A** A *buckle* fastens a *belt*. A *lace* fastens a *shoe*.

49. **B** A *wolf* is a part of a pack, and a *flower* is a part of a garden. A lawyer works in a courtroom but is not part of a courtroom, so eliminate (A). A puddle is not part of an ocean, so eliminate (C). A school is not part of a fish: this is the opposite relationship. Eliminate (D). Division is not part of a country, so eliminate (E). A country may be divided into different sections, but the divisions themselves are not part of the country. The correct answer is (B).

50. **D** A good actor must be talented. A good weight lifter must be strong.

51. **C** *Agony* is the opposite of *pleasure*. *Interference* is the opposite of *cooperation*.

52. **B** To *connive* is to *scheme*. To *grow* is to *flourish*.

 If you don't know the meaning of *connive*, work backward. None of the pairs in (A), (C), (D), and (E) are by definition related. Select (B).

53. **C** A *page* is a part of a *website*. A *photo* is a part of a *portfolio*.

54. **A** *Dubious* means *doubtful*. *Idiosyncratic* means *peculiar*.

 If you don't know the meaning of *dubious*, work backward. None of the pairs in (B), (C), (D), and (E) are by definition related. Select (A).

55. **E** *Qualm* is the opposite of *conviction*. *Compliment* is the opposite of *criticism*.

 If you don't know the meaning of *qualm*, work backward. *Yank* is the same as *pull*. Can something be the same as *conviction*? Sure, so keep (A). *Box* is the same as *carton*, so now eliminate (A) and (B), which have the same defining relationship and cancel each other out. *Manager* and *owner* are not by definition related, so eliminate (C). *Joy* is a stronger version of *pleasure*. Can something be a stronger version of *conviction*? Yes, so keep (D). *Compliment* is the opposite of *criticism*. Can something be the opposite of *conviction*? Yes, so keep (E). You should always guess when you are down to two.

56. **B** A *breeze* is a very light version of a *hurricane*. A *whirlpool* is a very light version of a *maelstrom*.

 If you don't know the meaning of *maelstrom*, use process of elimination. *Warmth* is not a very light version of *coldness*, *day* is not a very light version of *week*, *downpour* is not a very light version of *drizzle*, and *gold* is not a very light version of *silver*, so eliminate (A), (C), (D), and (E).

57. **B** Something that is *debilitated* cannot be *strengthened*. Something that is *neglected* cannot be *cultivated*.

 If you don't know the meaning of *debilitate*, work backward. *Eradicate* is the same as *destroy*. Could a word be the same as *strengthen*? Sure, so keep (A). *Neglect* is the opposite of *cultivate*. Could a word be the opposite of *strengthen*? Yes, so keep (B). *Bend* and *snap* are not by definition related, so eliminate (C). *Decorate* is the same as *adorn*, which means that you can eliminate (A) and (D), which share a defining sentence and cancel each other out. *Simulate* is the same as *pretend* and likewise cancels out. If you don't know one or more of *eradicate*, *cultivate*, *adorn*, and *simulate*, keep the answer or answers because you should never eliminate a word you don't know. Depending on how many answers you cannot eliminate, you may need to skip this question.

58. **A** A *yell* can be preceded by a *glare*. A *kiss* can be preceded by a *pucker*.

59. **A** *Dishonest speaking* has a negative connotation. *Noxious gas* has a negative connotation.

 If you don't know the meaning of *noxious*, use process of elimination. *Muggy* is an adjective that describes weather, not *summer*.

60. **E** *Subtle* is a lesser version of *obvious*. *Possible* is a lesser version of *guaranteed*.

Section 4

1. **C** Divide the number of staplers by the amount in each box to find that $\frac{17}{4} = 4\frac{1}{4}$. Since there is more than 4, she needs to buy 5 boxes to have enough staplers.

 Test the answers starting with (C). At 4 staplers per box, there would be 20 staplers, which is more than enough. Test (B) to see if that answer works. Now there are only 16 staplers, one too few, so the answer must be (C).

2. **B** Convert $39\frac{3}{4}$ to a decimal and subtract, taking care to borrow as needed.

 First subtract 39 from 100 which gives you 61. Now subtract the $\frac{3}{4}$ from 61.

3. **C** First, convert yards to feet for an apples-to-apples comparison. $8\frac{2}{3} \times 3 = \frac{26}{3} \times 3 = 26$. Now divide 26 by 2 to yield 13.

4. **C** Substitute the values given and solve. $10(4) + (5)^2 = 40 + 25 = 65$.

5. **B** Begin by multiplying 15 bouquets by $12 to yield $180. The four additional bouquets cost $16 each, so $4 \times \$16 = \$64$. Add $180 + $64 to yield $244. The correct answer is (B).

6. **D** Add the whole numbers first to find that $4 + 3 + 4 = 11$. Now add the fractions to find that $\frac{3}{4} + \frac{1}{4} + \frac{3}{4} = \frac{7}{4}$ or $1\frac{3}{4}$. Add 11 and $1\frac{3}{4}$ to find $12\frac{3}{4}$. Another way of solving is to convert the numbers to decimals before adding. $4.75 + 3.25 + 4.75 = 12.75$. The correct answer is (D).

 First add the whole numbers $4 + 3 + 4 = 11$. Now add the first two fractions $\frac{3}{4} + \frac{1}{4} = 1$. The two sums so far yield 12. Finally, add the final fraction.

7. **D** Let a and b represent the length of the two female hamsters, and set up the average equation: $\frac{a+b}{2} = 4.1$. Multiply both sides by 2: $a + b = 8.2$. Next, let c, d, e, f, g, and h represent the length of the six male hamsters and set up the average equation: $\frac{c + d + e + f + g + h}{6} = 5.3$. Multiply both sides by 6 to find that $c + d + e + f + g + h = 31.8$. Now, set up the average equation for all six hamsters and substitute the values you have determined: $\frac{a + b + c + d + e + f + g + h}{8} = \frac{8.2 + 31.8}{8} = \frac{40}{8} = 5$.

A good way to think of average is Total = Average × Number (TAN). Here, the number of female hamsters is 2, and the average is 4.1. Thus, the total length of the hamsters is 4.1 × 2 = 8.2. Likewise, the number of male hamsters is 6, and the average is 5.3. Thus, the total length of these hamsters is 5.3 × 6 = 31.8. Finally, the total length of all the hamsters is 40, and the number of hamsters is 8, so the average length is 5.

8. **D**   Turn the improper fraction $-\dfrac{15}{4}$ into a mixed number using long division and finding the remainder: 4 goes into 15 evenly 3 times with a remainder of 3, so the mixed number is $-3\dfrac{3}{4}$.

9. **D**   According to the chart, the percent of suburban people who selected dalmatians is about 80 − 15 = 65. Reduce $\dfrac{65}{100} = \dfrac{13}{20}$.

10. **A**   First, determine what percentage of suburban and rural people selected bulldogs, which is 20%. The percent of the rural people is the lighter shaded region to the left of the suburban people on the chart, which is roughly 5%. Therefore, the percent of suburban people must be 20% − 5% = 15%. Next, find how many people that is. 20% of 20,000 people translates into (0.20)(20,000) = 4,000. To find how many rural people selected bulldogs, simply subtract the suburban people, $\dfrac{3}{4}$ of the 4,000, from 4,000. Since there are 3,000 suburban people, the rural people must be the remaining $\dfrac{1}{4}$ of 4,000, which is 1,000. Take the difference of the two numbers to see how many more suburban people there are. 3,000 − 1,000 = 2,000. The correct answer is (A).

11. **D** The sum of a series of n evenly spaced numbers where S_1 is the first number and S_n is the last number is given by the expression $\left(\dfrac{S_1 + S_n}{2}\right)n$. In this case, you are told that there are 26 evenly spaced numbers and that the first number is 20 cents. You need to figure out the last number. The pattern shows that the day (1, 2, 3, etc.) is multiplied by 20 cents, so on the 26th day the value is \$5.20. Plug these values into the formula (using dollars or cents): $\left(\dfrac{0.2 + 5.20}{2}\right)26 = \$70.20$.

 If you have time, writing out the donations and adding them up is another valid way to solve this problem. Never fret forgetting the formula.

12. **C** Translate each element, *five times a number* is 5x, *two times a different number* is 2y, *is less than or equal to* is ≤, and *44* is 44.

13. **D** Set up an equation. $2s + 4s = 24$. Combine like terms and divide by 6 to get $s = 4$. Plug 4 into $4s$ to get 16.

 Test the answers, starting with (C). If $4s = 12$, $s = 3$ and $2s = 6$. Since $12 + 6 = 18$, it is less than 24. Eliminate (C) as well as (A) and (B). Try (D). If $4s = 16$, $s = 4$ and $2s = 8$. Since $8 + 16 = 24$, this is correct. The correct answer is (D).

14. **B** Follow PEMDAS. First, raise –5 to the second power: 25. Now, multiply the result by –2 to get –50.

15. **E** Of the 24 squares, 18 are shaded: $\frac{18}{24} = \frac{3}{4}$, which is 75%.

16. **D** Start by writing the average equation which is $\frac{P + Q}{2} = 80$. Then multiply both sides by 2: $P + Q = 160$. Check the answers. None of (A), (B), and (C) match the equation you wrote. Manipulate (D) to see if it matches, by adding P and 80 to both sides. It does.

 Plug in numbers for P and Q, following the restrictions given, such as $P = 60$ and $Q = 100$. Only (D) is valid when you plug P and Q into the answer choices.

17. **C** Let x represent the number of baseball cards Alice has. When she gives away 40% of those cards, she has 60% left or $0.6x$. She then gives away 40% of $0.6x$, which is $(0.4)(0.6x)$ or $0.24x$. Thus, she has $0.6x - 0.24x$ left, or $0.36x$. That is 36% of the original amount.

 Since the original amount is not given, plug in a number, such as 100. If she gives Luke 40% of her collection, she gives away 40 baseball cards, leaving Alice with 60 baseball cards. If she gives Luke 40% of the 60 cards she has left, she gives away 24 of her cards, leaving Alice with 36 baseball cards. Since she started with 100, 36 represents 36%.

18. **E** Multiply $72.75 by 0.55 to get $40.0125. Choice (E) is closest in value.

 Use ballparking here. Round $72.75 to $73 and 55% to 50% to make the math easier. Half of 73 is 36.5. Since 55% was rounded down instead of up, the answer should be a little more than this, making (E) the most likely answer.

19. **E** Use bite-sized pieces to solve this problem. First, work with the x^4 terms since every answer choice contains $2x^5$. $-(-x^4) = x^4$, so eliminate (A) and (B). Next, $-2x^3$ is the only term to the power of 3, so eliminate (D). The only difference is the x^2 term. $-(3x^2) = -3x^2$, so eliminate (C). The correct answer is (E).

20. **D** The base of the rectangle is given as b. If the height of the rectangle is 4 less than the base, then the height is $b - 4$. A perimeter is the sum of the sides, or $2(b + h)$, the perimeter of the rectangle is $2(b + b - 4) = 2(2b - 4) = 4b - 8$.

 Plug in a value for b, such as $b = 10$. As the height is 4 less than the base, the base is 6. The perimeter (all sides added) is 32. Only (D) yields 32 when 10 is plugged in.

21. **D** Combine like terms, starting with the coefficient: $\frac{12}{30} = \frac{2}{5}$. Next address k, remembering that when you divide common bases, you subtract the exponents: k^2. The s elements cancel out. Finally, address u, again applying the divide/subtract rule: u. Thus, the remaining elements are $\frac{2k^2u}{5}$.

22. **D** Trace your pencil along the lines to find out which cannot be drawn without lifting the pencil or retracing. If visual perception is not your strong suit, skip this question without guessing.

23. **E** The average of evenly spaced numbers is also the median of those numbers. Thus, the median here is 12. As the numbers are even, the next number after 12 is 14, followed by 16.

24. **A** If $p + q$ is divisible by 13, then (A) must also be divisible by 13 because you can factor out a 3: $3(p + q)$. It must be the case that 3 times a number divisible by 13 is also divisible by 13.

 Plug in numbers for p and q, ideally avoiding numbers that individually are divisible by 13. A good pair would be $p = 6$ and $q = 7$. Test these numbers in the answer choices to see which will be divisible by 13. Only (A) works.

25. **A** This question requires you to guess and check. Begin with the units digit. Q can be 0 or 5, as $0 + 0 = 0$, and $5 + 5 = 10$. Proceed to the tens digit. There is no number that when added to itself will yield an odd number. Thus, we need to carry a 1 from the sum of the units digit. We now know that Q is 5. Now, N can be 3 or 8, as $3 + 3 + 1 = 7$, and $8 + 8 + 1 = 17$. Finally go to the hundreds digit. M + P can be any combination that adds up to 6. If N = 3, M + P can be any combination that adds up to 6. If N = 8, and the 1 was carried from the tens place, then M + P + 1 = 6. Therefore, M + P = 5. Since the letters must be different digits, M could be 2 and P could be 3. Therefore the sum for $2 + 3 + 8 + 5 = 18$. So, the two sets of numbers are (1) Q = 5, N = 3, and M + P = 6, or (2) Q = 5, N = 8, and M + P = 5. The two possible sums of digits are 14 and 18. 18 is the only offered answer, so the correct answer is (A).

ISEE Practice Test

Section 1
Verbal Reasoning

| **40 Questions** | **Time: 20 Minutes** |

This section is divided into two parts that contain two different types of questions. As soon as you have completed Part One, answer the questions in Part Two. You may write in your test booklet. For each answer you select, fill in the corresponding circle on your answer document.

Part One – Synonyms

Each question in Part One consists of a word in capital letters followed by four answer choices. Select the one word that is most nearly the same in meaning as the word in capital letters.

SAMPLE QUESTION:

GENERIC:

    (A)   effortless
    (B)   general
    (C)   strong
    (D)   thoughtful

Sample Answer

Ⓐ ● Ⓒ Ⓓ

Go on to the next page. ➡

VR

Part Two – Sentence Completion

Each question in Part Two is made up of a sentence with one or two blanks. One blank indicates that a word is missing. Two blanks indicate that two words are missing. Each sentence is followed by four answer choices. Select the one word or pair of words that best completes the meaning of the sentence as a whole.

SAMPLE QUESTIONS:

<u>Sample Answer</u>
Ⓐ Ⓑ ● Ⓓ

Always ------, Edgar's late arrival surprised his friends.

- (A)   entertaining
- (B)   lazy
- (C)   punctual
- (D)   sincere

<u>Sample Answer</u>
Ⓐ Ⓑ ● Ⓓ

After training for months, the runner felt ------ that she would win the race, quite different from her ------ attitude initially.

- (A)   confident . . . excited
- (B)   indifferent . . . concern
- (C)   secure . . . apprehensive
- (D)   worried . . . excited

STOP. Do not go on until told to do so. STOP

Part One – Synonyms

Directions: Select the word that is most nearly the same in meaning as the word in capital letters.

1. LIBERATE:

   (A) establish
   (B) free
   (C) manage
   (D) read

2. TANGIBLE:

   (A) concrete
   (B) endearing
   (C) orange
   (D) popular

3. INNATE:

   (A) dreary
   (B) native
   (C) ordinary
   (D) primitive

4. DELIBERATE:

   (A) affect
   (B) enjoy
   (C) reflect
   (D) tease

5. PIOUS:

   (A) distant
   (B) joyful
   (C) prejudiced
   (D) devout

6. PLEA:

   (A) aggravate
   (B) corrupt
   (C) pretend
   (D) request

7. DISPERSE:

   (A) advertise
   (B) calm
   (C) expand
   (D) scatter

8. RENOWN:

   (A) application
   (B) fame
   (C) intellect
   (D) recollection

9. VENERATE:

   (A) baffle
   (B) establish
   (C) respect
   (D) ventilate

10. PLUNDER:

   (A) descend
   (B) frighten
   (C) roar
   (D) steal

11. VORACIOUS:

   (A) enlarged
   (B) frenzied
   (C) gluttonous
   (D) nasty

12. BELLIGERENT:

   (A) argumentative
   (B) frantic
   (C) illegible
   (D) lovely

Go on to the next page. ➞

13. OMINOUS:

   (A) fragrant
   (B) informed
   (C) pompous
   (D) worrisome

14. ZEALOUS:

   (A) envious
   (B) ordinary
   (C) passionate
   (D) treasonous

15. BENEDICTION:

   (A) blessing
   (B) greeting
   (C) insult
   (D) provision

16. DISPARATE:

   (A) amoral
   (B) imperfect
   (C) indifferent
   (D) unequal

17. AGGRANDIZE :

   (A) exaggerate
   (B) fabricate
   (C) generate
   (D) habituate

18. DISTINGUISH:

   (A) differentiate
   (B) elevate
   (C) personify
   (D) question

19. EQUIVOCAL:

   (A) ambiguous
   (B) dull
   (C) rapid
   (D) similar

20. MALCONTENT:

   (A) drifter
   (B) dissident
   (C) irritant
   (D) prisoner

Go on to the next page. ➞

Part Two – Sentence Completion

Directions: Select the word or word pair that best completes the sentence.

21. When Elise learned of the tragedy that had befallen her oldest and most beloved brother, she felt utter sorrow, even ------.

    (A) anguish
    (B) envy
    (C) fear
    (D) relief

22. Troy is ------ as a pianist thanks to years of lessons and practice, but he lacks the tremendous talent needed to join a major symphony orchestra.

    (A) adept
    (B) musical
    (C) joyous
    (D) openhanded

23. When I ------ that Carmen had left the fruit basket out on purpose, she did not realize that I was making an accusation.

    (A) complained
    (B) fabricated
    (C) insinuated
    (D) verified

24. Always ------, Barclay showered his friends with gifts and gave his time to mentoring children in need.

    (A) active
    (B) generous
    (C) lenient
    (D) suspicious

25. Roxie's enthusiasm for the project seemed unending, as no matter how many obstacles the team encountered, her positive attitude never ------.

    (A) argued
    (B) diminished
    (C) fathomed
    (D) lasted

26. In the ------ decision *Plessy v. Ferguson,* the Supreme Court established the false doctrine of "separate but equal," which legalized racial segregation for many decades until the court finally corrected this grave injustice.

    (A) complicated
    (B) ignoble
    (C) isolated
    (D) opaque

27. If it is true that some people can be fooled all of the time, then Matthew must be one such person, as he is so naive that no matter how unlikely the ------, he will believe it is true.

    (A) bargain
    (B) enigma
    (C) quality
    (D) ruse

28. The two sides were optimistic that they would reach agreement, but their final issue could not be resolved, leaving the talks at an ------.

    (A) ambivalence
    (B) emergency
    (C) impasse
    (D) opinion

Go on to the next page. ➡

VR

29. While Jennifer was moody nearly to the point of seeming perpetually miserable, Hamilton was always in high spirits, sometimes merely happy while other times outright ------.

    (A) elegant
    (B) jubilant
    (C) opulent
    (D) systemic

30. Different art forms appeal to different senses: while the auditory tones of an orchestra appeal to our ears, the ------ activities of dancers appeal to our eyes.

    (A) difficult
    (B) frugal
    (C) kinetic
    (D) soulful

31. Howard had none of his sister's ------: while she could speak powerfully and expressively in front of strangers, Howard was barely able to ------ even to friends.

    (A) charm . . . administer
    (B) curiosity . . . preach
    (C) eloquence . . . verbalize
    (D) practicality . . . pass

32. The best way to train a dog is not, as many people ------, to criticize unwanted behavior; rather, the owner who ------ welcome behavior will see faster results.

    (A) believe . . . separates
    (B) demand . . . punishes
    (C) manage . . . questions
    (D) suppose . . . extols

33. Esther's ------ effort to put the cabinet together only ------ her friends' belief that she was unable to do anything involving hand-eye coordination.

    (A) awkward . . . changed
    (B) hurried . . . continued
    (C) lengthy . . . factored
    (D) maladroit . . . perpetuated

34. Because Kurt's ------ interaction with animals was quite different from the nasty way he treated people, his parents reacted with ------ when he quit his job as a veterinarian in order to work in the customer service industry.

    (A) benign . . . chagrin
    (B) entertaining . . . apathy
    (C) kind . . . excitement
    (D) ingenuous . . . alarm

35. A person should write not only clearly but also ------, because a lack of brevity often has the effect of ------ the author's hope that people will read what the author has written.

    (A) basically . . . encouraging
    (B) concisely . . . undermining
    (C) obviously . . . depressing
    (D) succinctly . . . elevating

36. Patrick insisted that his hurtful statement was unintended rather than ------, but his effort to ------ the situation ended in failure when he repeated his offensive statement.

    (A) considerate . . . mitigate
    (B) involuntary . . . assess
    (C) malicious . . . ameliorate
    (D) spiteful . . . aggravate

37. Because Rodrigo was a loyal friend, he worked ------ to ------ any belief that the rumors about Erica were true, ending these efforts only after he was sure he had accomplished his goal.

    (A) amiably . . . terminate
    (B) fleetingly . . . question
    (C) persistently . . . dispel
    (D) tirelessly . . . construct

Go on to the next page. ➡

38. Christopher was ------ to have Consuela as a ------, because it is rare for an artist to find someone who is willing and able to provide financial support.

    (A) amused . . . teacher
    (B) fortunate . . . benefactor
    (C) lucky . . . surrogate
    (D) required . . . patron

39. Steadman's ------ comments during class impressed his teacher, as few students can express the type of clever ------ that came so naturally to Steadman.

    (A) astute . . . insights
    (B) contrite . . . questions
    (C) laudatory . . . perceptions
    (D) shrewd . . . obstructions

40. As the ocean ------ between low and high tides, David contemplated the vast ----- that separates humans and the creatures that live on the coral reefs beneath the water's surface.

    (A) endures . . . gap
    (B) fluctuates . . . chasm
    (C) rests . . . concern
    (D) swings . . . peculiarity

STOP. If there is time, you may check your work in this section only. STOP

NO TEST MATERIAL ON THIS PAGE

Section 2
Quantitative Reasoning

| 37 Questions | | Time: 35 Minutes |

This section is divided into two parts that contain two different types of questions. As soon as you have completed Part One, answer the questions in Part Two. You may write in your test booklet. For each answer you select, remember to fill in the corresponding circle on your answer document.

Any figures that accompany the questions in this section may be assumed to be drawn as accurately as possible EXCEPT when it is stated that a particular figure is not drawn to scale. Letters such as x, y, and n stand for real numbers.

Part One – Word Problems

Each question in Part One consists of a word problem followed by four answer choices. You may write in your test booklet; however, you may be able to solve many of these problems in your head. Next, look at the four answer choices given and select the best answer.

EXAMPLE 1:   <u>Sample Answer</u>

What is the value of the expression   Ⓐ Ⓑ ● Ⓓ

$5 + 3 \times (10 - 2) \div 4?$

(A) 5
(B) 9
(C) 11
(D) 16

The correct answer is 11, so circle C is darkened.

Go on to the next page. ⟶

QR

Part Two – Quantitative Comparisons

All questions in Part Two are quantitative comparisons between the quantities shown in Column A and Column B. Using the information given in each question, compare the quantity in Column A to the quantity in Column B, and chose one of these four answer choices:

(A)   The quantity in Column A is greater.
(B)   The quantity in Column B is greater.
(C)   The two quantities are equal.
(D)   The relationship cannot be determined from the information given.

EXAMPLE 2:

Column A	Column B	Sample Answer
50% of 40	20% of 100	Ⓐ Ⓑ ● Ⓓ

The quantity in <u>Column A</u> (20) is the same as the quantity in <u>Column B</u> (20), so circle C is darkened.

EXAMPLE 3:

y is any real non-zero number

Column A	Column B	Sample Answer
y	$\dfrac{1}{y}$	Ⓐ Ⓑ Ⓒ ●

Since y can be any real number (including an integer or a fraction), there is not enough information given to determine the relationship, so circle D is darkened.

STOP. Do not go on
until told to do so.

STOP

Part One – Word Problems

Directions: Choose the best answer from the four choices given.

1. Nate is n years old. If Blair is 6 years younger than Nate, which of the following gives Blair's age, in years?

   (A) $6 - n$
   (B) $n - 6$
   (C) $6 + n$
   (D) $\dfrac{n}{6}$

2. During her bowling competition with Paul, Krissi scored a total of 320 points in 4 matches. During her fifth match, she scored 75 points. What was Krissi's average score for the five games?

   (A) 75.00
   (B) 77.50
   (C) 79.00
   (D) 80.00

3. The graph shows the distance Enrico was from the beach over a period of time during his walk home.

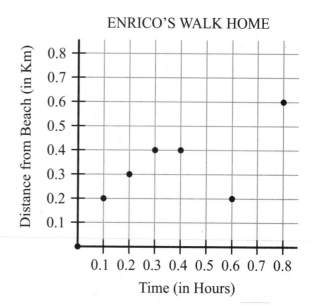

During the walk, Enrico worried that he had left his keys at the beach. He paused to look through his beach bag, did not find the keys, and started to walk back to the beach. Before he arrived at the beach, he realized that the keys were in his pocket, so he turned back around and went home. What was the total extra distance that Enrico walked because of his mistake?

   (A) 0.2 kilometers
   (B) 0.3 kilometers
   (C) 0.4 kilometers
   (D) 0.5 kilometers

Go on to the next page. ⟶

QR

4. Let $\ddagger x = 3x - 7$. What is the value of $\ddagger 6$?

   (A) 11
   (B) 17
   (C) 20
   (D) 25

5. If x is an even integer, then which of the following CANNOT be an integer?

   (A) $x - 2$

   (B) $2x + 3$

   (C) $\dfrac{x + 1}{2}$

   (D) $\dfrac{x}{2}$

6. If the length of the base of a parallelogram is decreased by 30% and the height is increased by 20%, what is the percent decrease in the area of the parallelogram?

   (A) 16%
   (B) 20%
   (C) 24%
   (D) 28%

7. If $(x + 6)^2 = x^2 + nx + 36$, what is the value of n?

   (A) 3
   (B) 6
   (C) 12
   (D) 36

8. If a and b each has a remainder of 4 when divided by 5, then which one of the following also has a remainder of 4 when divided by 5?

   (A) $a - b$
   (B) $2a - b$
   (C) $2a + b$
   (D) $a + 2b$

9. If the sum of the integers from 1 to 499, inclusive, is r, what is the sum of the integers from 1 to 497, inclusive, in terms of r?

   (A) $r - 499$
   (B) $r + 499$
   (C) $r - 997$
   (D) $r + 997$

10. If y is a non-zero number, which one of the following can NEVER be true?

    (A) $\sqrt{169 - y^2} = 12$

    (B) $\sqrt{169 - y} = 12$

    (C) $\sqrt{169} - \sqrt{y^2} = 13 - y$

    (D) $\sqrt{169 + y^2} = 13 - y$

11. What is the value of $\dfrac{2(4^2 + 4^3)}{4(2 + 8)}$?

    (A) 1
    (B) 4
    (C) 8
    (D) 16

Go on to the next page. ➡

12. Trapezoid *GHJK* is similar to trapezoid *WXYZ*.

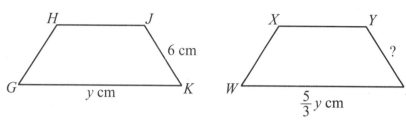

Note: Figures not drawn to scale

What is the length of side *YZ*?

(A) 6 cm
(B) 6*y* cm
(C) 10 cm
(D) 10*y* cm

---

13. Stewie knows that *y* is an integer greater than 4 and less than 10, and Peter knows that *y* is an integer greater than 5 and less than 12. If they share their information about *y*, then they know that *y* must be

(A) one of exactly 2 possible values
(B) one of exactly 4 possible values
(C) one of exactly 5 possible values
(D) one of exactly 7 possible values

14. If $3x + 2y = 8$ and $2x + y = 12$, what is $5x + 3y$?

(A) −20
(B) −8
(C) 16
(D) 20

15. After grading her students' tests, Ms. Schuyler added a bonus of 5 points to each test. If the range of the test scores before the bonus was 82, what is the new range of the test scores?

(A) 82.00
(B) 84.50
(C) 85.50
(D) 87.00

16. If $x^2 + y^2 = 65$ and $xy = 28$, what is the value of $(x + y)^2$?

(A) 37
(B) 93
(C) 121
(D) 784

Go on to the next page. ➡

17. A cube is shown.

Which one of the following nets could represent the cube?

(A)

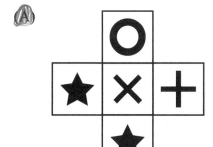

(C)

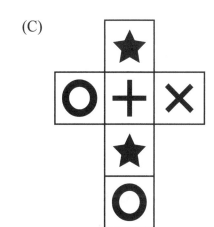

(B)

(D)

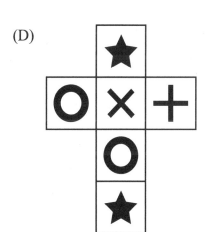

Go on to the next page. ➡

18. If x is a factor of c and y is a factor of d, which of the following statements must be true?

(A) xy is a factor of cd
(B) x is a factor of d
(C) xy is a multiple of cd
(D) y is a multiple of c

19. Use the diagram below to answer the question.

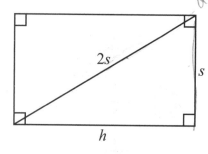

Given the lengths of the base and diagonal of the rectangle above, what is the length of height h, in terms of s?

(A) $s\sqrt{3}$
(B) $s\sqrt{5}$
(C) $3s$
(D) $3s^2$

20. Use the chart below to answer the question.

MARBLES IN A BAG

Color	Number
White	20
Black	30
Beige	40

There are also purple marbles in the bag. Which of the following can NOT be the probability of randomly selecting a purple marble from the bag?

(A) $\dfrac{1}{10}$

(B) $\dfrac{1}{4}$

(C) $\dfrac{2}{5}$

(D) $\dfrac{7}{15}$

Go on to the next page. →

QR

Part Two – Quantitative Comparisons

Directions: Using all information given in each question, compare the quantity in Column A to the quantity in Column B. All questions in Part Two have these answer choices:

(A) The quantity in Column A is greater.
(B) The quantity in Column B is greater.
(C) The two quantities are equal.
(D) The relationship cannot be determined from the information given.

	Column A	Column B			Column A	Column B
21.	$\dfrac{1}{1+3}$	$\dfrac{1}{1+\frac{1}{3}}$		24.	$\left(\dfrac{1}{12}\right)^{-2}$	$\left(\dfrac{1}{12}\right)^{-\frac{1}{2}}$

  ⓑ

  Ⓐ

Town A is 300 kilometers due north of Town B and Town C is 75 kilometers due west of Town B.

A bag contains 3 green buttons, 5 black buttons, 6 purple buttons, and 9 red buttons. Two buttons are removed randomly from the bag without replacing the first button.

	Column A	Column B
22.	The shortest distance between Town C and Town A	375 miles

ⓑ

	Column A	Column B
25.	The probability that both buttons are green	The probability that at least one button is green

Ⓐ

$y < 5$

	Column A	Column B
23.	$5y + 11$	$6y + 6$

Ⓐ

$$\frac{x}{y} = \frac{4}{7}$$

	Column A	Column B
26.	$\dfrac{x}{y}$	$\dfrac{x+4}{y+7}$

ⓒ

Go on to the next page. ➡

The product of three consecutive whole numbers is 504.

Column A	Column B
27. The smallest of the three numbers	6

Carl's average score on 5 tests is 88 and the mode is 89.

Column A	Column B
28. The score Carl would need on a sixth test to raise his average to 89	The median score after the sixth test if Carl raises his average to 89

The formula for the volume of a pyramid is $\frac{1}{3}Bh$, where B represents the area of the base of the pyramid and h represents the height of the pyramid. The volume of Pyramid A is 3 times the volume of Pyramid B.

Column A	Column B
29. The area of the base of Pyramid A	The area of the base of Pyramid B

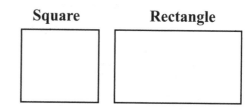

Square   **Rectangle**

Note: Figures not drawn to scale.

The perimeter of the square is 36. The perimeter of the rectangle is also 36.

Column A	Column B
30. The area of the square	The area of the rectangle

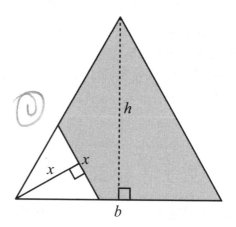

Note: Figure not drawn to scale.

Column A	Column B
31. The area of the shaded region	$\frac{1}{2}(bh - x^2)$

Go on to the next page. ➞

QR

②

Answer choices for all questions on this page.

(A) The quantity in Column A is greater.
(B) The quantity in Column B is greater.
(C) The two quantities are equal.
(D) The relationship cannot be determined from the information given.

Column A   Column B

32. 27^4 3^{12}

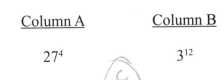

(C)

Daven has planted vegetable seeds in his rectangular garden with an area of 144 square feet. In order to prevent people from walking on the garden, he will enclose the perimeter of the entire garden with rope.

Column A	Column B
34. The number of feet of rope he needs	44 feet

(A)

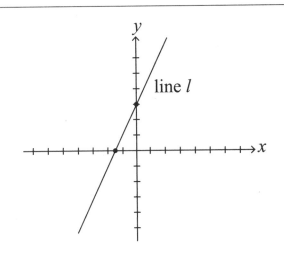

line l

$a < 0 < b < c$

Column A	Column B
35. $a + c$	b

(D)

Line l is the graph of $y = 2x + 3$.

Column A   Column B

33. The value of the y intercept when line l is reflected about the x axis

The value of the y intercept when line l is reflected about the y axis

(B)

Go on to the next page. ➡

The price of an item initially is $2.50. The price is then decreased by 20%, and the resulting price is then increased by 20%.

	Column A	Column B
36.	The final price of the item	$2.50

In a set of five numbers, the mode is 4, the median is 4, and the range is 4.

	Column A	Column B
37.	The average of the set of numbers	4

STOP. If there is time, you may check your work in this section only.

STOP

36 Questions

Time: 35 Minutes

This section contains six short reading passages. Each passage is followed by six questions based on its content. Answer the questions following each passage on the basis of what is <u>stated</u> or <u>implied</u> in that passage. You may write in the test booklet.

Questions 1-6

1   I still remember my visits to my
2 grandmother in Texas when I was young. When
3 I arrived, I was greeted by her little dog Charlie,
4 whom I named. I loved Charlie, and we played
5 for hours, chasing each other from room to
6 room. Then, I would give Charlie a vanilla
7 wafer as a treat. Sometimes, when I spent time
8 with my grandmother in her room before bed,
9 Charlie licked my hand over and over. I wanted
10 Charlie to sleep in my bed, but even though my
11 room was right next to my grandmother's room,
12 he refused to leave her bed.
13   During the hot summers, my uncle took
14 my brother and me to our cousin's house to
15 swim in her pool. At least I think she was a
16 cousin; I know her husband's parents and my
17 grandmother's parents were related in some
18 way. The pool was a beautiful, sparkling blue
19 color, and I was content to spend an entire
20 afternoon in the water, swimming and playing
21 with the floating rafts. I tried to teach my
22 brother how to dive—he always jumped into
23 the pool or even walked down the steps at the
24 shallow end—but after a while I gave up.
25   Before arriving at the pool, my uncle,
26 brother, and I went to a local hamburger
27 restaurant to pick up lunch and bring it back
28 to the pool. The owner of the restaurant was a
29 callous man who yelled at the customers. I was
30 quite frightened of him, but the hamburger with
31 the special sauce was delicious, so I always
32 wanted to go there for lunch. Years later, I found
33 out that my grandmother and her cousin liked
34 going there for the hamburgers because they
35 thought the owner's rude behavior was funny!
36   When I wasn't swimming or playing with
37 Charlie, I spent time with my grandmother.
38 We watched TV, went shopping for toys,
39 visited her friends (who always had cookies
40 for me and my brother), and talked. Staying
41 with her was so much fun, and when it was
42 time to say goodbye to her and return home, I
43 always felt a bit sad.

Go on to the next page. ➡

RC

1. This passage can best be characterized as

   (A) a person's pleasant recollections of his visits with family.
   (B) a child's description of one particularly memorable summer.
   (C) a story from the narrator's youth and the lesson that he learned.
   (D) a fictional account of two brothers traveling across America.

2. According to the passage, the narrator went to the local hamburger restaurant even though he was

   (A) aware that he should not swim for 30 minutes after lunch.
   (B) concerned that eating too many hamburgers was unhealthy.
   (C) unable to find hamburgers with special sauce at home.
   (D) intimidated by the owner of the hamburger restaurant.

3. The use of the phrase "but after a while I gave up" in line 24 suggests that

   (A) the author bored easily and rarely completed a task.
   (B) the author did not succeed in teaching his brother to dive.
   (C) the author's brother was more interested in reading than swimming.
   (D) the author's brother resented the author's efforts to teach him to dive.

4. In line 29, the word "callous" most nearly means

   (A) entertaining.
   (B) insensitive.
   (C) lumpy.
   (D) terrified.

5. The author mentions his grandmother in line 33 in order to

   (A) emphasize the delight he took in spending time with her during his summer visits.
   (B) question the truthfulness of her stated motivation for going to the hamburger restaurant.
   (C) contrast the perceptions of the narrator as a boy with his understanding as an adult.
   (D) highlight the contrast between his fear and her enjoyment of the restaurant owner's discourtesy.

6. The narrator's attitude toward Charlie is one of

   (A) concern.
   (B) devotion.
   (C) indifference.
   (D) resentment.

Go on to the next page. ➞

Questions 7-12

1   Coral reefs are underwater structures
2 created by very small animals called corals.
3 Coral reefs are home to amazingly diverse
4 ecosystems: although together they would fill
5 less space than half of France, nearly a quarter
6 of all marine species live on these reefs. Of the
7 109,800 square miles of coral reefs, over 90%
8 are located in the Indo-Pacific region, which
9 includes Australia, Indonesia, Fiji, and many
10 other countries lying on the Indian and Pacific
11 oceans. Less than 8% of the world's coral reefs
12 are found in the Atlantic Ocean or Caribbean
13 Sea.
14   Some coral reefs are massive barrier
15 reefs extending along part or all of an entire
16 coastline. The largest is the Great Barrier Reef
17 of Australia, running 1,600 miles. Given the
18 scarcity of Atlantic and Caribbean reefs, it may
19 come as a surprise that the second and third
20 largest barrier reefs are the Belize Barrier Reef
21 in Central America (620 miles), and the Great
22 Florida Reef, a 4-mile wide, 145-mile long
23 reef system that follows the arc of the Florida
24 Keys. A barrier reef is actually made of many
25 individual reefs that run together; the Great
26 Florida Reef contains over 6,000 individual
27 reefs. Nearly 1,400 distinct species live on the
28 Great Florida Reef, including 500 species of
29 fish and 40 species of coral.
30   The Great Florida Reef consists of two
31 ridges on the eastern side of the Hawk Channel.
32 The White Bank, closer to the Florida Keys,
33 is mostly sand and sea grass with patches of
34 coral reefs; this area is also known as the patch
35 reef community. The Florida Straits are farther
36 out to sea; this ridge forms distinctive barrier
37 reef formations and is known as the bank reef
38 community. Even closer to the shore is an area
39 known as the hardbottom community. This
40 first community is populated mostly by algae,
41 sea fans, and stony coral. Lobsters and other
42 crustaceans are plentiful here, as are groupers
43 and barracuda, among other fish species.
44   The White Bank community, with dome-
45 shaped coral structures growing up in giant
46 mounds, hosts a broad range of stunning fish
47 species, from wondrously shaped parrotfish
48 and puffer fish to brightly colored angelfish and
49 damselfish. The relatively shallow part of the
50 Florida Straits (less than six feet deep) take on
51 spur and groove formations—rows and rows
52 of reefs separated by white sand. Farther out
53 to sea are giant reefs that plunge into the deep.
54 In addition to fish similar to those in the patch
55 reefs, the giant reefs are also frequented by
56 large "pelagic" fish such as sharks.
57   The most frequently visited part of the
58 Great Florida Reef lies off of Key Largo, in
59 and around the protected John Pennekamp
60 Coral Reef State Park. Each year hundreds of
61 thousands of divers come to witness this unique
62 and marvelous part of America.

Go on to the next page. ➡

7. The passage is primarily concerned with

(A) providing details about the annual number of visitors to John Pennekamp Coral Reef State Park.

(B) describing the structure of barrier reefs and the types of fish species that inhabit these reefs.

(C) analyzing the reasons for the relative scarcity of reefs in the Atlantic Ocean and Caribbean Sea.

(D) giving information about coral reefs and more detailed information about a particular reef system.

8. In lines 18-19, the author indicates that "it may come as a surprise" that

(A) two of the largest barrier reefs are located in areas not known to hold many of the world's reefs.

(B) the Great Florida Reef is so much smaller than the Great Barrier Reef in Australia.

(C) a relatively small reef is inhabited by such a large and diverse number of fish species.

(D) a reef system containing 6,000 individual reefs is at the same time an important barrier reef.

9. In line 55, "frequented" most nearly means

(A) attacked.
(B) documented.
(C) repeated.
(D) visited.

10. The Florida Straits reefs are known for each of the following characteristics EXCEPT

(A) giant, plunging reefs.
(B) lobsters and crustaceans.
(C) spur and groove formations.
(D) sharks and other large fish.

11. In the last paragraph, the author mentions the John Pennekamp Coral Reef State Park in order to

(A) demonstrate that an excessive number of divers visiting reefs have required efforts to protect those reefs.

(B) explain that Key Largo, more than the other Keys, contains particularly beautiful parts of the Great Florida Reef.

(C) change the discussion from a general description of the structure of a large reef system to a specific location within that system.

(D) convince divers that other areas of the Great Florida Reef are also worthy of their attention.

12. The author's tone when discussing the fish species on the White Bank community (lines 44-49) is best described as

(A) analytical.
(B) concerned.
(C) delighted.
(D) irritated.

Go on to the next page. ➡

Questions 13-18

When former United States Supreme Court Justice Sandra Day O'Connor graduated from Stanford Law School, the prestigious California law firms of the day would not hire her as a lawyer. Despite the fact that she graduated third in her class, the only job offer she received was as a legal secretary. While women today are an integral and equal part of the legal community, Justice O'Connor's experience was far from unusual. Indeed, women struggled for centuries to be accepted in the legal community.

While there were some isolated exceptions, women were prohibited from practicing law during the seventeenth and eighteenth centuries. At first, women were not allowed admittance to law schools. Later, once women began to attend and graduate from law schools, they were not permitted to join the state "Bar." A lawyer who is not admitted to the Bar may not give legal advice or represent a client in court.

In 1872, Myra Bradwell was denied admission to the Illinois Bar. She appealed to the United States Supreme Court, arguing that the decision violated her rights under the "privileges and immunities" clause as a citizen of the United States. The Supreme Court agreed that she was a citizen, but rejected her argument that the "privileges and immunities" clause offered her protection. In a separate opinion supporting the vote of his colleagues, Joseph Bradley expressed the typical male view of the time:

Man is, or should be, woman's protector and defender. The natural and proper timidity and delicacy which belongs to the female sex evidently unfits it for many of the occupations of civil life. The constitution of the family organization, which is founded in the divine ordinance, as well as in the nature of things, indicates the domestic sphere as that which properly belongs to the domain and functions of womanhood. The harmony, not to say identity, of interest and views which belong, or should belong, to the family institution is repugnant to the idea of a woman adopting a distinct and independent career from that of her husband.

Twenty years later, the Supreme Court similarly ruled against Belva Lockwood, who challenged Virginia's refusal to admit her to the state Bar, even though she had been admitted to practice before the Supreme Court.

Even so, the tide was changing. Belle Mansfield of Iowa became the first woman admitted to a state Bar in 1869. Likewise, in 1872, Charlotte Ray of Washington, D.C. became the first black woman to be admitted to the Bar—although it appears the admissions committee was unaware that "C. E. Ray" (as she wrote on the application) was a woman. By the 1890s, though, admission of women to state Bars became increasingly common—even if prestigious law firms would not be ready to hire the likes of Justice O'Connor for decades to come.

Go on to the next page. ➡

13. The primary purpose of the passage is to

    (A) compare the careers of Myra Bradwell and Belva Lockwood with the career of Belle Mansfield.
    (B) analyze the Supreme Court's opinion concerning Myra Bradwell's rejection by the state Bar.
    (C) provide a history of women's struggles for equal protection under the laws.
    (D) describe some of the struggles women lawyers have faced over the years.

14. It can be inferred from the third paragraph that Joseph Bradley was

    (A) married to Myra Bradwell.
    (B) Myra Bradwell's lawyer.
    (C) a Supreme Court Justice.
    (D) a well-regarded journalist.

15. Lines 1-7 imply that Sandra Day O'Connor did all of the following EXCEPT

    (A) succeeded as a student in law school.
    (B) worked as a secretary for a law firm.
    (C) applied to prestigious law firms for employment.
    (D) served on the U.S. Supreme Court.

16. The author quotes Joseph Bradley in order to show that

    (A) the "privileges and immunities" clause had no bearing on whether women should be admitted to practice law.
    (B) some men of the time often believed that the role of women was incompatible with a woman's pursuit of a career.
    (C) Belva Lockwood was foolish to ask the Supreme Court to force the State of Virginia to admit her to the Bar.
    (D) Myra Bradwell deserves praise for her courage and perseverance in trying to establish new legal rights for women.

17. Why does the author mention in lines 52-53 that Belva Lockwood was admitted to practice before the Supreme Court?

    (A) to emphasize the extent of the Supreme Court's unwillingness to override State laws concerning women's right to practice law
    (B) to praise the Supreme Court for its willingness to hear arguments from women at a time when most State courts would not
    (C) to express admiration that the Supreme Court admitted women to that Court before many State courts admitted women to practice law
    (D) to place women's struggle for the right to practice law in the larger context of the pursuit of equal rights for women

18. According to the last paragraph, the increased frequency with which women were admitted to state Bars in the late nineteenth century

    (A) was inevitable following Belle Mansfield's admission to the Iowa Bar.
    (B) came as a relief to Myra Bradwell, who finally realized her dream.
    (C) did not necessarily mean that women would be hired by law firms.
    (D) paved the way for the admission of black men to state Bars.

Go on to the next page. ➡

Questions 19-24

1   Liu Xiaobo was in a Chinese jail when he
2 was awarded the Nobel Peace Prize in 2010.
3 The President of the Independent Chinese
4 Center and the magazine *Democratic China,* he
5 was charged with, and convicted of, "inciting
6 subversion of state power" and sentenced to
7 a prison term of 11 years in 2009. His crime:
8 advocating political reforms in China, such as
9 ending the Communist Party's complete control
10 of the political system and media. The Nobel
11 committee acknowledged his "struggle for
12 fundamental human rights in China."
13   In his early years as an academic, his
14 future role as dissident was not apparent. He
15 spent many years studying literature, earning
16 a Master's degree in 1984, when he was
17 29. He became a teacher at Beijing National
18 University, married, and had a son. In 1986,
19 however, during his work towards a Ph.D., he
20 began publishing what were radical opinions in
21 China. His 1987 book *Criticism of the Choice:*
22 *Dialogues with Li Zehou,* for example, offered
23 a pointed critique of the Chinese tradition of
24 Confucianism, and his doctoral thesis was
25 entitled "Aesthetic and Human Freedom." In an
26 interview, Liu explained his view that:
27   Modernization means whole-sale
28   westernization. Choosing a human life
29   is choosing the Western way of life. The
30   difference between Western and Chinese
31   governing system is humane versus
32   in-humane; there is no middle ground.
33   Westernization is not a choice of a nation,
34   but a choice for the human race.

35 In addition, he has demanded free markets,
36 multi-party elections, and separation of powers.
37 These are radical concepts in politically
38 repressed China.
39   Liu has also been a staunch supporter of
40 military action by the United States intended to
41 expand human rights: "The free world led by
42 the US fought almost all regimes that trampled
43 on human rights … The major wars that the US
44 became involved in are all ethically defensible."
45 He has also supported the United States' support
46 of Israel and the war in Iraq that led to Saddam
47 Hussein's downfall. He predicted that "a free,
48 democratic and peaceful Iraq will emerge."
49   But his efforts as a human rights activist
50 in China have earned him notoriety in the eyes
51 of the government and four arrests relating to
52 his writings. Ignoring the threat of prison and
53 more than one earlier prison term, he continued
54 to publish critiques of China anytime he was
55 free. His works were banned in China, and by
56 the late 1990s, the government was said to be
57 reading everything he wrote on the Internet and
58 listening to all of his phone calls. His works
59 have long been banned in China and when he
60 was working on a human rights report on China
61 in 2004, his computer and all of his documents
62 were confiscated by the government.

Go on to the next page. →

RC

19. The primary purpose of the passage is to

    (A) disapprove of the Chinese government for its lack of political freedoms and its retaliation against those who criticize it.
    (B) celebrate the awarding of the Nobel Peace Prize to Liu Xiaobo for his willingness to stand up for freedom and human rights.
    (C) provide information about the political views of a person and the consequences he has faced for expressing those views.
    (D) compare Liu Xiaobo's opinions about policies of China with his opinions about policies of the United States.

20. In line 50, the word "notoriety" most nearly means

    (A) admiration.
    (B) awards.
    (C) riches.
    (D) villainy.

21. The purpose of the third paragraph (lines 39-48) is to

    (A) briefly digress from the author's main focus.
    (B) provide evidence to support an earlier opinion.
    (C) point out an exception to a person's political views.
    (D) disagree with some of a person's political views.

22. The crimes that Liu Xiaobo has been accused of can best be described as

    (A) financial.
    (B) political.
    (C) vehicular.
    (D) violent.

23. According to the passage, Liu Xiaobo's view on American involvement in wars such as the United States' war in Iraq is one of

    (A) opposition, because he understood that no weapons of mass destruction would be found and he believed that America was interested only in Iraq's oil.
    (B) uncertainty, because he was in jail when American troops entered Iraq and he therefore lacked sufficient information to form an opinion.
    (C) indifference, because he is concerned with efforts to change China to a politically free country, not with the problems of other countries.
    (D) support, because he believes that one of America's roles is to bring freedom to people who suffer under tyrannical governments.

24. The passage suggests that during the early 1980s, Liu Xiaobo

    (A) engaged in frequent protests against the Chinese government.
    (B) supported the Chinese government until he was first arrested.
    (C) was not yet engaged in writing about politics and human rights.
    (D) was not yet interested in the problems of ordinary Chinese citizens.

Go on to the next page. ➡

Questions 25-30

1 More familiarly known as the Black Plague, the Black Death was one of the most deadly outbreaks of disease in history. Beginning in China sometime in the 1340s, it followed China's trade routes all the way to Europe. During the course of the Black Death, which saw its worst years in Europe between 1348 and 1350, as much as 60% of Europe's population succumbed to the disease. It would take 150 years for the population to recover.

11 The Black Death was the second of three major recorded plagues. The first was the Plague of Justinian in the 500s and 600s. Killing about 40% of Constantinople's population and nearly half of Europe's, the plague did not disappear until the mid 700s. The third, called the Third Pandemic, arrived in the 1800s; this plague, unlike the two that preceded it, was limited to China and India. But it is the Black Plague that continues to fascinate historians of disease, perhaps because after its first wave in the 1300s, it reappeared from time to time all the way through the 1700s. While a virulent plague will die out quickly as a population is decimated, it can recur because the bacteria continue to live in fleas.

27 The bacteria species that is believed to have caused the Black Death, *Yersinia pestis,* spread with ease, as it was carried by fleas that infested rodents. Medicine was not advanced during the Black Plague. In France, the King was informed that the plague was caused by astrological events such as the aligning of three planets. Moreover, during the Black Plague, personal hygiene was not considered important, and this surely helped the spread of the disease—ticks and fleas hopped from animals to people in the dirty streets. In addition to turning to astrology for answers, people of the time blamed earthquakes and, unfortunately, the Jewish people, whose communities in some towns were massacred not by the plague, but by other people.

44 The Plague had many names, including the Great Pestilence and Great Mortality. It was not until the sixteenth century that the color black attached to the name. Conventional wisdom holds that "black" referred to the grisly symptoms that appeared as the disease progressed, such as blackened skin. However, it is just as likely that the term was being used in the sense of "terrible." Ultimately, this question, along with what caused the plague and how many people died, will never be answered conclusively. The records from the time are simply not detailed enough to allow for confident answers. Hypotheses and extrapolations will have to do.

Go on to the next page.

25. The primary purpose of the passage as a whole is to

(A) question the reliability of information about the Black Death.

(B) criticize fourteenth-century people for their reaction to the Black Death.

(C) provide an overview of current beliefs about the Black Death.

(D) argue that the Black Death is more harmful than current diseases.

26. According to the passage, some people in the fourteenth century attributed the Black Death to

(A) planetary phenomena.

(B) fleas and rodents.

(C) *Yersinia pestis.*

(D) lack of cleanliness.

27. One possible reason the Black Plague is particularly interesting to those who study diseases is that

(A) its limitation to China and India allows for greater scientific understanding of its causes.

(B) the name Black Death evokes both the color of the symptoms and the horror of the disease.

(C) its repeated recurrence for several hundred years makes it a particularly devastating plague.

(D) the bacteria that caused it and the mode of transmission remain present today in many areas.

28. In line 25, "decimated" most nearly means

(A) armed.

(B) destroyed.

(C) infected.

(D) treated.

29. The sentence "Hypotheses and extrapolations will have to do" (lines 57-58) refers to

(A) the incomplete nature of present-day knowledge about the Black Plague.

(B) the scientific method, which relies on the experimental testing of hypotheses.

(C) the particular symptoms that many victims of the Black Plague suffered.

(D) whether the bacteria *Yersinia pestis* continues to exist today.

30. The author mentions Jewish people in line 41 in order to show that

(A) no group of people was immune to the devastating effects of the Black Plague.

(B) not all groups of people looked to the stars to explain the reasons for the Black Plague.

(C) some people's lack of understanding of the cause of the Black Plague led them to violent acts.

(D) their belief that earthquakes caused the Black Plague had disastrous consequences for them.

Go on to the next page. ➡

Questions 31-36

The Inuit appear to have been the first people to build an igloo. The Inuit are indigenous people living in the arctic regions of Alaska and Canada. In the Inuit language, the word igloo means house, even though many people suppose it has a more precise definition: snow house. Quite the contrary, anything from a tent to a building can be called an igloo by the Inuit. To other indigenous peoples, however, igloo does refer only to a snow house, and we shall proceed using this more narrow and conventional definition.

Making a house out of snow in the freezing arctic may seem strange, but the air pockets trapped within the snow work to trap heat inside the igloo. The igloo's inhabitants' body heat is enough to warm the space inside an igloo to as much as 60 degrees under some circumstances, all the while the outside temperature could be as low as –50 degrees. Not any snow will do, however. The snow must be quite heavy. Wind-blown snow is particularly well-suited to igloo construction, because the ice crystals in the snow become more compact and interlocked. The compacted snow is used to create the familiar igloo dome. Even without a supporting structure, a well-built igloo can support the weight of a man standing on it.

There are a number of types of igloos, each built for a specific purpose. Small igloos are used for temporary housing, perhaps for two or three days. Such igloos are built during hunting trips or other short journeys. Larger igloos form permanent homes. While just a single room, these igloos are large enough to accommodate one or even two families. A group of such igloos in a small area forms a village. The largest igloos have more than one room and can house as many as 20 people. Some of the large igloos are several small igloos connected together, while others are actually single structures.

In addition to body heat, stone lamps and small stoves are used to warm an igloo. While the stone lamp may cause the interior to melt a bit, the water refreezes, which serves to strengthen the igloo. For additional light, a hole is cut in the igloo, and a block of ice is inserted in the hole. Animal skins are used in place of a front door to keep warm air in, while caribou fur is used as a warm blanket on a bed made of snow. The bed is placed in a raised area, because warmer air rises.

Go on to the next page. ➡

③

31. Which sentence best expresses the main idea of the passage?

   (A) The term igloo refers more to a broader category of home than merely to homes made of snow.

   (B) Igloos come in a variety of sizes, and all are able to keep people inside them warm.

   (C) Igloos made of snow by the Inuit are known to be particularly well constructed.

   (D) Outside of the arctic regions of Alaska and Canada, igloos are no longer built.

32. According to the passage, which is true about igloos?

   (A) Igloos cannot maintain warmth without a stone lamp or stove.

   (B) A bed in an igloo is often placed higher than the entrance of the igloo.

   (C) A larger igloo is better suited to maintaining a warm environment.

   (D) Only the Inuit still make igloos from snow today.

33. The author of the passage appears to be most interested in

   (A) the number of igloos contained in a typical village.

   (B) how many people can live in igloos of various sizes.

   (C) the most effective way to maintain warmth in an igloo.

   (D) how igloos are designed and used by indigenous arctic people.

34. According to the passage, a stone lamp can have the effect of

   (A) ensuring that only a limited number of animal skins and furs are required to keep the igloo's inhabitants warm.

   (B) further strengthening the igloo through a process of partially melting and re-freezing the snow from which the igloo is constructed.

   (C) allowing the parents of Inuit children to have sufficient light by which to read the historical accounts of their ancestors.

   (D) providing an alternative to the use of small stoves to ensure that igloos are brought to a comfortable temperature for sleep.

35. Which of the following describes the organization of lines 31-44?

   (A) A statement is made and supporting examples are provided.

   (B) An opinion is offered and then contradicted with facts.

   (C) Types of igloos built today are compared with igloos from the past.

   (D) Reasons are given for the way igloos of different sizes are constructed.

36. The author implies that some igloos

   (A) can be constructed with materials other than snow.

   (B) can be moved from one location to another during a hunting trip.

   (C) cannot be built to a size sufficient to accommodate more than one family.

   (D) cannot be brought to temperatures of 60 degrees without an external heat source.

STOP. If there is time, you may check your work in this section only.

NO TEST MATERIAL ON THIS PAGE

MA

Section 4
Mathematics Achievement

Each question is followed by four suggested answers. Read each question and then decide which one of the four suggested answers is best.

Find the row of spaces on your answer document that has the same number as the question. In this row, mark the space having the same letter as the answer you have chosen. You may write in your test booklet.

SAMPLE QUESTION:

Sample Answer

Ⓐ ● Ⓒ Ⓓ

What is the perimeter of an isosceles triangle with two sides of 4 cm and one side of 6 cm?

(A)   10 cm
(B)   14 cm
(C)   16 cm
(D)   24 cm

The correct answer is 14 cm, so circle B is darkened.

STOP. Do not go on
until told to do so.

STOP

1. Which of the following is not equal to $\frac{1}{3}$?

(A) $\dfrac{1.5}{4.5}$

(B) $\dfrac{0.5}{1.5}$

(C) $0.\overline{33}$

(D) 0.333334

2. If the circumference of a circle is 12π, what is the area of the circle?

(A) 144π
(B) 36π
(C) 12π
(D) 6π

3. For which value(s) of x is it true that
$$\dfrac{x^2 - 36}{(x + 3)(x - 4)} = 0 ?$$

(A) $x = 2$ and $x = 3$
(B) $x = 6$ only
(C) $x = -6$ and $x = 6$
(D) $x = 2$, $x = 3$, and $x = 6$

4. What is the value of $\dfrac{4.2 \times 10^7}{6.0 \times 10^{-3}}$?

(A) 7.0×10^3
(B) 7.0×10^4
(C) 7.0×10^9
(D) 7.0×10^{10}

5. The area of each grid square in the rectangle shown below is 4 in².

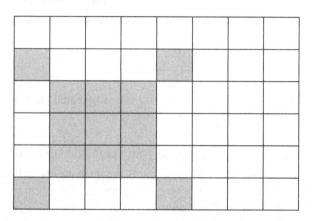

What is the area of the shaded region?

(A) 26 in²
(B) 46 in²
(C) 52 in²
(D) 62 in²

6. If p and q are prime numbers, what is the greatest common factor of $4p^8q$ and $10p^5q^4$?

(A) $2p^8q$
(B) $2p^5q^4$
(C) $2p^5q$
(D) $20p^8q^4$

Go on to the next page. ➡

④

7. The chart shows the inputs and outputs at a factory.

Inputs	Outputs
1	0
2	2
3	4
4	6
5	8
•	•
•	•
•	•
x	y

If the pattern shown is continued, then what is the value of y?

(A) $2(x - 1)$
(B) $2x - 1$
(C) $2x + 1$
(D) $2(x + 1)$

8. What is the slope of a line with coordinate points $(2, 5)$ and $(7, 3)$?

(A) $-\dfrac{5}{2}$

(B) $-\dfrac{2}{5}$

(C) $\dfrac{2}{5}$

(D) $\dfrac{5}{2}$

$$\frac{3-5}{7-2} = \frac{-2}{5}$$

9. The bar graph shown represents the number of miles Eleanor ran each week during an eight-week period.

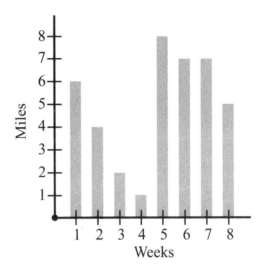

What is the median number of miles run?

(A) 3.0
(B) 4.5
(C) 5.5
(D) 7.0

10. If $x = (3.15 + 1.85)x$, what is the value of x?

(A) 0

(B) $\dfrac{1}{5}$

(C) $\dfrac{1}{2}$

(D) 5

Go on to the next page. ➡

11. Use the rectangle to answer the question.

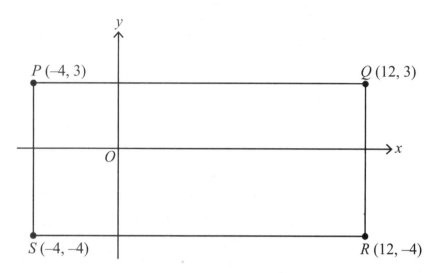

Which of the following distances is closest to 13?

(A) *PO*
(B) *QO*
(C) *RO*
(D) *SO*

---

12. What is the minimum value of *y* if $y = 3x^2 - 4$ for $-3 \le x \le 2$?

(A) -7
(B) -4
(C) 8
(D) 23

13. If point $(-1, 10)$ lies on a circle with center $(-6, -2)$, what is the radius of the circle?

(A) 7 grid units
(B) 8 grid units
(C) 12 grid units
(D) 13 grid units

14. What is the best unit to use when measuring the width of a television screen?

(A) inches
(B) kilometers
(C) pounds
(D) tons

15. What is the solution set to the inequality $-4 \le 3x - 1 \le 8$?

(A) $-1 \le x, x > 3$
(B) $1 \le x, x \ge 3$
(C) $-1 \le x \le 3$
(D) $1 \le x \le 3$

Go on to the next page. ➡

16. Mr. Lear recorded the number of inches of rain on each day during the month of February in the table below.

RAINFALL

Inches of Rain	Number of Days
0	3
1	5
2	12
3	3
4	5

What is the mode of the data?

(A)   2
(B)   3
(C)   5
(D)   12

17. From a club of 7 members, 3 will be chosen for president, vice president, and treasurer. How many different arrangements of members are possible for the 3 positions?

(A)   18
(B)   35
(C)   210
(D)   343

18. Use the diagram to answer the question.

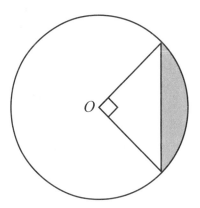

If the radius of Circle O is 6, what is the area of the shaded region?

(A) $9\pi - 18$
(B) $9\pi - 36$
(C) $12\pi - 18$
(D) $36\pi - 36$

19. If the number of students in a classroom is increased from 20 to 25, what is the percent increase in the number of students?

(A)   20%
(B)   25%
(C)   55%
(D)   80%

20. If x is the square root of a number that is not a perfect square, y is the square root of a different number that is not a perfect square, and neither x nor y is a factor of the other, which one of the following could be a rational number?

(A) $\dfrac{x}{y}$

(B) $\dfrac{\sqrt{x}}{y}$

(C) $\left(\dfrac{x}{y}\right)^2$

(D) $\dfrac{x}{\sqrt{y}}$

Go on to the next page. ⟶

21. Triangle ABC is similar to triangle PQR. The length of $\overline{AC}$ is 7 cm, and the length of $\overline{PR}$ is 4 cm. If the length of $\overline{PQ}$ is 16 cm, what is the length of $\overline{AB}$?

   (A) 28
   (B) 21
   (C) 14
   (D) 4

22. What is the value of $(x + 4)(x - 5)$?

   (A) $x^2 - 1$
   (B) $x^2 - 20$
   (C) $x^2 - x - 20$
   (D) $x^2 + x - 20$

23. The measures of three of the angles of a quadrilateral are shown in the diagram.

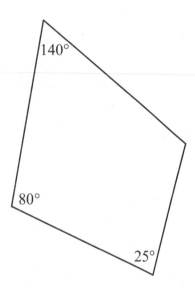

What is the measure of the fourth angle?

   (A) 105
   (B) 115
   (C) 205
   (D) 215

24. The equation $x = \dfrac{-4}{4 + x}$ is true for what value(s) of x?

   (A) -2
   (B) 0
   (C) all real numbers
   (D) There are no values for x that would make the equation true.

25. What expression is equivalent to $3a^3b^5 + 2a^2b^4 - (7a^2b^4 - 4a^3b^5)$?

   (A) $-4a^3b^5 + 6a^2b^4$
   (B) $5a^3b^5 - 3a^2b^4$
   (C) $-5a^3b^5 + a^2b^4$
   (D) $7a^3b^5 - 5a^2b^4$

26. If x is an odd number, which one of the following expressions is an even number?

   (A) $x(x + 8)$
   (B) $(x + 2)(x - 4)$
   (C) $x^2 - 2$
   (D) $x^2 - x$

27. The height of a tree is 30 feet, and it casts a shadow of 18 feet, as shown in the diagram.

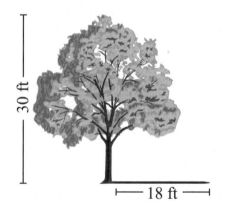

If Carmella is 5 feet tall, what is the length of her shadow at the same time of day?

   (A) 2 feet
   (B) 3 feet
   (C) 4 feet
   (D) 6 feet

Go on to the next page. ➡

28. What is the value of $\sqrt{64x^{36}}$?

   (A) $8x^6$
   (B) $8x^{18}$
   (C) $32x^6$
   (D) $32x^{18}$

29. The table below shows the results of a survey of 90 people at a movie theater. Each person was asked to name his or her favorite type of movie, by category.

FAVORITE MOVIE BY TYPE

Movie Type	Number of People
Comedy	60
Romance	11
Science Fiction	15
Other	4

   If this data is used to make a circle graph, what is the central angle of the portion of the graph representing Comedy?

   (A)   15°
   (B)   60°
   (C)   150°
   (D)   240°

30. There are 2 purple beads, 5 black beads, and 9 yellow beads in a bag. If 2 beads are selected at random without replacing the first bead, what is the probability of picking a yellow bead and then a purple bead?

   (A) $\dfrac{7}{16}$

   (B) $\dfrac{11}{16}$

   (C) $\dfrac{9}{16} \times \dfrac{2}{15}$

   (D) $\dfrac{9}{16} \times \dfrac{2}{16}$

31. Which one of the following expressions does NOT represent an integer?

   (A) $\sqrt{36 \times 9}$

   (B) $\sqrt{36} \div \sqrt{9}$

   (C) $\sqrt{36 + 9}$

   (D) $\sqrt{36} - \sqrt{9}$

32. Line l has a slope of $\dfrac{2}{3}$. If line m is perpendicular to line l, what is the slope of line m?

   (A) $-\dfrac{3}{2}$

   (B) $-\dfrac{2}{3}$

   (C) $\dfrac{2}{3}$

   (D) $\dfrac{3}{2}$

33. During an 80-minute musical, $\dfrac{1}{5}$ of the time was devoted to changes of scenery. If the average time it took to change the scenery was 40 seconds, how many times was the scenery changed?

   (A)   12
   (B)   16
   (C)   24
   (D)   96

Go on to the next page. ⟶

34. A solution set is shown on the number line.

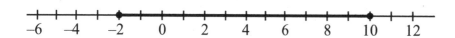

Which expression represents the solution set?

(A) $|x + 4| \leq 6$
(B) $|x + 4| \leq -6$
(C) $|x - 4| \leq 6$
(D) $|x - 4| \leq -6$

---

35. Sylvester is placing square tiles on his bathroom floor. If the measurement of the floor is 15 feet wide by 21 feet long, and the area of each tile is 1 yd², how many tiles will Sylvester need?

(A) 18
(B) 35
(C) 105
(D) 315

36. If $b^2 + 25 = 0$, which represents all possible values of b?

(A) 5
(B) ±5
(C) 5i
(D) ±5i

37. Which of the following is the result of the expression $\begin{bmatrix} 1 & 4 \\ 2 & 1 \end{bmatrix} + \begin{bmatrix} 2 & 5 \\ 6 & 1 \end{bmatrix}$?

(A) $\begin{bmatrix} 3 & 5 \\ 6 & 1 \end{bmatrix}$

(B) $\begin{bmatrix} 3 & 9 \\ 8 & 2 \end{bmatrix}$

(C) $\begin{bmatrix} 3 & 9 \\ 6 & 1 \end{bmatrix}$

(D) $\begin{bmatrix} 3 & 5 \\ 8 & 2 \end{bmatrix}$

38. If $ab + 3 = xb - a$, then $b =$

(A) $\dfrac{a + 3}{x - a}$

(B) $\dfrac{a - 3}{x - a}$

(C) $\dfrac{a + 3}{a - x}$

(D) $\dfrac{x - a}{a - x}$

39. Use the stem-and-leaf plot to answer the question.

Stem	Leaf
0	1 1 2 2
1	1 4
2	2 5 6
3	7
4	1 8 9
5	5
6	2 3 6 7

Which of the following can be determined based on the data above?

(A) mean only
(B) mean and median only
(C) mean, median, and mode only
(D) mean, median, mode, and range

Go on to the next page. ➡

40. If a sausage 26 inches long were cut into 2 pieces so that one piece was 8 inches longer than the other piece, what would the length be, in inches, of the shorter piece?

(A)   5 in
(B)   9 in
(C)   17 in
(D)   21 in

41. Use the diagram below to answer the question.

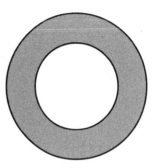

If the radius of the smaller circle is 6 cm and the radius of the larger circle is 10 cm, what is the area of the shaded region?

(A) 16π cm^2
(B) 36π cm^2
(C) 64π cm^2
(D) 100π cm^2

42. The box-and-whisker plot below shows the number of days without sunlight in a remote village in northern Alaska during winter last year.

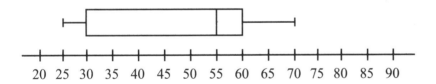

What is the range of the data?

(A)   30
(B)   45
(C)   55
(D)   70

Go on to the next page. ➡

43. If there are 5,280 feet in a mile, and a dog runs 14 miles per hour, which of the following expressions shows the dog's speed in feet per minute?

(A) $\dfrac{14 \times 60}{5,280}$

(B) $\dfrac{5,280}{14 \times 60}$

(C) $\dfrac{60}{14 \times 5,280}$

(D) $\dfrac{14 \times 5,280}{60}$

44. There are 7 orange jelly beans, 5 pink jelly beans, 3 green jelly beans, and 4 brown jelly beans in a bag. Graciela randomly removes two jelly beans from the bag without replacing the first jelly bean. If the first jelly bean Graciela removed was brown, what is the probability that the second jelly bean she removed was pink?

(A) $\dfrac{4}{19} \times \dfrac{5}{19}$

(B) $\dfrac{4}{19} \times \dfrac{5}{18}$

(C) $\dfrac{5}{19}$

(D) $\dfrac{5}{18}$

45. Triangle *LNM* is shown. The measure of angle *LNM* is 50°, and the length of *MN* is 5 cm.

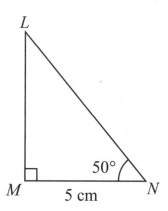

Side length $\overline{LM}$ is equal to which one of the following expressions?

(A) 5 tan 50°

(B) 5 sin 40°

(C) $\dfrac{5}{\tan 50°}$

(D) $\dfrac{5}{\sin 40°}$

Go on to the next page. ⟶

46. The height of the cone shown is 3 times its radius. The formula used to find the volume of a cone is $V = \frac{1}{3}r^2h\pi$, where r is the radius of the cone and h is the height of the cone.

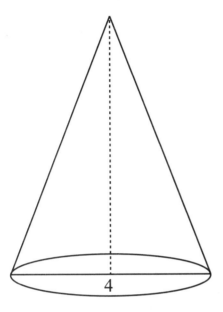

If the diameter of the cone is 4 cm, what is the volume of the cone in centimeters^2?

(A) 8π
(B) 24π
(C) 32π
(D) 48π

47. The normal number of days of rain per year in City A is 20, and this year's number of days of rain was within 5 days of the normal number. If this year's number of days of rain was R, which one of the following best describes this scenario?

(A) $|R - 5| \leq 20$
(B) $|R - 5| \geq 20$
(C) $|R - 20| \leq 5$
(D) $|R - 20| \geq 5$

STOP. If there is time, you may check your work in this section only.

STOP

NO TEST MATERIAL ON THIS PAGE

Essay

You will have 30 minutes to plan and write an essay on the topic printed on the other side of this page. **Do not write on another topic. An essay on another topic is not acceptable.**

The essay is designed to give you an opportunity to show how well you can write. You should try to express your thoughts clearly. How well you write is much more important than how much you write, but you need to say enough for a reader to understand what you mean.

You will probably want to write more than a short paragraph. You should also be aware that a copy of your essay will be sent to each school that will be receiving your test results. You are to write only in the appropriate section of the answer sheet. Please write or print so that your writing may be read by someone who is not familiar with your handwriting.

You may make notes and plan your essay on the reverse side of this page. Allow enough time to copy the final form on to your answer sheet. You must copy the essay topic onto your answer sheet, on page 3, in the box provided.

Please remember to write only the final draft of the essay on pages 3 and 4 of your answer sheet and to write it in blue or black pen. Again, you may use cursive writing or you may print. Only pages 3 and 4 will be sent to the schools.

Directions continue on the next page.

Essay Topic

Name a living person you would like to meet and describe what you would like to discuss with that person.

- Only write on this essay question
- Only pages 3 and 4 will be sent to the schools
- Only write in blue or black pen

NOTES

A living person I would like to meet is Elon Musk. Two things I would discuss with him is his booming company, Tesla, and how he got to such a prosperous time in his life. The reason to talk to him on such topics is the hope to one day lead a luxurious life like his.

As I mentioned, the first thing I would talk about is his company, Tesla. This is one thing that has truly made his place in world. A couple things or questions I would ask are about his inspirations for his company. I would also ask about how his friends and family felt about this choice he made, considering it was a big investment.

The second thing I would talk about was his life. I wanted to ask how he got to the prestigious level at which he is. I also want to learn his interest development into the topics that he has advanced present time.

Therefore, I would like to meet Elon Musk to learn about his company and his life. This would help me come to live an educated and prosperous life.

ISEE Practice Test: Answers and Explanations

ANSWER KEY

VR		QR		RC		MA			
1.	B	1.	B	1.	A	1.	D	25.	D
2.	A	2.	C	2.	D	2.	B	26.	D
3.	B	3.	C	3.	B	3.	C	27.	B
4.	C	4.	A	4.	B	4.	C	28.	B
5.	D	5.	C	5.	D	5.	C	29.	D
6.	D	6.	A	6.	B	6.	C	30.	C
7.	D	7.	C	7.	D	7.	A	31.	C
8.	B	8.	B	8.	A	8.	B	32.	A
9.	C	9.	C	9.	D	9.	C	33.	C
10.	D	10.	D	10.	B	10.	A	34.	C
11.	C	11.	B	11.	C	11.	C	35.	B
12.	A	12.	C	12.	C	12.	B	36.	D
13.	D	13.	B	13.	D	13.	D	37.	B
14.	C	14.	D	14.	C	14.	A	38.	A
15.	A	15.	A	15.	B	15.	C	39.	D
16.	D	16.	C	16.	B	16.	A	40.	B
17.	A	17.	C	17.	A	17.	C	41.	C
18.	A	18.	A	18.	C	18.	A	42.	B
19.	A	19.	A	19.	C	19.	B	43.	D
20.	B	20.	D	20.	D	20.	C	44.	D
21.	A	21.	B	21.	B	21.	A	45.	A
22.	A	22.	B	22.	B	22.	C	46.	A
23.	C	23.	A	23.	D	23.	B	47.	C
24.	B	24.	A	24.	C	24.	A		
25.	B	25.	B	25.	C				
26.	B	26.	C	26.	A				
27.	D	27.	A	27.	C				
28.	C	28.	A	28.	B				
29.	B	29.	D	29.	A				
30.	C	30.	D	30.	C				
31.	C	31.	C	31.	B				
32.	D	32.	C	32.	B				
33.	D	33.	B	33.	D				
34.	A	34.	A	34.	B				
35.	B	35.	D	35.	A				
36.	C	36.	B	36.	A				
37.	C	37.	D						
38.	B								
39.	A								
40.	B								

VR

1. **B** To *liberate* is to *free* something.

2. **A** *Tangible* means *touchable* or *concrete*.

3. **B** *Innate* means *inborn* or *native*.

4. **C** To *deliberate* is to *consider* or *reflect*.

5. **D** *Pious* means *virtuous* or *sacred*.

6. **D** To *plea* is to *request*.

 The word *please* shares the same root.

7. **D** To *disperse* is to *scatter*.

8. **B** *Renown* means *fame*.

9. **C** To *venerate* is to *respect*.

10. **D** To *plunder* is to *steal*.

11. **C** *Voracious* means *having a huge appetite* or *gluttonous*.

12. **A** *Belligerent* means *argumentative*.

 The Latin root *bell* means *war*. The period before the Civil War is called the *antebellum* period. The word *rebel* comes from the same root.

13. **D** *Ominous* means *worrisome*.

14. **C** *Zealous* means *passionate*.

15. **A** A *benediction* is a *blessing*.

 The Latin root *bene* means *good*, and the root *dict* means *word*, so a *benediction* is a *good word*, a *blessing*.

16. **D** *Disparate* means *unequal*.

 The Latin root *dis* means not, and the root *par* means equal.

17. **A** *Aggrandize* means *exaggerate*.

18. **A** To *distinguish* is to *separate* or *differentiate*.

19. **A** *Equivocal* means *ambiguous*.

 The Latin root *equ* means *equal*, and the root *voc* means *voice*, so *equivocal* means *equal voiced*, which is to say *ambiguous* in meaning.

20. **B** A *malcontent* is a *grouch*.

 The Latin root *mal* means *bad*.

21. **A** *Utter sorrow* requires *anguish* (suffering) as the answer.

 Even if you do not know the word *anguish*, you can eliminate the other answers because the correct answer must mean *utter sorrow*.

22. **A** *Years of practice* and *lacks the tremendous talent* requires *adept* (able) as the answer.

 Even if you do not know the word *adept*, you can eliminate the other answers because the correct answer must reflect the result of *years of lessons* yet without *tremendous talent*.

23. **C** *Did not realize I was making an accusation* requires *insinuate* (hint) as the answer.

 Even if you do not know the word *insinuate*, you can eliminate the other answers because the correct answer must reflect that the speaker made an *accusation* that the listener *did not realize* was an accusation.

24. **B** *Showered his friends with gifts and gave his time* requires *generous* as the answer.

25. **B** *Enthusiasm* and *positive attitude never* require *diminished*.

26. **B** *False doctrine* and *injustice* require *ignoble* (shameful) as the answer.

 Even if you do not know the word *ignoble*, you can eliminate (A) and (C), as well as (D) if you know the word, because the correct answer must reflect *false doctrine* and *injustice*.

27. **D**   *Naive* and *unlikely, believe,* and *true* require *ruse* (trick) as the answer.

 Even if you do not know the word *ruse*, you can eliminate (A) and (C), as well as (B) if you know it, because the correct answer must reflect that Matthew is *naive* and will *believe unlikely* things are *true*.

28. **C**   *Could not be resolved* requires *impasse* (*stalemate* or *deadlock*) as the answer.

 Even if you do not know the word *impasse*, you can eliminate (B) and (D), as well as (A) if you know it, because the correct answer must reflect that an issue *could not be resolved*.

29. **B**   *Always in high spirits* requires *jubilant* (*joyous*) as the answer.

 Even if you do not know the word *jubilant*, you can eliminate (A), as well as (C) and (D) if you know them, because the correct answer must reflect *always in high spirits*. You may need to guess from three choices.

30. **C**   *Activities of dancers* requires *kinetic* (*relating to motion*) as the answer.

 Even if you do not know the word *kinetic*, you can eliminate the other answers because the correct answer must reflect *activity of dancers*.

31. **C** Both blanks must relate to *could speak powerfully and expressively*, thus requiring *eloquence* (well-spoken) and *verbalize* as the answer.

 Do one blank at a time. The first blank, which might seem easier, must reflect that the sister *could speak powerfully and expressively,* so you can eliminate (A), (B), and (D). The second blank must also relate to *could speak powerfully and expressively.* The Latin root *loc/loq* means speech.

32. **D** The first blank must mean *believe*, while the second blank must mean *praises*, thus requiring *suppose* and *extol* (praise) as the answer.

 Do one blank at a time. The second blank, which might seem easier, must mean *praise*, so you can eliminate (A), (B), and (C). The first blank must mean *believe*.

33. **D** The first blank must mean *bad*, while the second blank must mean *confirmed*, thus requiring *maladroit* (*clumsy* or *unskilled*) and *perpetuated* (*continued*) as the answer.

 Do one blank at a time. The first blank, which might seem easier, must reflect *unable to do anything,* so you can eliminate (B) and (C). The second blank must mean *confirmed,* so you can eliminate (A). The Latin root *mal* means *bad,* and *adroit* means *skilled.*

34. **A** The first blank must be the opposite of *nasty*, while the second blank must reflect how the parents *reacted* to bad news, thus requiring *benign* (*kindness*) and *chagrin* (*irritation*) as the answer.

 Do one blank at a time. The first blank, which might seem easier, must be the opposite of *nasty*, so you can eliminate (B), as well as (D) if you know it. The second blank must reflect how the parents *reacted* to bad news, so you can eliminate (C). You may need to guess between (A) and (C). The Latin root *ben* means *good*.

35. **B** The first blank must be the opposite of *lack of brevity*, while the second blank must reflect an unsatisfied *hope*, thus requiring *concisely* (*briefly*) and *undermining* (*weakening*) as the answer.

 Do one blank at a time. The first blank, which might seem easier if you know the word *brevity* (briefness), must be the opposite of *brevity*, so you can eliminate (A) and (C). If you don't know *brevity*, you cannot eliminate any first-blank answers. The second blank must reflect an unsatisfied *hope*, so you can eliminate (D), as well as (A) if you haven't eliminated it already. You may need to guess between (B) and (C).

36. **C** The first blank must mean *hurtful*, while the second blank must reflect Patrick's intent (ending in *failure*) to convince people he didn't mean to offend, thus requiring *malicious* (*hateful*) and *ameliorate* (*improve*) as the answer.

 Do one blank at a time. The first blank, which might seem easier, must mean *hurtful*, so you can eliminate (A) and (B). The second blank must reflect Patrick's intent (ending in *failure*) to convince people he didn't mean to offend, so you can eliminate (D). The Latin root *mal* means *bad*.

37. **C** The first blank must emphasize Rodrigo's *efforts*, while the second blank must reflect his *goal* as a *loyal friend* to end the *rumors*, thus requiring *persistently* (*tirelessly*) and *dispel* (*end*) as the answer.

 Do one blank at a time. The second blank, which might seem easier, must reflect his *goal* as a *loyal friend* to end the *rumors*, so you can eliminate (B) and (D). The first blank must emphasize his *efforts*, so you can eliminate (A) if you know it. You may need to guess between (A) and (C). The Latin root *ami* means *friend*, and *amiably* means *in a friendly way*.

38. **B** The first blank must reflect that Christopher received *rare support*, while the second blank must mean *financial support*, thus requiring *fortunate* and *benefactor* (*supporter*) as the answer.

 Do one blank at a time. The first blank, which might seem easier, must reflect that Christopher received *rare support*, so you can eliminate (A) and (D). The second blank must mean *financial support*, so you can eliminate (C) if you know the word. You may need to guess between (B) and (C). The Latin root *ben* means *good*.

39. **A** The first blank must mean *clever*, while the second blank must relate to a type of *comment* that is *expressed*, thus requiring *astute* (*clever*) and *insights* as the answer.

 Do one blank at a time. The first blank, which might seem easier, must mean *clever*, so you can eliminate (B) and (C) if you know the words. If not, you will have to rely entirely on the second blank. The second blank must relate to a type of *comment* that is *expressed*, so you can eliminate (B), as well as (D) if you know the word. You may need to guess.

40. **B** The first blank must reflect the swaying of *low and high tides*, while the second blank must mean *vast separation*, thus requiring *fluctuated* (*swung*) and *chasm* (*vast divide*) as the answer.

 Do one blank at a time. The first blank, which might seem easier, must reflect the swaying of *low and high tides*, so you can eliminate (A) and (C). The second blank must mean *vast separation*, so you can eliminate (D).

QR

1. **B** If Blair is 6 years younger than Nate, who is *n*, she is $n - 6$.

 Plug in a value for *n*, such as $n = 10$. If Nate is 10, Blair is 4. Only (B) yields 4 when you test 10.

2. **C** To calculate the mean of all 5 scores, add the scores and divide by the number of scores: $320 + 75 = 395$, and $395 \div 5 = 79$.

3. **C** The extra distance is represented by the part of the walk from when he turned back to the beach through the time he reversed to go back home up until he arrived back at the point at which he had turned around in the first place. Read the chart, and you will see that from time 0.4 to time 0.6, he was moving *closer* to the beach. That distance was from 0.2 km (from 0.4 to 0.2). Getting back to where he first turned around adds another 0.2 km, for a total of 0.4 km.

4.   **A**   A "weird symbol" defined to equal an equation is simply a different form of function notation, so plug in numbers as directed by the defined equation. As $\ddagger x = 3x - 7$, $\ddagger 6 = 3(6) - 7 = 18 - 7 = 11$.

5.   **C**   Choice (C) cannot be an integer because an even integer times any integer is even and that result plus an odd integer is odd. An odd number divided by 2 is not an integer.

   Plug in an acceptable value for x, such as $x = 4$. Only (C) yields a non-integer when you test in 4.

6.   **A**   Let b represent the original base, and let h represent the original height. As area of a parallelogram is given by bh, the original area is bh. As the base was decreased by 30%, the new base will be 70% of the original, or $0.7b$. As the height was increased by 20%, the new height will be 120% of the original, or $1.2h$. Thus the new area is $(7b)(1.2h) = 0.84bh$. Percent change is found by taking the difference, dividing that by the original, and then multiplying the result by 100: $\dfrac{h - 0.84bh}{bh} = \dfrac{0.16bh}{bh} = 0.16$, and $0.16 \times 100 = 16$.

   As no original values were given, they do not matter, so you can plug in. Assign 10 to the original base and the original height. Thus, the original area was 100. The new base is 7 (reduced by 30% or 3), and the new height is 12 (increased by 20% or 2). Thus the new area is 84. As the new area is 16 lower than the original, and the original was 100, the percent change is 16.

7. **C** Use FOIL (First, Outside, Inside, Last) on the two factors: $(x + 6)(x + 6) =$ $(x^2 + 6x + 6x + 36)$. Combine like terms: $x^2 + 12x + 36$. Thus, $n = 12$.

 Plug in a number for x, such as $x = 2$, and solve both sides of the equation: $8^2 = 4 + 2n + 36$, so $64 = 40 + 2n$. Combine like terms and divide by 2: $n = 12$.

8. **B** For a number to have a remainder when divided by 5, it must be some factor of 5 plus 4. So let a and b each equal $5x + 4$. Substitute this expression into each answer. For (A), the result is 0, which is not equivalent to some factor of 5 plus 4. For (B), the result is $2(5x + 4) - (5x + 4)$, which is $10x + 8 - (5x + 4)$, which is $5x + 4$. This is a factor of 5 plus 4. If you check (C) out of caution, the result is $2(5x + 4) + (5x + 4)$, which is $10x + 8 + (5x + 4)$, which is $15x + 12$. When 12 is divided by 5, the remainder is 2, not 4. Choice (D) yields the same result as (C).

 If you are given a denominator of a quotient and a remainder, you can plug in for the numerator by adding the denominator and the remainder. In this case, you can set both a and b equal to 9 (4 + 5). Plug 9 into each answer (for a and b) and divide each answer by 5 to find its remainder. Only (B) yields a remainder of 4.

9. **C** The sum of the integers from 1 to 497 will not include two numbers counted in the sum of all integers from 1 to 499, namely, 498 and 499. If the sum of all integers from 1 to 499 is r, then the sum of all integers from 1 to 497 will be r minus the sum of 498 and 499: $r - (498 + 499)$, or $r - 997$.

10. **D** To find out that (D) does not work, you should square both sides and solve the resulting equation for y, obtaining $169 + y^2 = 169 - 26y + y^2$. Subtract 169 and y^2 from both sides, leaving you with $0 = -26y$. This can only be true if $y = 0$, but the question states that y is a non-zero number. Another way to solve this problem is to use PITA. Choice (A) works when y is 5, so eliminate it. $169 - 25 = 144$, so when $y = 25$, the expression works. Eliminate (B). Eliminate (C) because it works when $y = 12$. Choice (D) only works with 0, which is not non-negative.

 Guess and check to find out what could be true. For (A), as $\sqrt{144} = 12$, try to come up with a y value that will make the value under the square root equal to 144. Setting y equal to 5 works. Repeat the process for (B); in this case, setting y equal to 25 works. For (C), $\sqrt{169} = 13$, so setting y equal to 12 works. Select (C).

11. **B** Start with the parentheses and exponents: $\dfrac{2(16 + 64)}{4(10)} = \dfrac{2(80)}{4(10)}$. Now, cancel the denominator against 80: $2(2) = 4$.

12. **C** Set up a proportion: $\dfrac{6}{y} = \dfrac{?}{\frac{5}{3}y}$. Cross multiply: $y? = 6 \times \dfrac{5}{3}y = 10y$. Divide both sides by y: $? = 10$.

 Plug in a value for y, such as $y = 3$. Now set up the proportion: $\dfrac{6}{3} = \dfrac{?}{5}$. Cross multiply and divide both sides by 3: $? = 10$.

13. **B** First, list out Stewie's integers: 5, 6, 7, 8, and 9. Now list out Peter's integers: 6, 7, 8, 9, 10, and 11. Finally, circle any that are on both lists: 6, 7, 8, and 9.

14. **D** Multiply both sides of the second equation by -2: $-4x - 2y = -24$. Stack the two equations on top of one another and combine like terms: $-x = -16$. Multiply both sides by -1: $x = 16$. Substitute 16 for x in either equation: $2(16) + y = 12$. Combine like terms: $y = -20$. Finally, substitute the values for x and y in the expression and solve: $5(16) + (3)(-20)$ $80 - 60 = 20$.

 Rather than solve the variables individually, stack the initial equations and combine like terms: $5x + 3y = 20$. The question is asking for the value of $5x + 3y$, so you are done.

15. **A** Adding 5 points to each student's score will not affect the range because both the lowest and highest scores are 5 points higher, leaving the difference the same.

16. **C** The common quadratic $(x + y)^2$ can be written as $x^2 + 2xy + y^2$. Rearrange the expression to $x^2 + y^2 + 2xy$ and substitute in the given values: $65 + 2(28) = 65 + 56 = 121$.

 You can guess and check to find numbers that work. If $xy = 28$, then x and y can be 1 and 28, 2 and 14, or 4 and 7. Testing these in $x^2 + y^2$ shows that 4 and 7 work. Therefore, $(x + y)^2 = (4 + 7)^2 = 121$.

17. **C**   If you unfold the cube, you will have a star above a plus sign and an X to the right of the plus sign. Note the orientation of the star. Since the bottom of the star must be above the plus sign, eliminate (A) and (B). Only (C) has the correct orientation of the star. The correct answer is (C).

18. **A**   Choice (A) is correct because if a factor of one number is multiplied by a factor of another number, the product of the factors will be a factor of the product of the other two numbers.

  Plug in values for all four variables, following the requirements. A proper set would be $x = 5$, $c = 10$, $y = 3$, and $d = 6$. Test each answer using these numbers. Only (A) is true.

19. **A**   Set up an equation using the Pythagorean theorem: $h^2 + s^2 = (2s)^2$. Distribute the exponent on the right and subtract s^2 from both sides: $h^2 = 3s^2$. Take the square root of both sides: $h = s\sqrt{3}$.

  If you realize that this is a 30-60-90 triangle, you could use the proportions of a 30-60-90 triangle. If you didn't realize this, here is a great opportunity to Plug In a number and solve for h. Plug in a value for s such as $s = 2$, and set up an equation using the Pythagorean theorem: $h^2 + 2^2 = 4^2$. Apply the exponents and subtract 4 from both sides: $h^2 = 12$. Take the square root of both sides and simplify the value under the square root sign: $h = \sqrt{12} = \sqrt{4 \times 3} = 2\sqrt{3}$. Only (A) yields this value when you test 2 for s.

20. **D** Let x represent the number of purple marbles in the bag. Thus, there are $90 + x$ marbles in the bag. Set up an expression for the probability of selecting a purple marble: $\frac{x}{x + 90}$. Set this fraction equal to the value of each answer, cross multiply, and solve for x. For (A), $x = 10$. For choice (B), $x = 30$. For (C), $x = 60$. Choice (D) does not yield an integer value.

 You can guess and check possible numbers of purple marbles, but this may be too time consuming. As an example, if you guess that there are 10 purple marbles, that would mean there are 100 marbles, and (A) would represent the probability of picking one of those 10 purple marbles.

21. **B** The value of Column A is $\frac{1}{4}$. The value of column B is $\frac{\frac{1}{4}}{3} = \frac{3}{4}$.

22. **B** Draw the figure, which is a right triangle. Column A represents the hypotenuse. Column B represents the sum of the two legs. The third side of a triangle must be less than the sum of the other two sides, so the value in Column B is greater.

23. **A** Plug In 5, since this is the upper limit which is not actually possible. In Column (A), $5(5) + 11 = 36$. In Column (B), $6(5) + 6 = 36$. Since these quantities are equal but not possible due to the inequality, eliminate (C) and try something close to this. For instance, try 4.9: $5(4.9) + 11 = 35.5$. $6(4.9) + 6 = 35.4$. Column (A) is greater, so eliminate (B). Try one more: $5(-1) + 11 = 6$ and $6(-1) + 6 = 0$. Column (A) is still greater. The correct answer is (A).

24. **A** A negative exponent tells you to write the reciprocal of the base and bring the exponent to the denominator as a positive value. Thus, the value of Column A is $\dfrac{1}{\left(\frac{1}{12}\right)^2}$, and the value of Column B is $\dfrac{1}{\left(\frac{1}{12}\right)^{\frac{1}{2}}}$. When you divide 1 by a fraction, the fraction flips and comes to the numerator. Thus, the value of Column A is 12^2, and the value of Column A is $12^{\frac{1}{2}}$. Raising a number to a power of $\dfrac{1}{2}$ means taking the square root of that number. While you may not know the exact value of $\sqrt{12}$, it is less than 12^2, which equals 144.

25. **B** When you need two separate probabilities to occur, you multiply the distinct probabilities (taking care to ensure that the probability of the second event assumes that the first event has occurred). Thus, the probability of picking two green buttons (Column A) is $\dfrac{3}{23} \times \dfrac{2}{22}$. The probability of picking only one button is $\dfrac{3}{23}$. This is all you need for Column B, because one button is sufficient, and the second pick doesn't matter. Column B is greater because $\dfrac{3}{23}$ times any value between 0 and 1 will be less than $\dfrac{3}{23}$.

 Use logic. You need more luck to pick two green buttons than to pick one, which means there is a greater probability of picking one.

26.   C   The value of Column A is $\frac{4}{7}$, as given. Finding the value of Column B requires a few steps. First, cross multiply the given equation: $7x = 4y$. Now isolate one of the variables by dividing both sides by the number in front of that variable. If you isolate y, the result is $y = \frac{7x}{4}$. Substitute $\frac{7x}{4}$ for y in Column B: $\dfrac{x + 4}{\frac{7x}{4} + 7}$. Simplify first by creating a common denominator for the elements in the denominator:

$\dfrac{x + 4}{\frac{7x}{4} + \frac{28}{4}} = \dfrac{x + 4}{\frac{7x + 28}{4}}$. Now further simplify the value in Column B by multiplying the numerator and denominator by the reciprocal of the denominator (which is

$\dfrac{4}{7x + 28}$): $\dfrac{4(x + 4)}{7x + 28}$. Factor out a 7 from the denominator: $\dfrac{4(x + 4)}{7(x + 4)}$. Cancel out

$(x + 4)$: $\dfrac{4}{7}$.

Plug in values for x and y, such that the value of $\dfrac{x}{y} = \dfrac{4}{7}$. Good values would be $x = 4$, and $y = 7$. The value of Column A is $\dfrac{4}{7}$, and the value of Column B is $\dfrac{4 + 4}{7 + 7} = \dfrac{8}{14} = \dfrac{4}{7}$. As the value of Column A is not *always* greater than the value of Column B, and the value of Column B is not *always* greater than the value of Column A, eliminate (A) and (B). Now try different numbers, always making sure that $\dfrac{x}{y} = \dfrac{4}{7}$. Try $x = -8$, and $y = -14$. The value of Column A is $\dfrac{-8}{-14} = \dfrac{4}{7}$, and the value of Column B is $\dfrac{-8 + 4}{-14 + 7} = \dfrac{-4}{-7} = \dfrac{4}{7}$. If you are not convinced the values of the two columns will *always* be the same and have the time, you can try one more number set.

27. A You might start by setting up an equation, but you will see that it quickly becomes ugly: $(x)(x + 1)(x + 2) = 504$, so $(x^2 + x)(x + 2) = 504$. So, try another approach, such as breaking 504 into its prime factors: $7 \times 2^3 \times 3^2$. This means that the three numbers are 7, 8, and 9. As $7 > 6$, (A) is correct.

 As there is an unknown value in one column and a known value in the other, test the known value against the unknown value. That is, assume that 6 is the least of the three numbers. The numbers would be 6, 7, and 8, with a product of 336. As $336 < 504$, the least of the three numbers is greater than 6.

28. A As 89 is the mode, at a minimum there are two scores of 89. Let x, y, and z represent the three unknown scores, and set up the average formula: $\frac{x + y + z + 89 + 89}{5} = 88$. Multiply both sides by 5 to find the sum of the five scores: $x + y + z + 89 + 89 = 440$. For Column A, let q represent the sixth score and set up another average formula: $\frac{q + x + y + z + 89 + 89}{6} = 89$. Multiply both sides by 6 to find the sum of the six scores: $q + x + y + z + 89 + 89 = 534$. Subtract the sum of the five scores from the sum of the six scores to find q: 94. Now that you know Column A is 94, proceed to Column B. The median will be the average of the middle two scores. For the median to equal or exceed 94, the remaining three numbers would have to be listed to the right of 94, which means their sum would be greater than the sum of the known numbers. Check: $89 + 89 + 94 = 272$, and $x + y + z = 534$ (the sum of the six) − 272: 262. Thus, 94 cannot be one of the middle numbers and is to the right of the middle numbers.

 A good way to think of average is Total = Average × Number (TAN). Here, the number of tests is 5, and the current average is 88. Thus, the total score when all 5 tests are added is 440 (88×5). For Column A, find the total score for the six tests, using TAN: $6 \times 89 = 534$. Thus, to raise the average to 89, an additional score of 94 points is needed ($534 - 440$). For Column B, follow the procedure set forth immediately above.

29. **D** Use logic. While it is possible that the reduction in area relates to the area of the base, it is equally possible that the height of Pyramid B is reduced by a factor of $\frac{1}{3}$ while the area base is unchanged. (Other arrangements are possible as well.)

30. **D** The perimeter of a square will have 4 equal sides. Therefore, the sides of the square will be 9, making the area 81. The question notes that the figure is not drawn to scale, so there are many ways of creating a rectangle with the same perimeter. Plug In 12 and 6: these add up to a perimeter of 36, and the area of the rectangle would be 72. Eliminate (B) and (C). Note that a square is a type of rectangle, so Plug In 9 for both sides of the rectangle. Now the shapes are equal in area. Eliminate (A) and the correct answer is (D).

31. **C** The area of the shaded region is the difference between the area of the large triangle and the area of the small triangle. The base of the large triangle is b, and its height is h, so the area of the triangle is $\frac{1}{2}bh$. The base of the small triangle is x, and its height is x, so the area of the triangle is $\frac{1}{2}x^2$. Thus, the area of the shaded region is $\frac{1}{2}bh - \frac{1}{2}x^2$. Factor out the $\frac{1}{2}$: $\frac{1}{2}(bh - x^2)$.

 Plug in values for b, h, and x, such as $b = 10$, $h = 8$, and $x = 2$. The area of the large triangle is $\frac{1}{2} \times 10 \times 8 = 40$. The area of the small triangle is $\frac{1}{2} \times 2 \times 2 = 2$. The area of the shaded region is the difference between the two areas: 38. Substitute the selected values into the variables in Column B: $\frac{1}{2}(10 \times 8 - 2) = 38$.

32. **C** To compare the values in the two columns, you need to create a common base. As $27 = 3^3$, the value in Column A is $(3^3)^4$. When you raise a power to a power, multiply the exponents: 3^{12}.

33. **B** In the figure, the x intercept is –2, and the y intercept is 3. When a line is reflected about the x axis, the x intercept stays the same, but the sign of the y intercept reverses. Thus, the value of Column A is –3. When a line is reflected about the y axis, the sign of the x intercept reverses, but the y intercept stays the same. Thus, the value of Column B is 3.

34. **A** Consider different possible lengths given the area provided. If the rectangular garden were a square, the lengths would be 12 on all sides. The perimeter would be 48. If the rectangular garden had a length of 144 and width of 1, the perimeter would be 290. There is no way to create a perimeter of 44. Remember that a square of a certain area will always have a smaller perimeter than a rectangle of the same area.

35. **D** Given that the absolute value of a and the absolute value of c are unknown, $a + c$ can be any real number, including a number less than, equal to, or greater than b.

 Plug in values for a, b, and c, following the restrictions, such as $a = -2$, $b = 2$, and $c = 3$. The value of Column A is 1, and the value of Column B is 2. As the value of Column A is not *always* greater than the value of Column B, and the values of the columns are not *always* equal, eliminate (A) and (C). Change up the numbers, trying to make the value of Column A greater if possible. Try $c = 10$, but keep a and b the same. Now, the value of Column A is 8, and the value of Column B is 2. As the value of Column B is not *always* greater than the value of Column A, eliminate (B) and select (D).

36. **B**   The initial price of $2.50 fell after a 20% decrease to $2.00: 0.20 × $2.50 = $0.50, and $2.50 − $0.50 = $2.00. The new price of $2.00 went up after a 20% increase to $2.40: 0.20 × $2.00 = $0.40, and $2.00 + $0.40 = $2.40.

  In this type of question, the original price does not matter, so plug in $100 to keep things simple. Subtracting 20% brings the price to $80. Adding 20% brings the price to $96. Thus decreasing a price by a percent and then increasing the price by the same percent will yield a price lower than the original amount.

37. **D**   Start with what you know and begin a list. The middle of five numbers is 4, and there are at least two 4s: _, _, 4, 4, _. (Note that the second 4 could be to the left of the median.) Given that the range (largest − smallest) is 4, there are a number of possibilities. Write one or two, just to get a sense of how things might look: 1, _, 4, 4, 5 & 2, _, 4, 4, 6. Now address Column B. A good way to think of mean is Total = Average × Number (TAN). Here, the number of numbers is 5, and the average is 4. Thus, the total of all five numbers when added is 20 (4 × 5). Put a number, such as 2, into the first list and find the average: $\frac{1 + 2 + 4 + 4 + 5}{5} = 3\frac{1}{5}$. As the value of Column A is not *always* greater than the value of Column B, and the values of the two columns are not *always* equal, eliminate (A) and (C). Now put a number, such as 4, into the second list and find the average: $\frac{2 + 4 + 4 + 4 + 6}{5} = 4$. As the value of Column B is not *always* greater than the value of Column A, eliminate (B) and select (D).

RC

When you arrive at a new passage, read it quickly if you are a faster reader, or read the first sentence of each paragraph if you are a slower reader. For each detail question, read about 10 lines of text and try to predict what you believe will answer the question. Evaluate the answers against your prediction and make sure that the answer you selected is fully supported by the text.

1. **A** The passage is narrated from the point of view of a person recollecting his summers with his family. Choice (A) matches the opening sentences of the passage. Eliminate (B) because it does not say that his recollections are from one particular summer. Eliminate (C) as well because the author never mentions lessons learned. Eliminate (D) because it is not a fictional account of two brothers. The correct answer is (A).

2. **D** The passage states, "*The owner of the restaurant was a callous man who yelled at the customers. I was quite frightened of him,* but the hamburger with the special sauce was delicious, so I always wanted to go there for lunch."

3. **B** The passage states, "*I tried to teach my brother how to dive*—he always jumped into the pool or even walked down the steps at the shallow end—but after a while I gave up."

4. **B** The passage states, "*The owner of the restaurant was a callous man who yelled at the customers.*"

5. **D** The passage states, "*Years later, I found out that my grandmother and her cousin liked going there for the hamburgers because they thought the owner's rude behavior was funny!*" The grandmother and the author contrast each other in their perceptions of the hamburger owner, who is rude. Eliminate (A) because it is irrelevant to the window of the passage. Eliminate (B) because the truthfulness of her statement goes beyond the passage. Eliminate (C) because it does not give any information about the grandmother, nor does it give the author's perception as an adult. Choice (D) is correct because the author was *quite frightened* by the owner in line 30 while the grandmother found the *owner's rude behavior funny.* The correct answer is (D).

6. **B**   The passage states, "When I arrived, I was greeted by her little dog Charlie, whom I named. *I loved Charlie, and we played for hours, chasing each other from room to room. Then, I would give Charlie a vanilla wafer as a treat.*"

7. **D**   The passage describes coral reefs generally and provides specific details about the Great Florida Reef.

8. **A**   The passage states, "*Given the scarcity of Atlantic and Caribbean reefs, it may come as a surprise that the second and third largest barrier reefs are the Belize Barrier Reef in Central America (620 miles), and the Great Florida Reef,* a 4-mile wide, 145-mile long reef system that follows the arc of the Florida Keys."

9. **D**   Fish and other sea creatures would "visit" a reef.

10. **B**   For (A), the passage states, "Farther out to sea are *giant reefs that plunge into the deep.*" For (C), the passage states, "The relatively shallow part of the Florida Straits (less than six feet deep) take on *spur and groove formations*—rows and rows of reefs separated by white sand." For (D), the passage states, "In addition to fish similar to those in the patch reefs, *the giant reefs are also frequented by large "pelagic" fish such as sharks.*" Lobsters and crustaceans are mentioned in the hard bottom area, lines 38–43. The correct answer is (B).

11. **C**   This paragraph focuses on one specific part of the Great Florida Reef, rather than the Great Florida Reef generally.

12. **C** The author's tone is positive.

13. **D** The passage describes several women lawyers and their struggles to practice law.

14. **C** The passage states, "*The Supreme Court* agreed that she was a citizen, but rejected her argument that the "privileges and immunities" clause offered her protection. *In a separate opinion for the Court, Joseph Bradley* expressed the typical male view of the time."

15. **B** For (A), the passage states, "When former United States Supreme Court Justice *Sandra Day O'Connor graduated from Stanford Law School*, the prestigious California law firms of the day would not hire her as a lawyer. *Despite the fact that she graduated third in her class*, the only job offer she received was as a legal secretary." For (C), the passage states, "When former United States Supreme Court Justice Sandra Day O'Connor graduated from Stanford Law School, *the prestigious California law firms of the day would not hire her as a lawyer.* For (D), the passage states, "*When former United States Supreme Court Justice Sandra Day O'Connor* graduated from Stanford Law School, the prestigious California law firms of the day would not hire her as a lawyer." Choice (B) is not supported; she was offered a job as a secretary, but the passage does not state that she accepted such a job.

16. **B** In discussing the Supreme Court opinion that denied a woman the right to be admitted to the bar, the author quotes Joseph Bradley's reasoning as *"the typical male view of the time."*

17. A  The passage states, "Twenty years later, *the Supreme Court similarly ruled against Belva Lockwood, who challenged Virginia's refusal to admit her to the state Bar*, even though she had been admitted to practice before the Supreme Court."

18. C  The passage states, "By the 1890s, though, admission of women to state Bars became increasingly common—*even if prestigious law firms would not be ready to hire the likes of Justice O'Connor for decades to come.*"

19. C  The passage provides a description of the political writings of Liu Xiaobo and the Chinese government's actions against him.

20. D  As the Chinese government arrested Liu Xiaobo, a word such as *dislike* (or *villainy*) is best.

21. B  In the third paragraph, the author provides an example of Liu's political beliefs: *"Liu has also been a staunch supporter of military action by the United States intended to expand human rights."* This example supports the author's general discussion of Liu's support of *"fundamental human rights."*

22. B 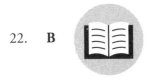 Liu Xiaobo was arrested for his political writings: "His crime: *advocating political reforms in China,* such as ending the Communist Party's complete control of the political system and media."

23. **D** The passage states, "Liu has also been a staunch supporter of military action by the United States intended to expand human rights: '*The free world led by the US fought almost all regimes that trampled on human rights … The major wars that the US became involved in are all ethically defensible.*' He has also supported the United States' support of Israel and the war in Iraq that led to Saddam Hussein's downfall. He predicted that "a free, democratic and peaceful Iraq will emerge."

24. **C** The passage states, "In his early years as an academic, *his future role as dissident was not apparent. He spent many years studying literature,* earning a Master's Degree in 1984, when he was 29."

25. **C** The passage provides information about today's understanding of the Black Death.

26. **A** The passage states, "In France, *the King was informed that the Plague was caused by astrological events such as the aligning of three planets.*"

27. **C** The passage states, "*But it is the Black Plague that continues to fascinate historians of disease, perhaps because after its first wave in the 1300s, it reappeared from time to time all the way through the 1700s.*"

28. **B** The plague ends swiftly after a population is destroyed.

29. **A** The passage states, "*Ultimately, this question, along with what caused the plague and how many people died, will never be answered conclusively. The records from the time are simply not detailed enough to allow for confident answers.*"

30. **C** The passage states, "In addition to turning to astrology for answers, *people of the time blamed earthquakes and, unfortunately, the Jewish people, whose communities in some towns were massacred not by the plague, but by other people.*"

31. **B** The passage describes different types of igloos and how they are constructed to maintain warmth.

32. **B** The passage states, "*The bed is placed in a raised area, because warmer air rises.*"

33. **D** Most of the passage describes the different designs and uses of igloos.

34. **B** The passage states, "*While the stone lamp may cause the interior to melt a bit, the water refreezes, which serves to strengthen the igloo.*"

35. **A** The paragraph begins with a statement—that there are a number of different types of igloos. The rest of the paragraph provides examples.

36. **A** The passage states, "In the Inuit language, the word igloo means house, even though many people suppose it has a more precise definition: snow house. *Quite the contrary, anything from a tent to a building can be called an igloo by the Inuit.*"

MA

1. **D**   Choices (A) and (B) are the same as $\frac{1}{3}$, as you can move the two decimals and reduce. Choice (C) is the decimal equivalent of $\frac{1}{3}$. Because $\frac{1}{3}$ generates a repeating decimal in (D), (D) is not equivalent.

  Numbers divided by 3, 6, 7, and 9 generate repeating decimals. If you know this fact, you can select (D) without additional work.

2. **B**   Find the radius by setting the given circumference equal to the formula for circumference: $12\pi = 2\pi r$, so $r = 6$. Substitute the radius into the formula for area: $\pi(6^2) = 36\pi$.

3. **C**   A fraction will equal zero if the numerator equals zero. Here the numerator will equal zero if $x^2 = 36$, as $36 - 36 = 0$. There are two values of x that satisfy the equation: ± 6.

  Test the answer choices. The numbers in (A) and (D) will not solve out to zero. While the number in (B) will, the answer is incomplete. Both numbers in (C) will solve out to zero.

4. **C**   First divide the coefficients: $\frac{4.2}{6.0} = \frac{42}{60} = \frac{7}{10} = 0.7$. Next divide the exponential terms, remembering that when you divide common bases, you subtract the exponents: $\frac{10^7}{10^{-3}} = 10^{10}$. As 0.7×10^{10} is not in proper scientific notation form, move the decimal forward once and decrease the exponent by one: 7.0×10^9.

5. **C** There are 13 rectangles. As each is 4 in², the total area is 13×4 in² $= 52$ in².

6. **C** Begin with the coefficients. As the factors of 4 are 1, 2, and 4, and the factors of 10 are 1, 2, 5, 10, the greatest common factor is 2. As p^5 is a factor of p^8, the greatest common factor of p^5 and p^8 is p^5. As q is a factor of q^4, the greatest common factor of q and q^4 is q.

7. **A** Plug values from the chart into the answers. Begin with $x = 1$ and $y = 0$. Only (A) works. The correct answer is (A).

8. **B** Use the slope formula: $\dfrac{y_1 - y_2}{x_1 - x_2} = \dfrac{5 - 3}{2 - 7} = -\dfrac{2}{5}$.

9. **C** List the numbers in order, being sure to use the y axis (miles): 1, 2, 4, 5, 6, 7, 7, 8. As there are an even number of numbers, the median is the average of the two middle numbers: 5.5.

10. **A** First add the terms inside the parentheses: $x = 5x$. For a number to equal five times that number, the number must be zero.

 Test the answer choices. Only (A) allows the equation to balance.

11. **C**   Use the distance formula for each answer: $\sqrt{(x_1 - x_2)^2 + (y_1 - y_2)^2}$, which because one of the points is (0, 0) is $\sqrt{(x_1)^2 + (y_1)^2}$. Choice (A) yields 5, (B) yields $\sqrt{153}$, (C) yields $\sqrt{160}$, and (D) yields $4\sqrt{2}$. As $13 = \sqrt{169}$, (C) is closest.

  Begin by estimating. Choices (A) and (D) are clearly too small. For the other two answers, draw in a line, creating a right triangle. While you can use the Pythagorean Theorem, you may recall that one of the Pythagorean triples is 5-12-13. Therefore, the triangle with legs of 12 and 4 will have a hypotenuse closer to 13 than will the triangle with legs of 12 and 3.

12. **B**   The smallest value of y is not necessarily determined by the smallest value of x, so try values of x on the ends and in the middle. If $x = 2$, then $3(2)^2 - 4 = 8$. If $x = -3$, then $3(-3)^2 - 4 = 23$. If $x = 0$, then $3(0)^2 - 4 = -4$. No value of x in the specified range will yield $y = -7$.

13. **D**   Use the distance formula: $\sqrt{(x_1 - x_2)^2 + (y_1 - y_2)^2}$. Plugging in the given points yields $\sqrt{(-1-(-6))^2 + (10-(-2))^2} = \sqrt{5^2 + 12^2} = \sqrt{169} = 13$.

  Plot the points in the coordinate plane and connect them. This line is the hypotenuse of a right triangle, so drawn in the two legs. Count the number of units left to right and the number of units bottom to top. Use these numbers in the Pythagorean Theorem.

14. **A**   Pounds and tons measure weight, so eliminate (C) and (D). Choices (A) and (B) can be used to measure linear distance, but one kilometer is over 3,200 feet, much larger than a television screen.

15.   **C**   When solving an equation with two inequality signs, perform the same operation to the two sides and the middle. Start by adding 1 to both sides and the middle: $-3 \leq 3x \leq 9$. Divide both sides by 3: $-1 \leq x \leq 3$.

16.   **A**   The mode is the number that appears the most. Be sure to focus on the number of times a certain number of inches of rain fell. Two inches of rain fell 12 times, so 2 is the mode.

17.   **C**   The number of arrangements possible when r are selected from n options is given by $\dfrac{n!}{(n-r)!}$. Here, the number of arrangements is $\dfrac{7!}{4!} = 7 \times 6 \times 5 = 210$.

    When dealing with orderings or combinations, you can set up slots for what you need and fill them with what is available. In this case we need three people, so we need three slots: ___ ___ ___. For the first slot, 7 people are available as a possible choice, while for the second slot only 6 people are available (as one is taken for the first slot), and for the third slot only 5 people are available (as another was taken away): _7_ _6_ _5_. To find the number of arrangements, multiply the numbers in the slots: 210.

18. **A** Questions seeking the area of a weird shaded region generally require you to subtract the area of one normal shape from the area of another normal shape. In this case, subtract the area of the triangle from the area of the quarter circle. The area of a quarter circle is $\frac{1}{4}\pi r^2 = \frac{1}{4}\pi(6)^2 = 9\pi$. As the triangle is a right triangle, the radii are also the base and height. The area of a triangle is $\frac{1}{2}bh = \frac{1}{2}(6)(6) = 18$. Choice (A) reflects the difference between the two areas.

 You can estimate that the area is a small fraction of the area of the circle, which is 36π or approximately 108. Choices (B) and (C) are negative, so you can eliminate them. Choice (A) is about 9, while (D) is about 72. Given that one quarter of the circle is about 72, (D) is too large.

19. **B** Percent change is calculated as follows: $\frac{difference}{original} \times 100$, so the number of students increased by 25%: $\frac{25-20}{20} = \frac{5}{20} \times 100 = 25\%$.

20. **C** A rational number can be expressed as a fraction. The square root of a number that is not a perfect square is irrational. The expression in (C) can be rational because squaring the square root of a number yields that number. Thus both x^2 and y^2 will be rational, so the quotient of those numbers will be rational.

 Plug in values for x and y following the restriction, such as $x = \sqrt{2}$ and $y = \sqrt{3}$. These numbers are both irrational, as they cannot be expressed as a fraction. Substitute these numbers into each answer choice to determine when the expression can be expressed as a fraction. Only (C) can.

21. **A**   Draw the triangles to make sure the corresponding vertices of the two triangles are aligned. Set up a proportion: $\dfrac{4}{7} = \dfrac{16}{x}$. Cross multiply and divide both sides by 4.

22. **C**   Use FOIL (First, Outside, Inside, Last) on the two factors: $(x + 4)(x - 5) = (x^2 + 4x - 5x - 20)$. Combine like terms: $x^2 - x - 20$.

  Plug in a number for x, such as $x = 6$, and solve: $(6 + 4)(6 - 5) = (10)(1) = 10$. Only (C) yields 10 when the value for x is plugged in.

23. **B**   There are 360 degrees in a quadrilateral. Add up the given angles and subtract the sum from 360: $360 - (140 + 80 + 25) = 360 - 245 = 115$.

24. **A**   First, multiply both sides by $(4 + x)$: $x(4 + x) = -4$. Distribute the x: $4x + x^2 = -4$. Add 4 to both sides and order the left side by leading exponent: $x^2 + 4x + 4 = 0$. Factor the left side of the equation: $(x + 2)(x + 2) = 0$. Set $x + 2$ equal to 0 and subtract 2 from both sides: $x = -2$.

  Test the answers. The value in (A) allows the equation to balance, so eliminate (B) and (D). Test any other number, and the equation will not balance. Eliminate (C).

25. **D** First, distribute the negative sign: $3a^3b^5 + 2a^2b^4 - 7a^2b^4 + 4a^3b^5$. Carefully combine like terms: $7a^3b^5 - 5a^2b^4$.

26. **D** As the square of an odd number is odd, and the difference between two odd numbers is even, (D) will yield an even number when x is odd.

 Plug an odd value for x, such as $x = 3$, into the answer choices. Only (D) is even.

27. **B** This question is testing the relationship between similar triangles. Set up a proportion: $\frac{30}{18} = \frac{5}{x}$. Cross multiply and divide both sides by 30.

28. **B** First take the square root of 64: 8. For the variable, you must use the rules of exponents. If the bases are the same, add the exponents when you multiply the terms. The term x^{36} represents a base of x that was squared, i.e., multiplied by itself. Thus the two exponents added were the same value and produced a sum of 36. $(x^{18})(x^{18}) = x^{36}$.

 To find the square root, divide the exponent in half. $\sqrt{x^{36}} = x^{18}$.

29. **D** The 60 people who chose Comedy represent $\frac{60}{90} = \frac{2}{3}$ of the survey participants. To represent this fraction in a circle graph, which has 360°, set up a proportion: $\frac{2}{3} = \frac{x}{360}$. Cross multiply and divide by 3.

30. **C**   Probability is always a fraction, $\dfrac{\text{what you want}}{\text{what you've got}}$. In the first reach into the bag of beads, we want a yellow bead (9) out of all the beads (16). Therefore, the first reach is $\dfrac{9}{16}$. For the second reach, we want a purple bead (2), but there is one less bead total, so the probability of getting a purple bead is $\dfrac{2}{15}$. When you need two probabilities to occur, you multiply the fractions.

31. **C**   As $36 + 9 = 45$, and $\sqrt{45}$ is not an integer, (C) is correct.

32. **A**   The slope of a line perpendicular to another line is the negative reciprocal of the other line's slope. The negative reciprocal of $\dfrac{2}{3}$ is $-\dfrac{3}{2}$.

33. **C**   First, determine how much time was devoted to changing scenery by dividing 80 minutes by 5: 16 minutes. Next, convert 16 minutes to seconds, so you have an apples-to-apples comparison, by multiplying 16 by 60: 960. Finally divide 960 by 40: 24.

34. **C**   Test the answers to determine which one yields the indicated graph. For each answer, there are two cases. For (A), first solve $x + 4 \le 6$. Subtract 4 from both sides: $x \le 2$. As this is not one of the indicated end points in the graph, eliminate (A). For (B), first solve $x + 4 \le -6$. Subtract 4 from both sides: $x \le -10$. As this is not one of the indicated end points in the graph, eliminate (B). For (C), first solve $x - 4 \le 6$. Add 4 to both sides: $x \le 10$. This is consistent with the graph. Now, solve $x - 4 \ge -6$. Add 4 to both sides: $x \ge -2$. This is also consistent with the graph, so (C) is correct.

35. **B** First, convert the length and width from feet to yards by dividing each number by 3: the measurements are 5 yards and 7 yards. Find the area: 35 yd^2. As each tile has an area of 1 yd^2, 35 tiles will be needed.

36. **D** First subtract 25 from both sides: $x^2 = -25$. Take the square root of each side, remembering there are two solutions for x^2: $x = \pm\sqrt{-25}$. Separate the 25 from -1: $\pm\sqrt{25 \times -1} = \pm 5\sqrt{-1}$. The square root of negative one is not a real number and is called the imaginary number i. Thus, $x = \pm 5i$.

37. **B** To add matrices, add the numbers that occupy the same position in each matrix. That is, add the top-left numbers, the top-right numbers, and so on. Here,
$$\begin{bmatrix} 1 & 4 \\ 2 & 1 \end{bmatrix} + \begin{bmatrix} 2 & 5 \\ 6 & 1 \end{bmatrix} = \begin{bmatrix} 1+2 & 4+5 \\ 2+6 & 1+1 \end{bmatrix} = \begin{bmatrix} 3 & 9 \\ 8 & 2 \end{bmatrix}.$$

38. **A** First, add a to both sides and subtract ab from both sides: $a + 3 = xb - ab$. Factor out b from the right side: $a + 3 = b(x - a)$. Divide both sides by $x - a$: $\dfrac{a + 3}{x - a} = b$.

 Plug in values for two of the variables, such as $a = 6$ and $b = 4$, and solve for x: $(6)(4) + 3 = 3x - 6$, so $24 = 3x - 6$, so $3x = 10$. Test the values for x and a in the answers to find the value for b. Only (A) works.

39. **D**   A stem-and-leaf plot shows the tens digit to the left of the vertical line and the units digits to the right of the vertical line. Thus, in the second row, the first number is 11, and the next is 14. Because all of the numbers of the data set are given, all statistical measures (mean, median, mode, and range) can be assessed.

40. **B**   Let x represent the smaller number and set up an equation: $x + x + 8 = 26$. Combine like terms and subtract 8 from both sides: $2x = 18$. Divide both sides by 2: $x = 9$.

  Test the answers, starting with (B) or (C). If you start with (C), the smaller piece is 17, so the larger piece is 25. The sum of these pieces is 42, which is too large. Proceed to (B). If the smaller piece is 9, the larger piece is 17. The sum is 26.

41. **C**   To find the area of an irregularly shaped shaded region, find the areas of the two normal shapes and subtract the smaller from the larger. As the area of a circle is πr^2, the area of the larger circle is 100π, and the area of the smaller circle is 36π. The difference is 64π.

  You can estimate that the area is a fraction of the area of the larger circle ($100\pi =$ approximately 300, as π is approximately 3). Estimate the values of the answer choices. Choice (A) is 48, which is too small. Choice (B) is 108, which might work. Choice (C) is 192, which might work. Choice (D) is the area of the larger circle, which is too big. While it may be difficult to determine whether the shaded region is about $\frac{1}{3}$ or $\frac{2}{3}$ of the larger circle, consider that farther out from the center takes up more area than closer to the center. Thus, (C) may be a safer bet.

42. **B** The vertical lines at either end of the box-and-whisker graph represent the lowest and highest data points. (The vertical line in the middle of the two boxes represents the median.) As range is calculated by subtracting the lowest value from the highest value, the range here is $70 - 25 = 45$.

43. **D** Begin by stating the speed as a fraction with the units marked: $\frac{14m}{1h}$. Now, convert the miles in to feet. As there are 5,280 feet in a mile, multiply 14 in the numerator by 5,280: $\frac{5,280 \times 14}{1h}$. Now, convert the hour into minutes. As there are 60 minutes per hour, multiply the 1 in the denominator by 60: $\frac{5,280 \times 14}{60}$.

44. **D** Probability is always a fraction, $\frac{\text{what you want}}{\text{what you've got}}$. The total number of jelly beans to begin with is 19, but Graciela removes a brown one, leaving 18 jelly beans behind, 5 of which are pink. Graciela's probability of removing a pink one is therefore $\frac{5}{18}$.

45. **A** Use SohCahToa. As $\overline{LM}$ is OPPOSITE TO the given angle, and $\overline{MN}$ is ADJACENT TO the given angle, use tangent: $\tan 50° = \frac{\overline{LM}}{5}$. Multiply both sides by 5: $5 \tan 50° = \overline{LM}$.

46. **A** As the diameter is 4, the radius is 2. The height—three times the radius—is 6. Substitute these numbers into the given formula: $\frac{1}{3}\pi(2^2)(6) = \frac{1}{3}\pi(4)(6) = 8\pi$.

47.   C   To determine whether a specified value is within a given range around a middle or normal value, subtract the middle value from the specific value, take the absolute value of that difference, and determine whether the result is less than or equal to the given range. That is $|specific - middle| \leq$ range. In this case, R is the specified value, 20 is the middle value, and 5 is the given range, so $|R - 20| \leq 5$.

 Plug in a permitted value for R, such as 22. Test 22 in each answer. For (A), $|22 - 5| \leq 20$. This is true, so keep (A). For (B), $|22 - 5| \geq 20$. This is false, so eliminate (B). For (C), $|22 - 20| \leq 5$. This is true, so keep (C). For (D), $|22 - 20| \geq 5$. This is false, so eliminate (D). As two answers remain, try a value for R that is not permitted, such as 13. In this case, the equation should fail, as 13 is not permitted. For (A), $|13 - 5| \leq 20$. This is true, so eliminate (A). For (C), $|13 - 20| \leq 5$. This is false, so keep (C).

Writing Sample

Give your essay to a parent or teacher, along with the prompt. Your reviewer should comment on whether someone working in an admissions office would think that you are nice, thoughtful, funny, or any other positive quality. Your reviewer should also focus on organization, grammar, spelling, and other aspects of good writing, but he or she should not hold you to the standard required of a well-polished essay. While glaring problems should be identified, very few people will write a perfect first draft in a timed setting.

NOTES

NOTES

NOTES